HISTORY
of
7th ARMOURED DIVISION

The Naval & Military Press Ltd

June 1943 — July 1945

Published by

The Naval & Military Press Ltd
Unit 5 Riverside, Brambleside
Bellbrook Industrial Estate
Uckfield, East Sussex
TN22 1QQ England

Tel: +44 (0)1825 749494

www.naval-military-press.com
www.nmarchive.com

In reprinting in facsimile from the original, any imperfections are inevitably reproduced and the quality may fall short of modern type and cartographic standards.

Foreword

IT is with great pleasure that I write this short foreword for the story of the 7th Armoured Division from June 1943 onwards.

The Division began its life in the Western Desert of Egypt; it went through all the varying changes of fortune in the desert campaigns; it fought its way across Africa and up to Italy; it landed in Normandy in June 1944 and fought its way across France, Belgium, Holland, and Germany; it was "in at the kill" in Germany in May 1945.

This is a fine record of which every officer and man in the Division can justly be proud.

Of all the Divisions that have served under my command the 7th Armoured Division has served with me the longest; I have had it under my command from August 1942 to the present time, except for a break from May 1943 to December 1943. I therefore feel that I know it well.

The Division has always given of its best at all times and has left its dead in many lands between Egypt and Germany. To those who have come through to the end I would quote the words of Pericles when speaking at the funeral of those who died in the defence of Athens:

> "To famous men all the earth is a sepulchre: for their virtues shall be testified not only by the inscription on stone at home but, in all lands wheresoever, in the written record of the mind, which far beyond any monument will remain with all men everlastingly. Be zealous therefore to emulate them."

B. L. Montgomery

Field-Marshal
Commander-in-Chief, 21 Army Group

Germany, July 1945

Introduction

THIS short history carries the story of the 7th Armoured Division from the end of the North African campaign, where the previous volume written by Lt.-Col. Carver left it, to the Victory Parade in Berlin on 21st of July.

It does not in any way pretend to be a detailed and final account of our battles from which lessons can be deduced. The intention is to present a general picture of the Division's deeds since the fall of Tunis, which, together with the photographs, may serve to revive memories and promote discussion amongst those who read it.

Our object has also been to produce this volume before demobilisation claims too many of the veteran "Desert Rats".

Though formation and unit commanders have been mentioned by name, the naming of others, who by their leadership and gallant deeds contributed so much to the success of the Division, has not been attempted. The sources of information available in the field and the time factor would have made the choice arbitrary and unrepresentative. It was therefore considered better to omit all mention of individuals by name. Their many deeds will no doubt be preserved for posterity when a fuller and more authoritative history of the 7th Armoured Division is written.

Finally, our thanks are due to all who have worked so hard to make the publication of this book possible and in particular Captain Martin Lindsay and Captain M. E. Johnston who have been responsible for the text and Captain N. B. Harris who has procured and arranged the photographs.

L. O. Lyne

Major-General
Commanding 7th Armoured Division

Germany, September 1945

CHAPTER I

AFTER TUNIS: A VISIT TO SICILY

May, 1943—September, 1943

After the capture of Tunis, the Division was looking forward after a long period out of contact with civilisation to exploiting such sources of amusement and relaxation as had been unearthed in the city. We were, therefore, somewhat shaken when, after a day or two, we were withdrawn into the heart of the desert again, the first stop being Bou Arada. Bou Arada is a wilderness with no sign of life other than the odd cactus; even here the Division was determined not to be deprived of its lawful pleasures—the conventional breakfast of soya links was more often than not replaced by a tumblerful of Tunisian brandy; and one trooper, asked for details of the events leading up to his appearance on sick parade, made the immortal remark, "Ee, it moost 'ave been woon of them Shepherdesses!"

From Bou Arada, the Division moved on to Homs on the coast East of Tripoli: this, it was learnt, was to be our permanent sojourn while we re-equipped and trained for operations in another theatre. There was again a little disappointment, particularly as it was learnt that some units were going back to the fleshpots of the Delta. But we all realised that the victory in Africa was only a beginning and that much hard work and hard fighting lay ahead; and there was no ill-feeling that was not quickly drowned in the particularly virulent type of date brandy for which Homs is celebrated.

There were three main problems confronting us. First, the Division had to be completely re-equipped in three months. All new equipment had to come from the Delta fifteen hundred miles away (and mostly by road). This was a major headache, but, thanks largely to the strenuous personal efforts of the Commander of 10th Corps, the task was completed just in time. Second, individual training, and particularly weapon-training, had been sadly neglected during the last few months of strenuous operations; and third, the Division had to re-train for a completely different type of warfare in close country. There was not yet much chapter and verse for this type of training; and when the Sicilian campaign started, its lessons had to be quickly assimilated. We also had to train for Combined Operations; a Landing Ship Infantry arrived in Homs harbour and everyone practised scrambling into and out of it.

Faced with the prospect of our having to spend three months in Homs, General Erskine was particularly anxious that it should be made habitable for the troops. There was one large and modern Albergo: this was turned into a Jerboa Club with facilities on a big scale for reading, writing and "brewing", the walls being adorned with frescoes showing tanks and armoured cars and (more important) English countryside scenes and Arab dancing girls. A cinema was established nearby, and a "Music for All" club in the local theatre (the sweltering heat made music very difficult). The old Roman Amphitheatre at Leptis Magna was used for ENSA concert parties—one of which included Vivian Leigh and Leslie Henson. A Leptis Magna steeplechase proved a great success: enormous sums passed through the Totalisator, and the local Sheikhs, who had been invited to take part, were tickled to death with the handsome presentation plaques constructed for the occasion by the Royal Electrical and Mechanical Engineers. Leave parties were organised for Tripoli: this town had a doubtful recreational value, being mainly noted for Bigger and Better queues—most of the Italian population had fled, leaving behind a mass of dubious gentry who delighted in charging fantastic prices for the trashiest of "Souvenirs" and announcing loudly that they were "Our Allies".

* * *

The Division participated in the Sicilian campaign to the extent of a Tactical Headquarters. General Erskine took with him a skeleton staff containing Operations, Intelligence, Supply, Medical and Royal Army Service Corps representatives, the idea being that the Independent Armoured Brigades in Sicily might require to be welded together and used as an Armoured Division, in which case we should assume control.

Our party sailed from Sousse on the 12th of July, 1943, and first sighted the Sicilian coast on the 14th of July. We sailed towards Augusta, hoping to land there, but some shells landing in the water nearby seemed to indicate that the enemy was still in possession, and our small convoy withdrew and made an orderly and peaceful entry into Syracuse harbour, our elaborately waterproofed vehicles driving straight off on to the quay.

After a few days of very pleasant waiting in the Syracuse area, it became apparent that our services were unlikely to be needed. The Italian formations in the Western half of the island were surrendering en masse with a rapidity which rendered the use of armour on our part superfluous; the Germans, who had gravitated to the Eastern end, were fighting like devils in the Catania area, in a type of country which precluded the deployment of large numbers of tanks. The Germans had meanwhile organised a most efficient ferry service to the Italian mainland; it was largely protected from the attention of our Air Force by the deployment of over three hundred flak guns, and the German troops were falling very slowly back towards it in a rearguard action, brilliantly organised by the staff of the Hermann Göring Division. For this most orderly evacuation of Sicily, General der Panzertruppen Hans Hube (one of the Division's better-class opponents) received well-earned Swords and Diamonds to his Ritterkreuz.

After about a fortnight, 7th Armoured Division "Tac" became definitely and officially superfluous and had with many regrets to return to Tripoli. But the period had certainly not been wasted: we were able to take back with us valuable lessons from operations in this new type of country, and being more or less unemployed in Sicily at this time of the year was not without its compensations (which included the sweetest and juiciest oranges known to man, sixteen different varieties of Marsala, and a gaggle of Artistes from the Italian version of ENSA, one of whom had been endowed by Nature with scarlet hair and green eyes).

CHAPTER II

THE ITALIAN CAMPAIGN AND RETURN HOME
September, 1943—December, 1943

On his return from Sicily, General Erskine knew that the Division was to take part in the Italian campaign. It was obvious that we were to be a "follow-up" formation and that a fair amount of planning ahead and study of the terrain would have to be undertaken. A small planning staff with Operational, Intelligence and Royal Engineer representatives installed themselves near the sea-shore in a large tent surrounded with barbed wire.

We were first of all to be prepared to take part in Operation "Buttress"—the Eighth Army's landing in South-West Italy. Accordingly, maps and a plaster model were prepared with names omitted and coastline altered at significant points, and these were used for Tactical Exercises Without Troops (on allegedly hypothetical terrain). Most officers participating in the TEWTs made it a point of honour to discover exactly to which part of the proper map the model corresponded, and as there were, strategically, not so very many alternatives, very few got the answer wrong. Their industry, however, proved to be completely wasted; the whole plan was changed, and we were switched to Operation "Avalanche"—the Fifth Army's landing in the Gulf of Salerno. This information was at first restricted to a very small circle, and the TEWTs were allowed to go on training with the old kit (and to go on congratulating themselves on their diabolical cunning in finding out the actual landing beach).

For the Salerno landing, the Division was to be for the first time under the command of an American Army, that of General Mark Clark. Planners soon found that our Allies had more lavish and variegated ideas about "Bumph" (United States "Poop") than those to which we had been accustomed, and one Staff Officer, grappling with a weighty and elegantly bound volume on the Ceramic Industries of the Lombardy Plain, was heard to enquire whether "Avalanche" referred to the actual operation or to the paper preceding it.

There were certain important factors that we had to consider in the planning of "Avalanche". The greater distance involved (the turn-round from Tripoli to Salerno was seven days) meant that our build-up would necessarily be very slow. For the first week or so our airfields would be a long way away from the scene of operations, and we might expect the enemy to have temporary local air superiority at times over the bridgehead. We had fairly accurate advance information on the enemy formations we might be expected to meet: we knew that 16 Panzer Division was already on the spot in the Battipaglia area, that the Hermann Göring Division had retired to Caserta to lick its wounds of the Sicilian campaign, that 3 Panzer Grenadier Division was ready to move at any moment from the Rome area, and that a lot of high-class troops, including 26 and 29 Panzer Grenadier Divisions, were retreating towards our sphere of operations from Eighth Army further South. Our order of embarkation was, therefore, planned on the assumption that things might well be fairly sticky in the bridgehead and that we might have to lend assistance. General Erskine decided to land first of all 131 Lorried Infantry Brigade Group with two infantry battalions, 5th Royal Tanks, a Battery of 3rd Royal Horse Artillery and a troop of Royal Engineers.

Operation "Avalanche" began on the 9th of September. With the assault Divisions went an advance party, consisting of Brigadier Whistler (commanding 131 Brigade) and representatives down to Company level of all the units in his Brigade Group, also the DAAG and Staff Captain "Q", whose task was to reconnoitre our Concentration Areas.

The first wave of our own Division contained a small Tactical Headquarters with General Erskine, the Commander Royal Artillery, the Commander Royal Engineers, the GII (Operations), the Intelligence Officer and the second in command Divisional Signals. There were no clerks, offices or messes, but the Headquarters could, and did, function by verbal and wireless means. The Lorried Infantry Brigade Group did not arrive quite as arranged, for some genius in the Movements Staff at Tripoli conceived the idea of loading the transport belonging to the two infantry battalions and leaving the bodies behind owing to lack of space. This might have had unfortunate consequences, but fortunately the Infantry in question were hastily stuck into a variety of miscellaneous ships and arrived three days later.

En route for Salerno, the wireless in our Landing Ship gave out daily a more gloomy communiqué, and at one point talked about the "sky being dark with planes locked in mortal combat". This had no effect on General Erskine who remained uniformly cheerful throughout, but some of the gloomier members of the party discussed the tactics of discharging the Landing Ship under spandau fire.

The party arrived on the evening of the 15th of September, and at first sight the beachhead appeared a far quieter place than the BBC would have had us believe. The sky in the area was indeed dark with planes, but these were, without exception, Fortresses, Lightnings and Spitfires, with (as far as the casual observer could discern) no foreign bodies "locked" to them. But in reality, the situation was far from easy. 46th and 56th Divisions had had some very tough fighting; the bridgehead was by no means large and their troops holding it were fairly thin on the ground. The harbour of Salerno could not yet be used, and the town itself was no health-resort. The whole of the bridgehead was under shellfire and the enemy, though apparently too clueless to do anything co-ordinated, was continually launching small vicious counter-attacks. General Erskine's White Scout Car broke a spring on its way to the Concentration Area, bedded down in a ditch for the night, was chased out of the ditch at four o'clock the next morning by a spirited counter-attack from 2 Battalion 67 Panzer Grenadier Regiment and withdrew at full speed with the sagging chassis tearing strips of rubber off the tyres.

The whole beachhead was crammed with equipment and, for the first few days after our arrival, extremely noisy, as there was precious little of it that was not a gun area. Enemy air activity was, in general, confined to the routine breakfast and suppertime visits, and considering that there was hardly a square yard of ground without some equipment parked on it, remarkably little damage was done. In the Battipaglia area, and especially round the large tobacco factory, which had been stubbornly defended by 26 Panzer Division, our air and naval bombardments had caused the most impressive devastation. The only thing to commend the beachhead in those days was the "Uva Fragola"—a large grape with a flavour of wild strawberries which hung in clusters over every leaguer.

By the 17th of September the approach, from the South, of Eighth Army had made the situation on our front appreciably looser, and 10th Corps could now turn its attention to preparing an attack through the passes North of Salerno to reach the Naples Plain. 46th Division attacked through the Vietri gap on the 22nd of September, and such of our Division as had arrived by that date was lined up on the road behind 46th Division to pass through them at twelve o'clock the next day. The enemy had excellent observation in clear air from the very high ground in front of us and made life unpleasant by shelling the road and mortaring the bridges. Due to the precipitous type of country ahead and the nature of the enemy troops (Hermann Göring and our old enemies 15 Panzer Grenadier), delays were inevitable, and, after waiting lined up on the road for twenty-four hours, we turned round and went away. It was actually not until the 28th of September that the Division was able to pass through. This proved to be a blessing, as, although our concentration was not fully complete until the 30th, we had by the 28th assembled enough of ourselves to function as a Division rather than a Battle Group. In general, for the fighting troops, this was a period of endless waiting on roads, enlivened only by severe rain-storms, which desert experience, quite wrongly, tended to regard as only a temporary inconvenience.

By the 27th of September it became clear that the time was ripe for us to pass through 46th Division. The plan was as follows: 46th Division was to clear the Vietri gap up to as far as Camerelle. The American Ranger Battalion, who had done so brilliantly in the Monte Chiunzi area, was to form a bridgehead through which the 23rd Armoured Brigade could debouch on to the Plain of Naples from the high ground North of Salerno and on our left. The 23rd and ourselves were to converge in the area of Scafati on the River

Sarno, and the 23rd were to come under our command. Thence the 23rd Armoured Brigade were to advance on Naples by the coastal road between Vesuvius and the sea, while the remainder of the Division was to pass round to the North of Vesuvius and advance towards the River Volturno in the Capua area. There was no convenient concentration area for us behind 46th Division, so we just had to line up and wait on the road, a process which revealed the interesting fact that at forty vehicles to the mile the Division occupied no less than fifty-five miles of road.

There was still difficult mountainous country ahead, and, even when we had reached the Plain, the roads were few and narrow and the country close and dotted with small thick orchards. It was decided that the lead must be taken by 131 Brigade with under command the 5th Royal Tanks, a Regiment of Royal Horse Artillery and a Troop of Royal Engineers.

Scafati

23rd Armoured Brigade moved off on the night of the 27th/28th of September, and at five-thirty on the morning of the 28th the 1/7th Queens advanced and quickly seized dominating high ground just outside 46th Division's final objective against opposition from a small but determined German rearguard.

We then advanced on the axis Cava dei Tirreni—Nocera—Scafati. In the lead were the 1/6th Queens whose commander, Lieutenant-Colonel M. Forrester, was well to the front keeping the whips out in the most spirited manner. The main bridge over the River Sarno in Scafati had been prepared for demolition and was guarded by the 2nd Hermann Göring Panzer Grenadier Regiment: but the 1/6th Queens made a lightning dash at the bridge which so unnerved Hermann Göring's satellites that the hand already resting on the switch refused to act: the bridge was captured intact, the charges removed and the rearguard killed or taken prisoner.

The rest of that day was spent in battalion battles in the streets of Scafati against enemy who counter-attacked again and again with tank support in desperate efforts to regain the bridge. But all these counter-attacks were beaten off; by the 29th, Scafati was finally cleared, and a Bailey bridge was built over the River Sarno to relieve the traffic in the Scafati bottleneck.

On the 29th and 30th, 23rd Armoured and 131 Brigades made slow progress; the roads were poor and the country between them had a sticky soil and was close enough to give the fullest scope to the German rearguards. Here we were once more up against the skilful and energetic organisation of the Hermann Göring Staff; the rearguard parties under their control generally consisted of one or two self-propelled guns protected by dug-in machine gun and rifle positions. An armoured car in front of the main position would give timely warning of our approach. The road would be mined and blocked by felled trees (at one point fifty large trees had been felled across the road) and the trees would probably be booby-trapped. From further back one or two troops of guns and probably some Nebelwerfers would bring down unpleasantly accurate fire on to the road. From the Göring Engineer Battalion (which had distinguished itself in the Sicilian campaign) we captured an order to destroy all roads, bridges, stations, water, gas and electricity installations, mills and factories that lay in the path of their retreat.

Opposition loosened on the 1st of October, and at nine-thirty that morning the King's Dragoon Guards entered Naples, from which for several days great columns of black smoke had been rising as the German demolition squads, harried and sniped by Italian patriots, carried out their evil work. 131 Brigade were also observing columns of smoke, but these had a more natural origin: Vesuvius had been reached and the Brigade closed up to Somma Vesuviana, the bottleneck on the North side of the great volcano.

The network of roads was now slightly less inadequate, and therefore on the 2nd of October General Erskine decided to hand the lead over to 22nd Armoured Brigade. Somma Vesuviana was a mass of rubble and demolitions, but the 1st Royal Tanks, under Lieutenant-Colonel R. M. P. Carver, persisted until they had found

The entry into Naples

a way through, and for the next two days fought a series of spirited battles against just the same type of determined and expert enemy rearguards, aided by the same type of demolitions and booby-traps. Melito di Napoli, Afragola, Cardito and Aversa, all fair-sized towns, were flushed of the enemy. Italian patriots were helpful and more than once acted as guides and led the way through orchards to the rear of small parties of Germans. 23rd Armoured Brigade on our left were temporarily held up by a bumper crop of demolitions at Qualiano.

This type of fighting, though less noisy, was infinitely more exhausting than African warfare. The vineyards were not the comparatively open hill-sides with prim rows of vines, of not more than shoulder height, associated with the advertisements of wine merchants, but on the contrary, tall and luxuriant growths reaching to twenty feet above the ground, festooned between the poplar trees which supported them. In between the rows were innumerable market garden crops, many of which seemed to require tall stakes, or else fields of maize which now reached above a man's head. In this country an anti-tank gun could knock out the leading tank of a column at a range of under a hundred yards, without the following tanks being able to detect its lair; and owing to the skilful way in which tanks, self-propelled guns and anti-tank guns were disposed so as to be mutually supporting, attempts by the remainder of a troop to manœuvre to a flank often only ran them on to a few well-placed mines or on to other guns. Much excellent work was done by scout car and carrier patrols in detecting areas which were held, but the enemy's well-trained gunners were not prepared to waste armour piercing shot on such small targets, and thus these patrols could not, as a rule, do more than indicate that enemy were located in such and such an area, from which our patrols had been engaged by small arms or grenades. They could give no information as to a more detailed layout. Moreover, dismounted reconnaissance by foot patrols was equally difficult, as the well-placed and well-concealed spandau posts made movement almost impossible. In consequence, these advances were made either by tanks fighting blind, or else on the result of night patrols by the motor companies, whose scope was naturally restricted to the distance they could walk. This patrolling added increasingly to the fatigue of the riflemen, since rest by day was impossible as the Regimental columns jerked spasmodically forward. It was, however, invaluable as much of the enemy's movement was carried out by night, and the country, although impossible to patrol silently, did make withdrawal considerably simpler if contact was gained. Much during this period depended on the Royal Horse Artillery, who were continually called upon for rapid fire support on suspected targets, and never failed to achieve the desired results. At times this activity developed into small battles, involving attacks in company strength. One such occasion was at Cardito, a small town surrounded by peculiarly thick vineyards, in which a number of self-propelled and anti-tank guns were in position, protected by machine gun posts on the Southern outskirts of the town. After one tank had been knocked out by an anti-tank gun which could not be located, and others reported guns firing which they could not see, "C" Company of the 1st Rifle Brigade were put in to attack supported by "CC" Battery, 5th Royal Horse Artillery. Before, however, they could get started, an enemy Observation Post, which must have been within a few hundred yards of them, from where he could see under the tangled vines, had reported them forming up on a narrow track, and a heavy concentration of both mortars and 105 mms was brought down, which, by causing casualties, particularly one Platoon Commander and another Platoon Sergeant, who was commanding a platoon, made it impracticable for "C" Company to carry on. (It must be remembered that the dismounted strength of a motor company at this time was only two platoons, rarely totalling more than thirty-five to forty all ranks.) "I" Company of the Rifle Brigade was accordingly brought up, to which were added the carriers and machine guns of "C" Company. The tanks of 1st Royal Tanks were to operate in direct support and to cover the flanks. The attack was a complete success. The barrage from "CC" Battery fell exactly where it was needed, and after some enterprising close-range fighting in which good use was made of the thick cover for assisting grenade throwers to approach spandau positions from flanks and rear, the town was occupied at surprisingly little cost. The only enemy met to the North was a single self-propelled gun, which, after damaging one of our tanks, was knocked out by two exceedingly well-aimed shots from the tank that had been hit.

On the 5th of October 1st Royal Tanks, in spite of all the bridges having been blown, forced a crossing over the Regi Lagni—a large drainage ditch South of the Volturno and one of many that made this area so unsuitable for armoured movement. We also knew that the Volturno bridges were all prepared for demolition, and the strip of country, completely bare except for occasional thick copses, between us and the river was so riddled with ditches and dykes that we had given up all hope of being able to repeat our Scafati "coup". A helpful Italian officer who had crossed the lines revealed that 15 Panzer Grenadier Division had moved down to the Volturno, and gave us a description of their general layout, which subsequently proved to be surprisingly accurate. The covering parties for the Volturno bridges in our sector were provided by an old enemy, Oberst Grell, who told his men that the bridges would be blown behind them (as indeed they were in the course of the next two days), and after that they would have to fend for themselves. However, we cleared from the Regi Lagni up to the Volturno without much further difficulty, and 131 Brigade then took over the line of the river from Santa Maria la Fossa to Grazzanise.

During this part of our journey, Divisional Headquarters sat in many leaguers that were in violent contrast to Homs, El Assa and other arid wastes we had grown to regard as our inevitable lot; the best of these leaguers was in the main square of Pompeii with the Armoured Command vehicles facing the cathedral, whose massive light-coloured Campanile towered above us in the sun-drenched air. Into this Cathedral square came endless bodies to be interrogated: two sixteen-year-old boys from Hermann Göring who were so bomb-happy that each question made them burst into tears; a bombardier from 15 Panzer who swore that his Battery Commander, firing a trial registration shot on the 9th of September, had accidentally sunk a British destroyer in the Gulf of Salerno; an Italian who was alleged to know where a platoon of German saboteurs commanded by a Colonel were hiding in the ruins of Pompeii, but whose actual wishes (somewhat distorted through language difficulties) proved to be nothing more than "cioccolata e biscotti" for his "dieci bambini". Considering the damage done by Allied bombing to some of the finest parts of the old ruined town, the population were remarkably friendly and indeed eager to excuse us by saying "there must have been some German guns hidden there".

The whole background of this part of our history must, indeed, remain a vivid and colourful memory to all who took part. Accustomed to sullen Arabs who cared less than nothing for the armies of either side except when they had "chai" to exchange for "eggis", the smiles and waving, the cheers and kisses warmed our hearts. General Erskine when travelling with his Tactical Headquarters bore with great fortitude the numerous well-meant bunches of grapes that sailed past his head or squashed themselves on his greatcoat, but was reported to have reached for his Tommy gun when one over-enthusiastic "vecchia mamma" scored a direct hit on his nose with a walnut. Undoubtedly the population had hated the humourless Germans (as far as the

Southern Italian has energy enough to hate anything), and most of them clung for some time to their illusion that all the lorries in our convoys were crammed with chocolate, cigarettes, white bread, farings in plenty and all for them.

Casaluce—Major-General Erskine and the orphans

One leaguer at Casaluce is especially rich in memories. We started off by arresting a small boy who had been riding along on a donkey behind the cable troop of our Signals, winding in the cable as fast as they laid it. Charged with being the Italian equivalent of a Werewolf, he tearfully referred us to his mother who assured us that she had packed him off that very morning "on a recce" charged in the strictest terms with procuring something she could use as a clothes-line. Her explanation was accepted and the boy let go. From then on our reputation was made. Villagers from far and wide flocked to an enormous Thanksgiving Service in the local church and loud and long expressed their amazement that Conquering Armies could show such justice and mercy. We increased our popularity by lending a three-tonner to fetch back to the village the famous Silver Virgin of Casaluce. Just before the invasion this statue had been lent to Aversa for an annual Festival, and the Casalucans were stung to the quick when the Aversans went about boasting that now there was a war on there'd never be any transport to cart the Silver Virgin back and they, the Aversans, meant to hang on to it for ever. Eventually a deputation arrived to ask the "Generale Inglese" to be present at eleven o'clock to receive a bouquet from the local Orphans: at eleven o'clock the local Orphans duly appeared, collars starched, hair slicked down, faces and hands scrubbed with yellow soap till they glowed; they bore a bouquet about the size of the Albert Hall, handed it over, then lined up and sang an Anthem (which appeared to have been specially composed for the occasion) about the "Generale magnifico" with his "Liberatori Arditi". This anthem had any number of verses and a distressing habit of suddenly going right back to the beginning, and by the time it really had ended, the hot sun had melted most of the NAAFI chocolate which General Erskine had been clutching in his hand to dole out later to the Orphans.

By the 6th of October, the country South of the Volturno had been cleared, the last enemy withdrawing on the morning of the 7th. On the Division's right, 56th (London) Division faced Capua, and on our left 46th Division held from Cancello to the sea. The task of each Division in 10th Corps was to find its own crossing, although later our crossing became, in fact, a diversion to help out 56th Division on the right. Between Capua and Cancello, the area of our front, the Volturno was a swift-running river, at this period varying in depth between nine inches on the shoals and six feet in the deepest parts, and surrounded by high banks, whose sides were thickly overgrown with brush-wood and trees. All the existing bridges, including Hadrian's at Capua, had been blown by the enemy as he withdrew, and the swift current, together with the width of the river, added to the difficulties of crossing. Moreover, the flat clay valley on either side, with its many ditches and canals, was completely open to observation from trees and houses standing above the level of the river banks. This was of more assistance to the enemy than to us, since while he had to stay where he was, we had not only to work hard improving roads, continually liable to collapse under the rains, and making improvised crossings over the drains, but also to carry out our concentration directly under the enemy's eyes. Only one advantage really remained to an attacking force, namely that the winding river, with its many loops, enabled crossings to be undertaken at points where the enemy's line necessarily jutted out towards ours, and it was for this reason that our attention was concentrated on the long tongue of land, some two thousand yards long by three hundred broad at its narrowest point, that juts towards the town of Grazzanise. This tongue had the additional advantage of being served by a minor road, which led to a bridge, demolished at both ends, but intact in the centre. The preliminary tasks, then, of 131 Brigade, to whom the operation was entrusted, were fourfold; first, to improve communications to the rear and plan all arrangements for the Engineer tasks of bridging and ferrying; secondly, to find out by patrolling all that could be known about the proposed crossing places, in which task infantry and Engineers co-operated; thirdly, to discover as much as possible about the enemy's defences; and fourthly, while the preparations were under way, to deceive the enemy as to our intentions by diversionary patrols and artillery fire.

The enemy, however, appreciated that, if a crossing was to be made on our front, the obvious crossing place was at Grazzanise, and his defences were disposed accordingly. On the banks he had numerous spandau posts, dug in below the crest, to watch the river itself. Behind these were further mutually supporting positions on the dykes whose fire could command the crests of the flood walls, and behind them again were numerous mortars, Nebelwerfers and guns, accurately ranged on the river banks and all likely targets behind. (In view of this, the importance of thorough reconnaissance was even greater for us, an Armoured Division, perhaps than for an Infantry Division, for we could not afford to sacrifice our few, and highly valuable, infantry to circumstances which had not been foreseen but which were foreseeable.)

The Engineer preparations went smoothly. In spite of shell-fire a crossing over the Canale di Fiumerella was constructed and much hard work done on the roads. Owing to the limitations of bridging equipment, nothing more ambitious could be attempted than the construction of two rafts and a possible make-shift utilisation of the remains of the wooden bridge with Bailey bridging. Tanks, if they were to cross at all, would have to wade. The difficulties of finding suitable rafting points were inevitable owing to the steepness of the banks, which, almost vertical, would have to be cut away in order to get vehicles down and up the far side. By the 10th, however, as a result of ceaseless patrolling, two places had been found, the best to the South of the bridge. But no suitable tank ford was located. Meanwhile, much was done to bring up preliminary stores and to conceal them in the woods along the bank. This task could only be accomplished in darkness as any movement behind Grazzanise brought down accurate artillery and mortar fire, though after the first few days the enemy became a little dubious about exposing his gun positions in strength to the observers of the 3rd Royal Horse Artillery. The only remaining task was to force the enemy to show his hand. This was undertaken by the battle patrol of 1/7th Queens who crossed in assault boats on the night of the 10th. They reached the other side successfully, working along the demolished bridge, but, within twenty yards of landing, were met by spandau fire and, in attempting to silence it, their attack was stopped by fire from supporting posts and the patrol commander killed. The patrol sergeant then attempted to withdraw to the river bank, fighting a fierce small arms battle and covered by the guns of the 3rd Royal Horse Artillery and the battalion's mortars. After fifteen minutes of this, the enemy, presumably imagining that the real attack had come, sent up a red verey light which immediately brought down his defensive fire, much of which was observed to fall on the best crossing site below the bridge. The battle patrol was finally extricated with very great gallantry at the cost of one man severely wounded and another slightly. In spite of the fire brought down on the companies of the 1/7th Queens, which had caused casualties, the patrol had succeeded in making the enemy reveal his dispositions, which then received a very severe handling from the guns of the 3rd Royal Horse Artillery.

By now the Brigade's task was no longer to achieve an assault crossing, but by patrolling, shelling and mortaring to distract attention from 56th Division's crossing at Capua. However, it was decided to continue with a plan to get the best part of two battalions across, 1/5th and 1/7th Queens, and some tanks if possible, and to occupy Brezzia to the East. On the night of the 12th/13th the 1/7th Queens attempted their crossings under cover of a barrage. Initially this landed on the river banks, and brought down the enemy's defensive fire as before. The barrage was then lifted but an attempt to cross brought down a heavy concentration of air-burst on the crossing site, with the result that it was postponed until three hours later when it met with complete success. By daylight, two platoons and a Machine Gun section were established on the North bank. The enemy did not react to this intrusion except by sporadic gun and mortar fire, and indeed did not

Royal Engineers bridge the Volturno River

appear to notice that it had taken place. The next night, in spite of shelling and mortar fire, a raft was constructed and six jeeps and four six pounder anti-tank guns brought across and man-handled up the bank. Meanwhile the 1/5th Queens cleared the banks by energetic patrolling. In the course of the next two days each battalion established a company on the far side and Brezzia was occupied. The construction of the bridge, however, was delayed by heavy shellfire, and it was decided to discontinue work during the night in order to avoid casualties as our own gunners were capable of mastering the enemy during day-time. Eventually the bridge was completed on the 15th, just in time, for a fall in the level of the water made the ferry unworkable. This did, however, bring to light a tank crossing near the bridge and on the 16th, after energetic work by a squadron of the 4th County of London Yeomanry, who shovelled away the river bank, and the construction of a gap by bull-dozer on the other side, the tanks got across. At dawn on the 16th, with the 1/5th and 1/6th Queens, they set out to clear the bridgehead between the river and the canal two thousand yards to the North. This was mainly an infantry task, for a torrential downpour had made movement for the tanks impossible off the roads, and, in any case, mines and demolitions greatly hindered their progress. Isolated spandaus and mortars were eliminated and by night-fall the entire area was clear and contact established with 56th Division on our right.

56th Division eventually withdrew, as did we, crossed the Volturno higher up and came down to clear Capua from the North-West. While they turned North to the mountains flanking the Volturno valley, the Division kept along the low ground, advancing along Highway 7. The enemy was making his usual slow withdrawal to his next line along the Garigliano and Monte Cassino, demolishing the numerous bridges and culverts as he went. To the South-West on the plain, 11th Hussars were able to make good progress, for, by the 19th, the enemy had virtually withdrawn to the line of the Savone River, with rearguards well supported by artillery, still fighting in the mountains, and occupying an outpost line around Francolise and Sparanise and in the hills above. Enemy resistance on the ground was not severe, but attempts to work forward by patrols brought reaction from 88's and mortars. On the 22nd, Sparanise was found abandoned, and the 5th Royal Tanks Group occupied it and sent patrols into the mountains beyond. Observation Posts were also cleared from the hills above Sparanise in a spirited attack by "I" Company 1st Rifle Brigade. These advances continued steadily, meeting few enemy, but being continually shelled, until by the 26th, the Division was firmly established on the line of the River Savone. It was a period of tiring and uneventful fighting, entailing much patrolling, and hard work for the Royal Engineers in organising diversions and in clearing mines. Casualties had not been heavy and prisoners few, mostly in fact deserters.

At the end of October, the Division moved South-East to take over the line of the Regi Agnena near the sea. The move, as were all moves in a country so ill-equipped with roads and evacuated by an enemy so well equipped with explosives, was as tedious as ever, the main obstacle being the bridge at Capua, which throughout this period could only take one tank at a time. The Rifle Brigade took over the line, scattered in woods and along the banks of dykes and patrolled vigorously by night. In front of us was an expanse of marshy plain with behind it the bulk of the Monte Massico rising abruptly above. The enemy's main position was on the mountain, from which he was replenished through the railway tunnel, but he also held the coast road, leaving, between the mountain and the sea, a few self-propelled guns, covering his demolitions and mining parties. From the mountain he had excellent observation and "swanning" tank officers, doing reconnaissances in the forward defended localities of the Rifle Brigade, with immaculate white belts and large map cases, were not popular, however they might have considered that their presence instilled confidence into the infantry man in his slit trench. Their visits were invariably followed by an unpleasant half-hour from mortars and self-propelled guns.

Meanwhile, reconnaissance had revealed a fordable crossing for tanks near the beach, which had been heavily mined, and it was decided to send a squadron of the 5th Royal Tanks by this route, while the remainder of the Regiment supported the 1/6th Queens in an attack on Mondragone and the high ground beyond. This attack, which went in at dawn on the 1st of November, was highly successful. A few tanks were lost on mines near the beach, but Mondragone was found to be clear and the Massico Ridge was occupied at small cost, a company spending a most unpleasant night in bitter cold and subject to sporadic mortar fire from the hills beyond. To add to their miseries, their ration parties which had attempted to find them in the mountains, wandered all night with their dixies full of nourishing stew, only to find, when eventually the company was located at dawn the next morning, that the strain, exhausting enough for the ration parties, had proved too much for the stew, which had gone bad. As a consolation, they were, the next morning, relieved by a company of the Rifle Brigade, who, apart from getting a front view of the battle in the plain below, suffered no further inconvenience, as the enemy were clearly withdrawing over the Garigliano three miles beyond.

The tanks, though heavily shelled, and much hampered by demolitions, continued to work round between the mountains and the sea and next day pushed on towards Cicola, finally captured after a sharp fight, and towards Sessa Aurunca, where we joined up with 46th Division who had taken the mountain route.

This was the last action the Division fought in Italy. 1st Battalion the Rifle Brigade took over a scattered line, some four thousand yards from the Garigliano, with two motor companies, having virtually to build a road to get them there. The remainder of the Division less a squadron of 5th Royal Tanks and 11th Hussars remained behind the Massico in reserve. There was no intention of crossing the Garigliano on our part, and we rather came to the conclusion that the enemy held the same opinion. We were prepared to concede him the right of shelling the road as it came out from behind the Massico, because it was extremely dusty and in full view from the mountains behind

Approaching the Garigliano River

Minturno, but towards the end of our stay he sent both standing and fighting patrols across, resulting in several engagements—scarcely fair tactics against troops who, although not officially informed, firmly believed that they were going home, rumour asserting that various other regiments had been told officially. Possibly to compensate for this disagreeable activity, the enemy very sportingly arranged a small mortar concentration near a party, conspicuous in white corduroy trousers, who were endeavouring to flush the duck in the marshes near the river mouth. Whether this was the intention, we shall never know; it may only have been bad shooting, but the effect upon the duck was truly remarkable.

On the 7th, the last of the Rifle Brigade left the line to rejoin 22nd Armoured Brigade around Aversa. Everyone was in excellent spirits, for the great news of our imminent return home had been officially proclaimed. Vehicles were handed over to the 5th Canadian Armoured Division, somewhat to the surprise of the latter, for some of the "B" vehicles had been with the division since the previous February, when they had been obtained second hand from 4th Indian

Division. Several thousand miles, mostly over open desert, had not subsequently improved them. However, all that could be done was done, and it was a misfortune that the crews, who had worked so hard to freshen up tanks and vehicles as much as possible, should have had to hand them over in a field several inches deep in mud.

The Division then moved to concentrate on the Northern side of the Sorrento Peninsula, which had been completely untouched by the war. Billets were comfortable and life agreeable. although the amenities of this resort were, for the most of the time, obscured by rain. In a short time, the Division, in spite of the shortage of new battledress, returned to the peaceful glory of gleaming brasses and white equipment. Little could be done in the way of training, and not even every man possessed a rifle, but to the astonishment of the Italians, who clearly had little use for martial exercises, parades and physical training were carried out in the narrow streets and piazzi of the coastal towns.

Recreation was naturally limited, but a lucky, and usually rather wet, few undertook trips to Capri, by courtesy of the Navy, and also to Ravello and Amalfi on the South coast. Meanwhile, the remainder went into Naples to buy up what little was left in the shops at fantastic prices, to visit the cinema and other sources of entertainment, whose dangers were frankly exposed by the area authorities on large hoardings. Cinemas were established in all the towns but dances were not a success as the Italians were either too nervous of being unable to compete against the soldier's charm, or too conscious of female frailty to allow their women folk to attend. Indeed, the principal recreation was scanning the bay for the convoy that was to take us home, in which various coasters, and two Liberty ships, anchored permanently off Castellamare, played a leading part. Meanwhile, advance parties had already arrived at the docks to supervise the loading of the three ships in the convoy. The baggage officer on each ship had the hardest part, for the amount of baggage per man, and particularly per officer, bore little relation to the official scale. However, by the time we sailed the cases of oranges, lemons, and nuts had been safely stowed away, in some cases on top of the baggage of those units that had disembarked from the ships that we were to use. Early on the 20th, the Division, after a short night's rest in a wet and uncomfortable camp, moved down from Casoria to embark, spending the greater part of the morning in an almost stationary queue through the streets of Naples. By four o'clock in the afternoon all were on board and the convoy weighed anchor.

The voyage home was uneventful. The celebration of Christmas and New Year on board passed comparatively quietly, although the ships could scarcely be described as "dry" except from the official point of view. In one ship, the permanent Officer Commanding Troops was distinguished by a passion for boat drill, and for heartening addresses on this subject, an enthusiasm which was scarcely shared by his charges. Fortunately these constant rehearsals for abandoning ship were not put into practice, in spite of the enemy's promise to prevent the return home of the 7th Armoured Division, declared over Rome wireless.

On the 7th of January, 1944, the Division docked at Glasgow. The trains were already waiting, and it was not long, considering the delays necessarily imposed by military ocean travel, before we were on our way to Norfolk.

CHAPTER III

ENGLAND: TRAINING AND RECREATION

January, 1944—May, 1944

131 Brigade were well cared for in the choice of billets, being for the most part quartered in civilisation around King's Lynn.

The Armoured Brigade was perhaps less fortunate in the Brandon area. Our misgivings had already been aroused by the publication of an article in "Country Life" which, while attributing to the district considerable importance for both archæology and ornithology, made it clear that it possessed few, if any, other amenities. "Country Life" was right. Eager watchers, at the windows of the long troop trains, saw flat black fenland give way to sandy heath; Brandon station gave a glimpse at least of houses and a pub; but the Troop Carrying Vehicles into which we were detrained carried us inexorably away from this brief vision of paradise, farther and farther into the waste, depositing us mercilessly into groups of decayed Nissen huts, clustered beneath the tall pines. The 4th County of London Yeomanry were perhaps the most unfortunate, the greater part of their camp having been constructed well below the water-level for the district, and they glared enviously at their neighbours, perched on their sandy islands above the waste. NCOs complained of the inadequacy of one hut for their Platoons or Troops; Colour Serjeants enquired bitterly how they were expected to put the stores into "that there 'ole there", and deep inroads were made into the coal stocks before it was discovered that this commodity was, in England, severely rationed.

Meanwhile, throughout the Division, officers and NCOs attempted to solve the mysteries of home documentation; victory was achieved, and within three or four days the Division went on leave. Sunburnt faces and white equipment startled barmen with their harsh cries in Arabic, and Military Policemen with the slight vagaries in their dress; occasionally old ladies, with memories of an earlier invasion, enquired anxiously whether our "Kangaroos" meant that we were Australians. It was a month before the majority of the Division was reassembled, and, in the intervening period, much had been done to organise administration. Cooks had to be taken off water-trucks and forced to cook within the limitations of home ration and coal issues; the NAAFI, the local breweries and wine merchants throughout the country cajoled into accepting new customers; week-end leave trains were extracted from the LNER as a special concession, and leave transport was organised to Wisbech, March and King's Lynn. Quartermasters and Colour Serjeants returned, not without affection, to home exactitude in accounting for stores and barrack damages.

Until we should be concentrated for the invasion, units had to be re-equipped and trained with new, and in some cases unfamiliar, vehicles and weapons; trained in the workings of a European war establishment; trained and practised in combined operations at the Divisional School at Yarmouth, and made to relearn the old lessons of training from a troop or platoon to a regimental or battalion level. On the 11th of February, Major-General Erskine addressed all officers of the Division at Mumford Cinema, and told them the nature of the coming battle, a rough outline of the plans, and the training which was to be carried out.

New tanks and other vehicles arrived slowly, frequently having to be driven on their tracks long distances in order to reach the Divisional area. When they did arrive it was found that in order to make them battle-worthy by our standards, vital modifications had to be carried out, as for example to the escape hatches of the Cromwells. The home war establishment obliged us to receive vehicles, such as Loyd carriers, which we could not consider suitable for the tasks required of them, or else imposed restrictions which we felt to be unworkable. Units had to train with vehicles which, in the case of the 1st Rifle Brigade, were of a type totally different to those they would be using in battle; and in most cases were continually hampered by shortages in supply and by the uncertainty of war establishments. Ranges were inadequate, and in some cases far distant, continually involving an anxious battle for rail-flats. Training areas were restricted. Moreover, to add to our problems, on arrival at home, the 11th Hussars, who had been with us so long, were replaced by an Armoured Reconnaissance Regiment, the 8th Hussars, equipped substantially as an Armoured Regiment, but without any armament heavier than a 75 mm, and with a higher proportion of light reconnaissance vehicles. In fact, we soon got the 11th Hussars back and the 8th Hussars, in practice, functioned as a fourth armoured regiment within the frame-work of the armoured brigade.

This was also a period of visitations, by both royal and other distinguished persons. On the 17th of February the Commander-in-Chief of the Twenty-first Army Group, General, as he was then, Montgomery toured the Division, a day of bitter cold and snow. On the 24th of February, more fortunate in his weather, His Majesty the King inspected us, and in many cases Colonels-in-Chief and Colonels of units took the opportunity to pay them a visit.

Time and the training facilities available precluded much activity on large-scale exercises, and in addition we were also responsible for the training of the 8th and 33rd Armoured Brigades. But apart from nights in the cold and wet by individual Battalions and Regiments, 131 Brigade contrived to get through two aptly-named exercises, "Shudder" and "Shiver", and even Divisional Headquarters, not to be outdone, indulged, with a similar sense of the appropriate, in an exercise "Charpoy"*. We also succeeded in impressing the Russian Military Mission with the smartness of the Guard of Honour from the 1/5th Queens at King's Lynn, and the speed with which the Commander Royal Engineers succeeded in bringing up his bridgelayer at an exercise held for 33rd Armoured Brigade, in spite of the unkind assertion that, having had prior information as to the location of the obstacle, he had prudently concealed his bridgelayer behind an adjacent bush. We concluded with a large-scale TEWT (Tactical Exercise Without Troops) extending from the Wash to Thetford, which included, in addition to the Division, 8th and 33rd Armoured Brigades and 56th Infantry Brigade, and was in fact a rehearsal of what we were required to do in Normandy.

For most of us this period of training was agreeable enough. We were not overworked and had considerably greater opportunities for leave and recreation than those to which the home army were accustomed, but for Commanders and their Staffs the uncertainty and difficulty of these problems added much to their already heavy enough responsibilities in the planning of future operations.

* Hindustani: "a bed".

Chapter IV

THE INVASION OF EUROPE: FIRST BATTLE OF VILLERS BOCAGE AND SUBSEQUENT DEFENCE OF THE BRIDGEHEAD

May, 1944—the 1st of July, 1944

The place selected for the invasion of Europe, namely the stretch of coast between the mouths of the rivers Orne and Vire, was perhaps one of the best kept secrets of the war. Before describing the Division's part in the planning and the execution of the initial battles, it is worth while to review briefly the enemy's situation, and the country to be fought over, in order to understand the reason for this choice and the nature of the subsequent fighting.

By the end of 1941, having lost the battle for air supremacy, the Germans abandoned all plans to force a decision in the west by offensive sea-borne operations. The initiative was now in the hands of the Allies, and to counter it, the Germans set to work to fortify the coast of Europe from Norway to the Bay of Biscay, and also along the North Mediterranean. Clearly it was impracticable to fortify every mile with the same degree of strength, even excluding those areas in which natural obstacles needed no reinforcement. They were therefore forced to concentrate upon the ports and those areas which seemed the most likely objectives for a landing: in their view the beaches of the Pas de Calais and Flanders, from which the British Army had been evacuated in 1940. By the beginning of 1944, however, steps had been taken to secure a more even distribution of defensive strength, and much work was put into building new defences, in addition to improving existing obstacles along other sections of the coast. But time and the necessary equipment were insufficient and we found that many emplacements on the Normandy coast, designed for coastal artillery, in fact contained only field guns.

The enemy's plan was to defend the coast-line with tired, second-rate Divisions containing a high proportion of foreigners. Behind them were field infantry divisions for immediate counter-attack, and concentrated in strategic areas to the rear were the Panzer, Parachute and Infantry divisions of the counter-offensive force. It was hoped that the coastal defences would hold up the landing and subsequent build-up sufficiently long to allow the counter-offensive forces to be assembled for a crushing blow which would drive the invaders into the sea. Thus by "D" Day, the coastal crust on Second Army's front was held by one second-line infantry division, with two of its regiments in the line occupying static concrete positions scattered along the coast at intervals of approximately 2000 yards. Behind them, South-West of Bayeux, was 352 Infantry Division. The two nearest Panzer Divisions, 12 SS and 21 Panzer Divisions, were within easy reach at Falaise and Bernay respectively; while two further Panzer Divisions, 17 SS South of the Loire and 2 Panzer at Amiens, would probably get into position by the evening of D+1. These Divisions were equipped mainly with Panther and Tiger Tanks, both more heavily armoured than our own tanks, and mounting a gun which, in the case of the Panther, was the equal of our 17 pounder, with the additional advantage that it could fire HE, and, in the case of the Tiger, superior to any tank or anti-tank gun we possessed. In the Normandy fighting their heavy armour and

Bayeux

armament amply compensated for any disadvantage they might have had due to their lack of speed, though this latter factor, coupled with a lower standard of mechanical reliability, was to tell heavily against the enemy during the great advances.

The Normandy countryside is sharply divided between the "campagne" and the "bocage", with a narrow belt of marsh-land running along the greater part of the sea-shore. The "campagne" consists mainly of open, rolling plain, almost entirely under crops, intersected by narrow and well-wooded river valleys. Its villages are of compact, solid, grey-stone buildings centred around the tall towers of their rich churches, and ringed with orchards. Trees are few and mostly confined to the roads or occasional woods. From the coast this belt is at its narrowest around Bayeux, gradually widening out slightly South of the main Bayeux—Caen road and extending to a broad belt between the rivers Orne and Dives as far as Falaise. To the West and South-West of Bayeux was the "bocage". If viewed from above it appears almost continuous forest, but in fact it is a maze of small fields and numerous orchards, surrounded by high-banked hedges of pollarded trees. Apart from the main roads, endless narrow, muddy tracks, almost tunnels between the tall hedges of thorns, briars, gorse, broom and hazel, connect the hamlets and small farms. The "bocage" is not, however, everywhere so impenetrable, and South-East of Caumont towards Aunay and the Orne valley is a pleasant country of open pasture and cornland interspersed with numerous small woods and orchards. Above all towers Mont Pinçon, its lower slope covered in thick woods, chestnuts, beeches, oaks and firs, and its summit open heather and gorse, a ridge which was to be our objective for so long. When we did finally ascend it we found that, owing to the close nature of the countryside, its tactical value for observation was negligible.

Briefly then, the coast of Calvados was selected as being the most suitable accessible beach with a reasonable road-net behind. The only approaches on the enemy's side lay over the Seine or the Loire, whose bridges had received the full attention of the RAF, and on the West flank lay the tempting prize of Cherbourg at the head of the narrow Cotentin peninsula. The Allied plan was to land on a front of some thirty miles, protected by initial air-borne landings, with the Americans making for the crossings over the Vire and thence for Cherbourg, and the British securing the crossings over the Orne and the road centres of Bayeux and Caen. In particular, on Second Army's front, three main landings were to be made, following the initial Commando and Airborne landings, whose objective was the crossings over the River Orne, North of Caen; on the left-hand sector 1st British Corps with 3rd British and 3rd Canadian Divisions, supported in each case by an Armoured Brigade; on the right-hand sector, on the Arromanches and le Hamel beaches, 30 Corps with 50th Division, supported by 8th Armoured Brigade. The subsequent build-up, in the absence of a natural harbour, was to be operated from a pre-fabricated artificial port —the "Mulberry".

Planning at the Divisional level for these operations comprised, first, the operational and intelligence plans; secondly, the shipping plan.

"Mulberry"

For this purpose a Tactical Headquarters was set up with Second Army at Ashley Gardens, near Victoria Station, an arrangement that permitted the cares of planning, at least for the junior staff, to be lightened by other attractions.

There was much work to be got through in a very limited period, in the analysis of air photographs, intelligence reports, and the preparation of maps and diagrams, arrangements for concentration areas near the embarkation ports, liaison with the naval forces involved, numerous conferences, and finally the continual stream of amendments to earlier plans inevitable in an operation of this kind.

The shipping plan, in essence, was simple enough. The Armoured Brigade, less 1st Battalion the Rifle Brigade, was to sail in assault landing craft, landing on "D" Day and D+1, whilst the Infantry Brigade, the operational section of the echelons and the bulk of the headquarters were to sail in Liberty ships and coasters. In theory, therefore, equipped with the knowledge of the number and the capacity of the ships it should have been possible to fill them in the most economical manner with those vehicles and men most urgently required. In fact, owing to constant fluctuations in the war establishments and shipping allotment, inevitable as different services and different formations struggled to secure the acceptance of their claims, no final decision was achieved until shortly before we moved to the concentration area. The loading of the landing ships and craft at Ipswich was arranged by the Divisional Principal Military Landing Officer and his harassed staff which was a considerable convenience, as, although he was equally involved in the sudden and unexpected appearance of strange and vital units of the Navy, Base RE or RAF in his ships, he was, at least, on the spot in both the planning and embarkation stages to make a final decision. The Liberty ships and coasters were to have been loaded in accordance with the tables prepared by the War Office, usually supplied by formations with inadequate data of the types and numbers of men and vehicles, but, in fact, their meticulous plans were, as far as the Division was concerned, sometimes ignored by knowledgeable men in bowler hats who leant over the side of the ship shouting: "Bring on that one there; ———— what the bloody officers say, I bin loading ships for forty years and know what they'll 'old." In fairness to the men in bowler hats they were right, and the caravans and cook-houses which, according to the War Office, were supposed to be some two feet less than their actual height, were accommodated without difficulty, even though this was little consolation for the ardours and anxieties of the previous few weeks. Meanwhile, the remainder of the Division stayed behind, waiting its turn in accordance with predetermined, but much amended, priority tables to fill those ships that returned from the Beaches. By all accounts this period was not wasted.

Early in May, the greater part of the Division moved down from Norfolk to concentrate and complete water-proofing. The Armoured Brigade went to join the fleet of landing craft at Ipswich, the Infantry Brigade, the supply services, and 1st Battalion the Rifle Brigade partly to West Ham, near the London Docks, partly to Brentwood, near the Tilbury Docks.

The Movement Control and Camp staffs probably suffered most by this, Middle East nonchalance proving an easy winner against English exactitude. Harassed Movement Control Officers, grasping damp and slightly uncontrolled masses of paper, would plough their way through a maze of ticks and counter-ticks to enquire what had happened to "one 3-tonner 4 by 4, GS" which was missing from some column, only to be met with the bland assurance that it was sure to be all right, and wasn't that one of the "buckshee" ones?

The water-proofing was carried out partly by Regiments themselves, partly by the Brigade workshops and, owing to the shortage of supplies and to the frequent failure of those responsible to insert vital parts in what were alleged to be complete kits, was a nightmare. It was hard, dirty and monotonous work, and it is to the credit of those concerned that not a single vehicle was "drowned" on landing for mechanical reasons.

Accommodation was indifferent, but fortunately the worst we had to suffer were dust-storms of an almost desert intensity which swirled round the tents, and the far worse enemy of rain never appeared to make us completely miserable. Moreover, as many of the Division were now quartered within easy reach of their homes, until the camps were "sealed", much could be endured. With the sealing of the camps more serious difficulties arose, as it was felt that, with an enormous army and an enormous fleet lying for all the world to see, particularly those civilians who journeyed every day to and from the concentration area, it required little imagination on the part of any enemy agent to work out the reasons. The troops had been told nothing, so there was no danger of a lapse in security on their part, and the sudden absence from the streets of London of large numbers of "Desert Rats" might only have served to confirm the suspicion that something was imminent in the near future. Large chalked notices appeared advertising the location of "Stalag Xb", and in one camp the troops made their own somewhat liberal interpretation of the "sealing" regulations by employing a steam-roller to destroy the wire.

By the 28th of May plans were complete and the General Officer Commanding briefed all officers in the garrison cinema at Brentwood. 22nd Armoured Brigade were to land on the beaches already secured by 50th (Northumbrian) Division and to concentrate around Ryes, some two and a half miles from the beaches, starting on the evening of "D" Day. Meanwhile, 50th Division were assumed to have captured Bayeux and secured the road from there to Tilly-sur-Seulles. 22nd Armoured Brigade, with as much of the Division as was available, was then to pass through to Mont Pinçon, via Villers Bocage and Aunay-sur-Odon. Having secured a firm base on the Mont Pinçon feature, the armour was then to turn East towards Thury Harcourt and the crossings over the Orne.

On the 4th of June, 22nd Armoured Brigade embarked at Felixstowe, followed shortly by the rest of the Division from the London

An Armoured Command Vehicle is lowered into an LCT

and Tilbury Docks. The worst sufferers were those men of the Armoured Brigades in the LCTs*, vessels originally designed for short passages only, and with no permanent accommodation for troops. The naval crews, however, co-operated magnificently to lighten their discomforts by sharing sleeping and cooking facilities. The other craft, LSTs† and Liberty ships, did have arrangements of a sort, and, although misgivings were inevitable on first viewing the cramped, murky holds in which we had to live, most of us got hot food and a space to lay our bodies. In any case, to a Middle East formation, the hardships of sea-faring were nothing new.

Waterproofed vehicles unload from LCTs

Meanwhile we lay at anchor watching the enormous assembly of ships, ranging from the trim warships to the oldest and dirtiest collier that would float, and watching more anxiously the sky. The barometer was falling and a South-West wind, with sharp rain-squalls, freshening all the time. We knew the invasion was being delayed, but the

* Landing Craft Tank. † Landing Ships Tank.

question was: would we have to endure the appalling anti-climax of waiting for next month's tides? Fortunately for everyone's morale, the decision was taken to ignore the weather and carry on, and we set sail for what proved to be, comparatively, a very uneventful journey, bearing in mind that the whole fleet passed under the Channel guns in broad daylight. Innumerable patrol vessels and aircraft dropped smoke-floats to screen us, but with the strong wind these were soon dissipated. For some twenty-five minutes after sighting the French coast not a gun fired, until at last the first huge splashes rose among the convoy, some three-quarters down its length, to be followed in a few seconds by a second salvo securing a hit for'ard on one of the Liberty ships, which started to "brew", until we left her far astern enveloped in black smoke. From then on to the beaches the voyage was unopposed, and this incident was typical of the voyage of almost every convoy in the early days.

The Armoured Brigade landed successfully in the morning of D+1, the 7th of June, having been delayed twelve hours by the weather, which steadily worsened until the landing programme was soon forty-eight hours behind. Nevertheless, few vehicles were lost. More and more ships congregated off the beaches, bombed at night with singularly little effect, and occasionally shelled as they came inshore by those batteries still holding out. Indeed, the unloading of the Liberty ships was a most hazardous operation. LCTs came alongside, rising six feet amidships with every wave and constantly yawing away. While the vehicles escaped with only some strain on their springs, their crews had to jump for it from a rope ladder, involving a considerable degree of physical and nervous agility, particularly to those whose occupation was normally sedentary.

Tanks land at Arromanches

The Armoured Brigade, less 1st Rifle Brigade and much of its transport, having successfully concentrated by the evening of the 7th of June, the next morning was required to take part in a series of what were, in fact, purely infantry operations until the 12th of June. 50th Division had been successful in their landing, had captured Bayeux intact, and advanced South on the Tilly and Caen roads for about three miles, with their flanks resting on the rivers Aure and Seulles. Enemy pockets, however, still remained North of Bayeux at Sully and Port-en-Bessin, which 56th Brigade, supported by 5th Royal Tanks, were given to clear. This task proved typical of all tank fighting in the bocage. The closeness of the country meant that tanks and anti-tank guns usually engaged at ranges of fifty yards and upwards. Infantry could approach unprotected tanks unseen, and once succeeded in boarding one of our tanks; and snipers, as often as not merely infantry soldiers offensively trained in the use of the rifle, were extremely active. However, the regiment, after much hard fighting, succeeded in destroying four 88 mm guns, one 75 mm gun and one self-propelled 20 mm. Meanwhile, 1st Royal Tanks and 4th County of London Yeomanry spent an uneventful day in defensive positions supporting 69th Infantry Brigade in the St. Leger area and 151st Brigade in the area of Jerusalem cross-roads.

By the 10th of June, it was considered that the build-up was sufficiently advanced for offensive operations by armour directed on Tilly-sur-Seulles and Villers Bocage. No unexpected enemy formations had so far been identified, except for two battalions of cyclists with a few self-propelled guns whose intervention North-West of Bayeux, after an exhausting pedal, had had no appreciable effect upon the battle. 352nd Infantry Division were in front of us and 12 SS fighting on our left, North-West of Caen. 8th Armoured Brigade had made good progress and were now in the outskirts of St. Pierre less than a mile from Tilly. Accordingly, the plan was to pass 22nd Armoured Brigade through 50th Division, and to follow up with 56th Brigade who came under command for this operation. 5th Royal Tanks were to advance on the right to Verrières, through Blary, Ellon and Folliott, and 4th County of London Yeomanry, on the left, down the main road to Tilly and Juvigny. 1st Royal Tanks, as the Regiment most behind hand in the build-up, was to stay behind, guarding the bridges over the Seulles. The artillery available was our own two Royal Horse Artillery Regiments, 86th Field Regiment and 64th Medium Regiment, and the infantry had under command a self-propelled Battery of the Norfolk Yeomanry, our Anti-tank Regiment.

The advance began at a quarter to six on the morning of the 10th, and the leading tanks of the 5th Royal Tank Regiment made slow progress down the sunken roads towards Ellon, although one troop, somewhat to its own astonishment, and to the considerable surprise of the enemy, succeeded in entering a German leaguer, where they destroyed a Mark IV. Once again, however, the tanks were up against infiltrating enemy infantry, snipers, and a strongly held road-block near Ellon. An attempt to work round farther to the left towards Bernières Bocage met with no greater success, two Cromwells being lost to a Panther in the village. The next morning an attempt was again made towards Bernières Bocage. The reconnaissance troop worked on a mile beyond the village, and opposition seemed to have diminished; but enemy reinforcements with a self-propelled gun had come up into the woods, and destroyed one of the leading Honeys of the reconnaissance troop. A platoon of the Rifle Brigade which attempted to clear part of these woods without close tank support found itself rushed by forty infantry and suffered severe casualties. Clearly what was required was more infantry, and a company of the 2nd Battalion the Essex Regiment came up, cleared the village and the surrounding woods, while the advance continued through Ellon and Folliott until open cornfields were met East of the road Bernières Bocage to Folliott. Here the going seemed more promising, but Mark Vs were met, concealed in the thick woods East of Bernières Bocage; a Sherman 17-pounder was hit, and a German tank stalked the tanks of the right-hand troop along a sunken road, destroying two tanks with two rounds. Once again the Essex attacked and secured their objective, and although heavily counter-attacked during the night by a company of infantry, supported by two Mark IV flame-throwing tanks, they held their ground in spite of heavy casualties, and destroyed one tank with a Piat and damaged the other. Thereafter the 5th Royal Tanks, with the 8th Hussars and 2nd Essex, remained in position to cover the right flank.

On the left the 4th County of London Yeomanry were fighting the same sort of battle. Opposition was first met in the woods and houses around the cross-roads at Jerusalem. Three platoons of "A" Company

Jerusalem

the Rifle Brigade then led off to clear the area. A Mark IV was met on the road just to the North of the cross-roads and reported to the tanks, who destroyed it before it could fire. In the area of the houses, a further two tanks were met who engaged the riflemen, but after missing the tanks they moved away, probably nervous of the 5th Royal Tanks in the Ellon area, and the village was occupied. Sniping continued, however, all day, until in the evening the village was cleared by the 1st South Wales Borderers, a task which tanks alone could not undertake. Meanwhile, having secured the right flank towards the 5th Royal Tanks, the remainder of the Regiment attempted a flanking movement towards Ste Bazaire, some two thousand yards to the North-East of Jerusalem. The advance was at first hindered by 8th Armoured Brigade in the area of the river, who knocked out two tanks before recognition was established. In fairness to 8th Armoured Brigade, it had not been possible to send them a Liaison Officer from the Brigade as insufficient scout cars equipped with wireless were available, and the Cromwell tank, seen at intervals through the close country, bore a strong resemblance to the German Mark IV. Moreover, for some time, they had been virtually cut off by infantry and tanks who had infiltrated behind them. But eventually recognition was established and the advance continued. The Rifle Brigade, supported by 5th Royal Horse Artillery, occupied Ste Bazaire and later, closely supported by the tanks, worked down to the woods North of Bucéels.

It was clear by now that more infantry would be required to press the attack down the main road through Bucéels, and the 2nd Gloucesters, supported by "A" Squadron, entered the village and secured the bridges to the South, knocking out one Mark IV and taking some prisoners. But darkness was coming on, and with no very clear idea as to the enemy's strength in Tilly and to the North, it was decided to leaguer for the night, and push on over the bridges with the reconnaissance troop the next morning. The night passed without incident, and at first light the advance continued, meeting two Mark Vs and an anti-tank gun on the road some five hundred yards North of Tilly. One Mark V and the anti-tank gun were destroyed by the tanks from a flank, and the second Mark V attacked the infantry but was destroyed by a Piat. Further advance, after this promising start, proved impossible. The tanks attempted a flanking movement to the West, only to lose a complete troop to well-sited anti-tank guns, and the infantry were held in their attack from the North by the accurate fire of enemy mortars, guns, and small arms. A troop of tanks did, however, get across the main road to the East of the town and shot up some enemy infantry and an anti-tank gun. Meanwhile, the enemy had worked back round the bridges at Bucéels and the Regimental group, in the absence of further troops to protect their rear, had to withdraw to their positions of the preceding night. The next morning, a further attempt was made to work round Tilly to the West through Verrières. Enemy infantry were met in the outskirts of the village, reinforced by a tank and an anti-tank gun. The infantry were engaged with hand-grenades from the tanks, and the tank, after withdrawing into the village, returned to knock out one of our own. Finally, a last attempt was made, on the morning of the 12th, to continue towards Tilly and Hottot with two Battalions of 131 Brigade, who had by now arrived, supported by the 1st Royal Tanks, but this met with no more success than the attacks of the previous day.

By midday on the 12th of June, the Division's attack was virtually at a standstill. The enemy, who turned out to be Panzer Lehr Division, was well able to hold his own along the line Verrières-Tilly with his infantry, supported by tanks, and had inflicted upon us considerable losses in men and tanks, from the cover of the woods and villages. The Divisional Commander, therefore, was ordered to disengage and to attempt to expand the bridgehead by advancing along the network of secondary roads leading down to Villers Bocage between Balleroy and the valley of the Aure. Slightly to the West of this area, good progress was being made by the American 5th Corps who were reporting little opposition on their advance on Caumont, and there seemed at the time a good chance of turning the left flank of the Panzer Lehr Division by using the armour in an offensive as opposed to a supporting role.

8th Hussars, who up till now had been watching the right flank of the Division, were to lead, followed by the 4th County of London Yeomanry, with "A" Company of the 1st Rifle Brigade. The remainder of 22nd Armoured Brigade was made up as follows: a troop of the 4th Field Squadron, Royal Engineers, 5th Royal Horse Artillery, less a Battery, 1/7th Queen's Royal Regiment, 5th Royal Tanks, two Companies of the Rifle Brigade, and a battery of self-propelled anti-tank guns. Their objective was Villers Bocage and the high ground to the North-East on either side of the main Caen road. 131 Brigade, with the 1st Royal Tanks, were to step up behind the armour as required, and to be ready to do this by the morning of the 13th, by which time their remaining battalion, the 1/6th Queen's Royal Regiment, was due to arrive.

The route chosen was along steep and narrow country roads through typical Bocage country, through the villages of Trungy, St. Paul du Vernay, Ste Honorine de Duchy, La Mirerie, Livry and Briquessard, avoiding the two main roads running South from Bayeux to Villers Bocage, upon which, it was felt, enemy would certainly be met. By two o'clock in the afternoon 8th Hussars had got off to a good start, and it was evident that, in spite of the noise and the dust of the tanks, the enemy had been surprised. Livry, twelve miles on from Jerusalem, was the first village to be found held, with an anti-tank gun and some infantry, and it was not until eight o'clock, after "A" Company of the Rifle Brigade had put in a dismounted attack, that the village was captured. It was therefore decided not to push on farther and the column closed up and leaguered for the night. Meanwhile, contact had been made with 1st United States Infantry Division towards Caumont, and a Squadron of the 8th Hussars, protecting the left flank of the Division, had met enemy on the main road from Caumont to Caen.

At half-past five the next morning the advance continued through Briquessard and Amaye-sur-Seulles. Villers Bocage was entered without incident, although the 11th Hussars and the 8th Hussars had both contacted enemy on either side of the centre-line. "A" Squadron of the 4th County of London Yeomanry, and "A" Company of the 1st Rifle Brigade then pushed on according to plan towards the high ground to the North-East of the town. In order to clear the traffic on the roads behind, the column had to move out comparatively closed up, and it was this that gave a Mark VI tank, which suddenly appeared from a side road, its opportunity. Its first shot destroyed one of the Rifle Brigade half-tracks, thus blocking the road, and then at its own convenience, it destroyed the remainder of the half-tracks, some Honey tanks of the Reconnaissance Troop, four tanks of the Regimental Headquarters and the two OP tanks accompanying the squadron. Escape for the tanks, carriers and half-tracks was impossible, the road was embanked, obscured by flames and smoke from the burning vehicles whose crews could only seek what shelter they could from the machine gun fire, and our own tanks were powerless against the armour of the Tiger, with limitless cover at its disposal. Meanwhile "A" Squadron in the lead, with the Commanding Officer, were cut off. Their last wireless message, received at half past ten, reported that they were completely surrounded by tanks and infantry, that the position was untenable, and withdrawal impossible. Relief was equally impossible, as, in addition to the burning tanks and vehicles, the road was blocked by the same Mark VI which commanded all approaches.

What had happened was simple enough, namely, that the anticipated counter-attack by 2 Panzer Division, much delayed by our own and the United States Air Forces, was at last on its way. Both sides were using Villers Bocage as the most important road-centre South of Bayeux, and the Division, advancing from the North, had met the German armour coming up in the opposite direction. As a result, there followed the brilliant defensive battle of Villers Bocage which, although it obliged us to withdraw some seven miles, cost the enemy casualties quite disproportionate to this gain.

Meanwhile, with the forces available, a hasty defence of Villers Bocage was organised. "B" Squadron of the 4th County of London Yeomanry moved up to block the entrances to the village, and almost immediately found themselves engaged in a tank battle with Mark VIs and IVs. At the same time the 1/7th Queens had been ordered up from the high ground to the East. The anti-tank guns were hastily got into position, and as the leading company made contact with the reserve Squadron, "C", of the 4th County of London Yeomanry, a Tiger tank suddenly appeared from a side road and proceeded to blow down a corner house in the main square where the troops were assembled. The infantry dispersed into the houses with Piats, while the tanks and the six-pounders of the infantry disposed themselves to block all the

Knocked out Tiger in Villers Bocage

entrances to the main street. But superior fire-power told, and more tanks succeeded in getting through, only to be completely bottled up by particularly fine work on the part of a tank-hunting party of the Queens, the six-pounders and a troop of "B" Squadron. The fighting was at point-blank range, and at one time a Mark VI was being engaged through a shop-front by a Cromwell in a side-street. A Company of the Queens then attempted to work through to the railway station on the South-Western outskirts of the town, only to be met by more tanks, of which four Mark VIs were claimed as destroyed by their anti-tank guns. By four o'clock in the afternoon the village was still ours and the enemy had lost six Mark VIs and three Mark IVs. The tank attack having been smashed, a more serious threat, that of infantry infiltration, supported by heavy shell-fire, had developed, and this was a threat with which the slender forces available, the remains of two squadrons of tanks and the scattered men of a single infantry battalion, were unable to deal. Moreover, the enemy infantry were also pushing on towards the Eastern outskirts of the town. By this time the remainder of the Brigade, reinforced by the 1/5th Queens, had taken up a battle position on the high ground to the East of Tracy Bocage, with 131 Brigade, reduced to the 1/6th Queens and the 1st Royal Tanks, protecting the long open left flank to the East of Caumont. It was impossible to hold Villers Bocage with its present garrison, and to have reinforced the position with further infantry would have risked the entire force being cut off, as 50th Division had not succeeded in advancing beyond their positions of the previous morning. Accordingly, the decision was taken to withdraw the garrison into the area already held by the rest of the Armoured Brigade. Covered by fire from the 5th Royal Horse Artillery, the infantry withdrew first, followed by the tanks, whose final withdrawal was screened by smoke from the gunners.

The plan was to hold on East of Amaye-sur-Seulles until the advance of 50th Division on our left relieved us, and the bulk of the Division formed a tight "box", some two thousand yards from East to West, and one thousand five hundred yards from North to South. To the East the 1/7th Queens occupied the line of a sunken track running across a knoll of rolling corn-land, with a narrow valley behind; to the North of the valley were the 1st Rifle Brigade on a wooded feature astride the main road to Villers Bocage, with a company closing the gap between 1/7th and 1/5th Queens; and to the West the 1/5th Queens with the 4th County of London Yeomanry held a reverse slope, amid orchards and farm-buildings. During the day the 5th Royal Tanks occupied battle positions towards Villers Bocage and on the flanks of the infantry, withdrawing at night behind them. In reserve were two Squadrons of the 8th Hussars. The guns of the 5th Royal Horse Artillery were in position roughly in the centre, while from outside magnificent support was given by the 3rd Royal Horse Artillery, 5th Army Group Royal Artillery, consisting of medium and heavy guns, and the 186th United States Field Artillery Battalion, whose co-operation during this difficult period will always be remembered. For the most part the "box", owing to its narrow perimeter, was overlooked from all sides, and crammed with vehicles, while the woods and broken ground of the surrounding country gave ample scope for enemy infantry and tanks to approach and form up unseen.

The evening and night of the 13th passed anxiously but without undue incident, the enemy contenting himself with active patrolling against the Southern flanks of the position, sniping, and a little shelling. On the morning of the 14th, the 5th Royal Tanks once more moved out, and the remainder of the Brigade set about improving their positions and patrolling. Enemy were found on both flanks and across the road leading back to Briquessard. As the day progressed the shelling increased; one or two vehicles inside the box were "brewed up"; and enemy activity in the woods and orchards became considerably more noticeable, giving good targets for the artillery. By eleven o'clock this patrolling materialised into an attack, delivered on the left-hand company of the 1/7th Queens. Once more great execution was done by mortars and artillery, but the enemy succeeded in penetrating the area of one platoon, being driven off in a spirited counter-attack with Sten guns and grenades by the rest of the Company, which successfully discouraged further attempts on this flank. Thereafter he contented himself with accurate and heavy mortar fire on the exposed positions of the 1/7th Queens.

Meanwhile, 131 Brigade, on the morning of the 14th, set off to clear the road from Livry to the "island" as it came to be known. Briquessard was occupied successfully, and near Amaye the tanks of the 1st Royal Tanks made contact with a patrol of the 11th Hussars coming up in the opposite direction. A Squadron of the 8th Hussars had by now worked down to a commanding feature two thousand yards South of the road to Villers Bocage, and Amaye and the area round it were occupied by a Squadron of the 1st Royal Tanks and a company of the 1/6th Queens. The enemy were still both North and South of them, shelling and making constant attempts to probe their defences with infantry through the thick set hedges and orchards bordering the stream running through Amaye, and further West up the river valley from Cahagnes. But, having been repulsed in his attempt to break through the "island" from the direction of Villers Bocage, he now turned his attention to cutting the road behind it, and at four o'clock the tanks and infantry guarding the Southern approaches to Amaye saw infantry approaching to within a few hundred yards of their position through the orchards. These were immediately engaged by Besas when the commander of the left-hand tank spotted the muzzle brake of a tank moving along a hedge behind the infantry. It was fired upon but continued across the line of fire of the remaining tanks of the troop. Three hits forced the turret crew to bale out, and the tank was finally destroyed as the driver attempted to move it back to cover. Meanwhile a second tank appeared making for the high ground around Point 198, from which the 8th Hussars had by now been withdrawn. After attempting to find cover behind a bush, it was stopped as it tried to withdraw. The accompanying infantry still persisted, however, and were finally halted by the Besa fire of the tanks.

By now it was clear that nothing was to be gained by remaining in our precarious position with enemy both North and South, and little hope of a speedy advance by 50th Division, who were having a difficult time with Panzer Lehr. At four o'clock in the afternoon the Divisional Commander ordered a withdrawal to the Briquessard area, where we would be in contact with the Americans on our right and would be able to cover, at least by patrolling, the lightly-held enemy salient between our left and the right hand troops of 50th Division. 131 Brigade were to hold the road open while 22nd Armoured Brigade withdrew through them, dropping off the two infantry Battalions on their arrival to take up defensive positions in Briquessard and the wooded ridge running to the North. The 5th Royal Tanks, with a company of the 1/7th Queens carried on the tanks, were to form the rearguard, and the withdrawal was planned to start immediately after last light, at half-past eleven.

However, before the withdrawal could be achieved, the enemy made one last attempt to eliminate the "island" position entirely, this time from the South. At about half-past six a considerable increase in enemy patrol activity became noticeable, and tanks, mostly Mark VIs, were seen to be forming up. Half an hour later came the attack itself, by two battalions of Panzer Grenadiers supported by tanks. This attack was destroyed mainly by the artillery and mortars, and the few troops that did succeed in penetrating the forward positions of the 1/5th Queens were quickly destroyed by small arms fire and by the guns of two troops of the 4th County of London Yeomanry who came up to help. Owing to the country, it was a close range battle, and for a time "G" Battery, 5th Royal Horse Artillery, were engaging enemy infantry with air-burst and Bren guns at four hundred yards range. This attack cost the enemy some seven to eight hundred casualties, and, owing to the vigorous anti-tank defence of the close perimeter, eight Mark IV tanks were destroyed as they attempted to penetrate the position. By eight o'clock the enemy had recognised defeat, and at half-past midnight our own tired columns, without lights and in clouds of dust, set out. The noise of the tanks was for the most part drowned by artillery fire and the noise of a heavy bomber attack, and the 1st Royal Tanks, standing to all night inside their tanks waiting for 22nd Armoured Brigade to go through, were undisturbed by the enemy. He did indeed shell the centre line, causing casualties and destroying some vehicles, but as the first light of dawn appeared the 1st Royal Tanks drove out unmolested.

The battle of the "island" was a defensive victory of great importance. As we learnt later, 2 Panzer Division's intention was to drive a wedge between the British and American armies through Balleroy and the Forêt de Cérisy beyond. In fact, to their great surprise they met the Division at Villers Bocage, and were forced to fight an offensive battle in close country which undoubtedly favoured anti-tank defence, particularly the six-pounder anti-tank gun with Sabot ammunition which, in view of the short ranges imposed by the country, was probably the most effective anti-tank weapon we possessed. In order to support the Panzer Grenadiers, their tanks were forced to close with our anti-tank guns, but even so were unable to prevent the annihilation of the infantry by our concentrated artillery fire. The result was that, temporarily, 2 Panzer Division, at a crucial stage in the landings, when the build-up was much delayed by the weather, was severely crippled for a time as an effective offensive force. Our own losses had not been light, but bore no comparison with the enemy's. Of the prisoners taken quite a few managed to escape back to our own lines, including one Sergeant of the 8th Hussars, who succeeded in strangling one of his guards and brought the other one back with him in an amphibious Volkswagen. For the next three weeks the Division settled down to the uneasy stalemate of Bocage fighting, with its patrolling, sniping, shelling and mortaring, and our infantry, weary though they were, never lost the ascendancy gained at Villers Bocage.

By the middle of June, in spite of the weather, the battle for the bridgehead had been won, and for the Allies the decisive battles were being fought in the Cherbourg Peninsula, and by 8th Corps to the North-West of Caen. The Division's part in the fighting was limited to a defensive battle with the Infantry Brigade and 1st Battalion The Rifle Brigade in roughly the area to which we had withdrawn after Villers Bocage.

Originally, as we have seen, the plan was to hold Briquessard cross-roads and the ridge running thence to the North, an area which was "bocage" at its worst. However, on the night of the 16th, 2 Panzer Division made one more probing attack, after a very considerable amount of accurate shelling on the village. Two battalions of a Panzer Grenadier Regiment were involved, supported by a few Tigers. The enemy infantry worked their way through the orchards with considerable skill and forced the leading company of a battalion of the Queens to withdraw slightly, although not before a Tiger had been knocked out at a hundred and fifty yards range by one of the seventeen-pounders of the anti-tank regiment. Meanwhile, the defensive fire of the artillery, mortars and tanks was doing its customary execution, with the result that the second battalion of the Panzer Grenadiers never got started at all, and a rapid counter-attack was able to eject what remained of the enemy infantry in the village and to recapture the seventeen-pounder.

It was then decided that the advantage of holding Briquessard as a jumping-off place was outweighed by the casualties which would result, and the three battalions of Queens were reorganised along the reverse slope of the ridge, with the Rifle Brigade on their left around Le Pont Mulot. The five thousand yards between the left-hand companies of the Rifle Brigade and 50th Division East of St. Paul du Vernay were covered by the 8th Hussars, who did much excellent patrolling under difficult circumstances, owing to the noise and dust of the tanks, which made movement impossible to conceal. Later, a slight advance by 50th Division, which brought 56th Brigade into the area, did much to secure this flank, for, on one occasion, a Panther had suddenly appeared within eight hundred yards of Divisional Headquarters at St. Paul du Vernay, and foot patrols were not unknown in that area. There was no real task for the armour, which was withdrawn into reserve around Ste Honorine de Ducy. The enemy's policy was much the same. The villages to our front, Anctoville, St. Germain, Granville and Longraye, were held in some strength, with the tanks well back. The intervening areas were lightly held by a thin screen of machine-gun posts, which frequently changed their positions and were reinforced by night. In accordance with his usual policy he kept up harassing fire with mortars and artillery upon our forward positions, and occasionally on the rear areas as well, and carried out a considerable amount of patrolling.

For our infantry it was a trying period of living in slit trenches in the rain, of suffering a steady drain in casualties from shell and mortar fire, and occasionally from snipers, all the time enclosed in the damp prison of the Bocage, the line of sight bounded by a hedge two hundred yards away. At night there was the constant anxiety of patrolling to pin down an elusive enemy, through close hedges, which were often mined, waiting for the inevitable challenge and the quick bursts of a Spandau. Typical of these encounters was that of a patrol, consisting of eight men, led by an officer, who were moving silently down a hedgerow alongside a track. Suddenly, from the corn to the right, a bolt was heard to open and shut. The patrol

La Butte

leader immediately sprayed the field with his Sten gun and a groan was heard. The patrol withdrew slightly to listen for a few seconds, until a burst of Spandau fire came down the hedge from the direction of the wounded German, followed by two five-centimetre mortar bombs which fell just in front of them. Shortly afterwards, a Verey light went up, followed by artillery fire designed to cordon off the area. Meanwhile, the patrol, who were beating the hedge and cornfield, found the German, and their task being completed, then withdrew. Naturally, not all were as eventful as this. As often as not, patrols went out, found mines or a trip wire, were fired on from a distance with the tracer going wide and high, or found and heard nothing except the enemy's echelons moving up in the distance; but the Bocage, with a perfect position for a machine gunner every few hundred yards, with its hedges, often only passable through one or two obvious gaps which could easily be mined, was very difficult country for patrolling.

It was with great relief that we handed over our positions on the 31st of June and the 1st of July to the 2nd United States Armoured Division and withdrew to a much needed rest and refit in the area West and North-West of Jerusalem, where our only enemy, in a country in which indoor billets were unobtainable, was the weather.

The only protection, for the most part, was that degree of shelter that each individual could devise with ground-sheets, gas-capes, ingenuity and "scrounging", for bivouacs and tents were unknown. Towards the end of an otherwise uneventful stay, harassing fire on the area occupied by 131 Brigade caused some casualties.

Beached LSTs at Arromanches

Thus ended, for us, the first stage of the Battle of Normandy. It had been a period of hard and bitter fighting, which, although it had achieved, as far as the Division was concerned, great defensive results, seemed to promise little from the point of view of armour as an offensive arm. Many valuable lessons had been learnt in the close co-operation of tanks and infantry, but, at the time, there seemed all too few signs of an answer to the problem of getting out in the face of the small numbers but highly effective equipment possessed by the enemy, with all the advantages that Normandy offered for its defensive employment. The only consolation appeared to lie in the still untried open country East of Caen, which offered scope for the deployment of tanks off the roads, and where, in fact, our next battle was to be fought.

Chapter V

ATTEMPTS AT BREAKING OUT OF THE BRIDGEHEAD: FIRST BATTLE OF CAEN: CAPTURE OF MONT PINCON

The 1st of July—the 14th of August, 1944

By the first weeks in July, the bridgehead had become a firm base for further offensive operations, and it had been admitted by General Dittmar that the enemy's intention was no longer to drive the invaders into the sea but to contain them where they were. To achieve this, the enemy's chief need was infantry, in order to spare the Panzer Grenadier Regiments of the Panzer Divisions a wastage that could not be controlled, and in order to concentrate his armour for decisive action. But, by the 1st of July, the infantry reserves of the Seventh Army had been exhausted. Four divisions had been cut off and virtually destroyed in the Cherbourg Peninsula, and a further

Tank cemetery at Villers Bocage

four had been reduced to the strength of Battle Groups. Reinforcements still remained with Fifteenth Army in the Pas de Calais and Belgium, and with Army Group "G" in the South of France, but these had each contributed two infantry divisions, and could scarcely provide more if they were to continue in their present commitment on the coasts. Of the armour, the four divisions that had originally been engaged in the battle, 12 SS, 17 SS, 21 Panzer and Panzer Lehr, were fit only to be reformed, and 2 Panzer was heavily committed to a shuttle service to and from threatened sectors of the front. By the 12th of July, the score of enemy tanks on Second Army's front alone was reckoned at 538 knocked out, of which 224 had been destroyed. Meanwhile, air attacks on the enemy's rear were also having their effect in reducing supplies as well as in hindering the movement of reinforcements.

From the Allied side, the most important event had been the capture of Cherbourg on the 24th of June. It was followed by the American offensives down the West coast of the peninsula and on to St. Lô, offensives which finally achieved the first break-through out of the bridgehead. On Second Army's front, in the centre, between Caumont and Tilly, little had changed. 50th Division was still fighting bitterly for every yard they gained, and, although Tilly had fallen, the enemy still held Hottot. Between Tilly and Caen, however, the most important fighting was taking place. On the 25th of June, 49th Division attacked South from West of Tilly. By the 1st of July,

Caen

they had reached Rauray cross-roads six thousand yards to the South-East. Here they met the first attempt at a large scale counter-attack by the enemy's armour, employing 1, 9 and 10 SS Divisions. The result was a severe defeat for the SS, who lost fifty-five tanks destroyed and two self-propelled guns, apart from considerable casualties inflicted on the Panzer Grenadiers. As a result, 8th Corps were soon over the Odon a few miles North-East of Evrecy. Meanwhile, by the 10th of July, the Canadians were in Caen, and 12th Corps were fighting hard between Carpiquet and Maltot to the West. Caen was the most sensitive spot in the German defences in the East end of the bridgehead, since a breakthrough down the main Caen to Falaise road would loosen their entire front to the West. In consequence, in the immediate neighbourhood of Caen, both West and East of the River Orne, the enemy had accumulated 1, 10 and 12 SS Divisions, 21 Panzer Division, and three Infantry Divisions, 16 GAF and 271 and 272, together with a large number of anti-aircraft 88 mm guns.

On the 17th of July, the Division moved over from the orchards around Jerusalem to concentrate in the open country North and North-West of Caen, and, from then onwards, lived either in the feet deep dust or mud of the "campagne" country, according to the weather. The operation in which we were to take part was designed to expand the tight Allied bridgehead on the East bank of the Orne to the South and East, in conjunction with an attempt by the Canadians to break out from Caen itself. This bridgehead had originally been secured by the 6th Airborne Division and a Commando

Colombelles factory—Caen

Brigade on "D" Day, and consisted of a strip of orchards and villages along the river valley, about ten thousand yards long, and between one thousand and three thousand yards in depth. It was served by one bridge that the Airborne Division had captured intact, and three Bailey bridges which were later built. The Southern sector was held by the 51st (Highland) Division, whose task was to clear the East bank of the Orne, particularly the factory area around Giberville. The three armoured Divisions concentrated for this operation, the Guards, 7th and 11th, were then to pass through, the 11th leading and going South-West across the main Caen—Falaise road towards Bretteville, the Guards turning South-East towards Vimont, and ourselves going through in the centre toward Falaise. The 3rd British Infantry Division was to advance due East to Troarn, in order to prevent the enemy's continued use of the high ground above the river valley for observation. The whole operation was to be covered by an intensive air support programme ranging from Lancasters to Typhoons.

On the 18th, the Division moved across the Orne in blinding dust, and the degree of traffic congestion which was to be expected from the movement of two armoured divisions (11th had already crossed) on a narrow front. That night we had a first taste of the Luftwaffe deployed in "strength", which, although not numerous by RAF standards, was able to make life on the bridges very unpleasant both for those crossing and for the traffic control personnel. Fortunately, casualties were small and damage slight, but the accuracy of the bombing, coupled with the volume of our own anti-aircraft fire,

Cuverville

probably exaggerated the moral, as opposed to the material, effect of the enemy's efforts.

At six thirty that morning our own bombing programme went in on the enemy's positions South and South-West of Giberville, and undoubtedly succeeded in destroying any great will to resist on the part of the infantry. 11th Armoured Division advanced successfully, though losing many tanks, as far as the main road to Falaise some four thousand yards South of Caen. 5th Royal Tanks were behind the last regiment of 11th Armoured, and, as this enormous mass of tanks moved slowly out of the gap, they were at first opposed only by an isolated Mark IV on the left, which, after knocking out two tanks, was destroyed by the concentrated fire of eight of our own. While the Guards got into Cagny, Grentheville was cleared by 5th Royal Tanks after a short action against a few infantry, and small groups of prisoners came in all the while, until they numbered about eighty. A troop of Nebelwerfers was also found abandoned. The occupation of Grentheville provoked a small counter-attack from the South-East by six tanks, which withdrew after two had been knocked out on each side. The night passed quietly except for shelling, the battlefield illuminated by numbers of burning tanks, and flares and tracer over the bridges. The next day this cautious advance continued. 4th County of London Yeomanry took over on the right from 11th Armoured, who were being pulled back to refit. Ifs, Bras and Hubert Folie were occupied, and patrols pushed on as far as Verrières. 5th Royal Tanks occupied Soliers with two platoons of the Rifle Brigade, and pushed on to Bourguebus with two troops,

Hubert Folie

who, entering the village at the same time as a small enemy tank force, destroyed two Tigers and a Panther for the loss of one Cromwell, and going in again on the 21st captured two Panthers intact and destroyed a Tiger without loss. On the left, 1st Royal Tanks occupied Four against minor infantry opposition, but against considerable and increasing fire from both field and anti-tank guns and Nebelwerfers.

By this time, such progress as had been made had been stubbornly contested all the way, and the opposition showed no signs of weakening. Our attack had reached stalemate, and from the 20th to the 24th of July, the situation remained virtually unchanged. The enemy, aided by the weather, was bringing up further reinforcements and, by now, had recovered from the shock of our earlier air bombardments which had caused considerable casualties to his artillery and Nebelwerfers. The Division was limited to offensive patrolling, based on a defensive position running along the reverse slope of a ridge some four thousand yards South of the suburbs of Caen. This afforded good observation for the artillery and the Royal Air Force contact car, which were able to engage enemy movement of tanks and infantry to good effect, particularly in Tilly, Bourguebus, La Hogue and the woods behind. For many of us it was our first opportunity of seeing, across open ground, the Typhoons diving, with a rapid succession of smoke-puffs as they released their rockets, followed by clouds of dust and often the encouraging black smoke of a "brew". For the infantry in the line and the tanks in support, it

Bourguebus

was, however, a most unpleasant period. The congestion of vehicles, artillery and men in an area only some four thousand yards wide by four thousand yards deep, since the Division's centre line now ran through Caen itself and the Guards had taken over our original area to the East of the town, gave the enemy air force, artillery and mortars excellent opportunities, which they were not slow to take. Not only had the enemy direct observation over part of the area, in which he was assisted by an unprecedented amount of air reconnaissance, but the advantages and limitations of the ground were as obvious to him as to our own troops. The remains of the villages had to be held, and there were no covered localities for reserves and artillery emplacements. Thus, harassing fire on the villages, and along and behind the crest of the ridge, where lay the slit trenches of the forward defended localities and the crowded reserve companies and squadrons, was certain to be effective. The tank crews were often virtually confined inside their tanks during daytime, while the infantry could only sit in their slit trenches, watching the first rounds throwing up their mushrooms on the ridge, the range increasing after every few salvos, and there was an inevitable steady and comparatively heavy drain of casualties. At last light, moreover, the enemy sent over, for him, considerable numbers of reconnaissance aircraft, of which quite a few were shot down or damaged by the concentrated fire of the light anti-aircraft Bofors. These were followed afterwards by one or two visits to the gun areas by a small number of medium bombers, which made up in accuracy what they lacked in numbers. Divisional Headquarters were particularly unfortunate in this respect, being sited on a bare ridge immediately outside the Faubourg de Vaucelles, in the midst of a large and completely uncamouflaged ammunition dump and a battery of medium guns. At first, the aircraft and artillery tended to concentrate on the guns and ammunition, and Divisional Headquarters received mainly the overthrows in the form of butterfly bombs and exploding ammunition, but once the Armoured Command Vehicles had been bulldozed in, with a glistening surround of white lime-stone, the bombers decided that a more profitable target was probably to be found in what from the air must have looked like emplacements for large calibre naval guns or secret weapons at the least. Fortunately however, casualties, in comparison with those of the infantry, were light, and in general were inflicted more upon the sleep of the staff and their assistants than upon their persons.

On the 25th, we were by now under command of 2nd Canadian Corps, and a further attack, preceded by air bombardment and a heavy artillery programme, went in against an enemy who had had plenty of time to prepare. The 2nd Canadian Division, on our right, had, as their first objective, the village of May-sur-Orne, while we, in support of 3rd Canadian Division, were to continue along the axis of the main road from Caen to Falaise. The enemy had his tanks and infantry well dug in, and the effect of our artillery barrage was to a certain extent minimised by shelling on our forward positions and gun areas as the attack was about to start. Progress was, therefore, slow and difficult, although the day started well with the destruction by the 4th County of London Yeomanry of four tanks just off the main road near Verrières. Verrières was taken and the 4th Canadian Infantry Brigade advanced five hundred yards towards Rocquancourt, where five anti-tank guns were knocked out, and two Panthers ceased firing after a Typhoon attack. The enemy tanks and infantry South-West of Verrières then counter-attacked East, a counter-attack which was repelled, although the "C" Squadron, 1st Royal Tanks lost eight tanks during this three hour battle in endeavouring to give close support to the harassed infantry, destroying in return one tank and a self-propelled gun. Verrières remained ours, although the position there was by now very unpleasant as the 2nd Canadian Division on the right had been unable to hold May-sur-Orne and enemy tanks were North-East of Verrières, hull down on a ridge, and also across the Falaise road to the East, so that the village was virtually isolated by their fire.

Rocquancourt

East of the main road, the attack towards Tilly-la-Campagne, by 5th Canadian Brigade, had been even more difficult. The Typhoon attack had failed to persuade the enemy tanks and infantry to move. Our tanks and infantry had a difficult time in securing a foothold, and by last light were not in occupation of the entire village, which was finally cleared during the night.

Once more, after advances of only a few thousand yards, the attack had reached stalemate. From the 26th to the 28th of July, the

Division remained in defensive positions with the 5th Royal Tanks in support of 4th Canadian Infantry Brigade at Verrières, 4th County of London Yeomanry astride the main road, 131 Brigade holding the triangle Tilly, Soliers and Hubert Folie, and 1st Royal Tanks concentrated in reserve. By now the enemy on the East bank of the Orne had elements of five Panzer or SS Panzer Divisions, considerably reinforced by artillery and night bombers. Thus, in spite of his shortage of infantry, with three hundred and fifty tanks, some one hundred and fifty self-propelled guns and three hundred anti-tank guns, on a very narrow front, the enemy was in a strong position to hold any attack in this sector. On the evening and night of the 26/27th of July, he attempted a few small-scale counter-attacks with tanks and infantry on Verrières, which were dispersed mainly by artillery fire. Subsequently he remained on the defensive, relying on artillery, mortars and night bombers to make life sufficiently unpleasant for us, while his infantry attempted to improve their positions, under cover of smoke and of his tanks, attempts which gave many good targets to our gunners.

On the 28th of July the Division was ordered back to rejoin 30th Corps in the Caumont sector, and we handed over our responsibilities on this very unpleasant sector to 4th Canadian Armoured Division. For very nearly a fortnight 8th Corps, 1st British Corps and 2nd Canadian Corps had been fighting hard, and suffering heavy casualties, to secure an advance of little more than six thousand yards at the furthest point. But, during this period, the Americans had broken out of the Cherbourg Peninsula, and the entire German line from Caumont to the sea was in danger of being turned. In the meantime, the enemy had been forced to keep the best part of five armoured divisions, much in need of rest and replacement, in action, suffering heavy casualties in men and guns, and a steady drain in tanks, particularly from air attack, as the weather improved. It would not be an exaggeration to say that the tank fighting on the Caen sector, however fruitless it might have appeared at the time, had a decisive effect on the battle of the bridgehead, in that it forced a vital delay on any plans to concentrate the German armour to meet the American threats.

On the 29th the Division moved across to our old concentration area South of Bayeux, and for the first time, perhaps, the woods and orchards of the Bocage appeared as a welcome change after the dust and mud of the Caen plain. The operation, in which we were to take part on the following day, was designed to clear up the obstinate German centre from the River Orne to the River Vire, which the increasing speed of the American advance to the West was making strategically untenable. 30th Corps, under whose command we came, were advancing South-East from Caumont with the Division, and South from Orbois, to gain which so many stubborn battles had been fought, with 50th Division. The eventual objective was to clear the Mont Pinçon feature down to Condé-sur-Noireau and Flérs. Meanwhile, 8th Corps were to do the same on the right, while 12th Corps secured a bridgehead over the Orne at Thury Harcourt in preparation for a final blow by the Canadians coming South from Caen.

The enemy on the Division's front were not expected to be in greater strength than an infantry division, supported by the usual numbers of tanks and self-propelled guns.

The Division itself was by this time considerably below strength in infantry, and the armour had had a very trying time at Caen, with no opportunity to rest or refit after their exhausting move over. At this period we received the 5th Royal Inniskilling Dragoon Guards, newly arrived out from England to see action once more for the first time since 1940. They took the place of the 4th County of London Yeomanry, who went to amalgamate with their 3rd Regiment in 4th Armoured Brigade. This was a sad parting, for 4th County of London Yeomanry had formed part of 22nd Armoured Brigade from the first days of the reconstituted 1st Armoured Division, went with them through the Desert, and came to us with 22nd Armoured Brigade when they replaced 7th Armoured Brigade in the Division after Knightsbridge, in the summer of 1942.

On the 31st the Division moved down from the concentration area North of Caumont, to fight its way against stubborn opposition from there to the Eastern extremity of the Mont Pinçon feature above Thury Harcourt. The start was a slow business, inevitable in the Normandy fighting, as we had to move out partly across 8th Corps' centre line and hopelessly confused with a part of 50th Division, who were also moving on the same centre line. On the 1st the Division was still not completely clear but was making slow progress down the main road from Caumont to Aunay against opposition, largely mines covered by small arms fire, in which the enemy were assisted by a thick morning mist. By the evening of the 2nd the 1st Royal Tanks had reached the important cross-roads at Robin, six thousand yards South of Caumont, against numerous bazookas and anti-tank guns, and had, with their motor company and a company of 1/7th Queens, cleared the woods to the South-East. Meanwhile, the infantry were still clearing the enemy from between the main road and Briquessard. Our opponents, 326 Division, although very disorganised, were comparatively fresh, and small pockets continued fighting long after they had been surrounded. They had, in the woods to the East of the triangle formed by the main roads from Villers Bocage to Vire and Aunay, and from Caumont to Aunay, a strong position well protected by mines, to which they clung with great determination, their tanks and some anti-tank guns being forward of this position covering the open corn-fields from the protection of the orchards and houses along the road.

By the morning of the 3rd the 1/6th Queens had secured the high ground around Sauques after a night attack, and were five thousand yards East of Aunay. The 5th Royal Tanks, however, farther to the East, were engaged with tanks, and being heavily shelled, on the high ground East of Aunay-sur-Odon, losing six tanks for the price of one Mark IV. In the course of the morning the 1/6th Queens were counter-attacked by a Battalion of 326 Division from the woods to the South, a counter-attack supported by self-propelled guns and accurate mortar fire. 1/6th Queens suffered heavy casualties among the two companies affected before the attack was stopped and the infantry reorganised in a strong point around the remaining Squadron of 5th Royal Tanks. At the same time enemy tanks, operating from cover, were causing casualties to the two squadrons of 5th Royal Tanks, eventually succeeded in isolating them completely, and infantry attacked with bazookas as soon as darkness came. Finally, the two squadrons, by now reduced to twelve tanks, charged their way through in the darkness, losing three on the way to rejoin the remainder of the Regiment with 1/6th Queens.

Aunay-sur-Odon

On the evening of the 4th, the 11th Hussars were sent to find a way round the opposition by taking the road to Villers Bocage and thence working down to the South. They succeeded in contacting 50th Division coming down from the North, near Villers Bocage, although 69th Brigade, advancing on Villers down our old centre line from Amaye-sur-Seulles, were experiencing considerable difficulty in getting forward. Meanwhile 8th Hussars, who had relieved 5th Royal Tanks East of Aunay, found progress difficult against many mines, anti-tank guns and bazookas. That night it was therefore decided to push the Armoured Brigade up to La Poste, a small village a few thousand yards West of Villers Bocage, thence across country along a route which the Sappers were clearing of mines (the town of Villers Bocage being impassable owing to rubble and mines), down the main Villers Bocage—Aunay road, from where they would carry out an outflanking movement to the East of Aunay, using the by-roads running South-East between Villers Bocage and the Mont Pinçon feature. This move carried on throughout the night and caused some delay to 59th Division, who had broken through to the Orne on the right, and whose centre line was seriously affected by it. For their task 22nd Brigade were given the 1/5th Queens, while the remainder of the Division remained in position West of Aunay, which was entered the following morning through mountains of rubble, well-sown with mines, by 50th Division advancing South from Villers Bocage.

By the 5th the enemy had clearly abandoned any hope of maintaining any coherent line West of the Orne, to which he was withdrawing, at the same time hoping to smash the American break-through with an armoured counter-attack. Owing to the danger from the air, however, he was unable to carry out these movements as quickly as he desired. As a result 22nd Armoured Brigade were quickly able to reach Bonnemaison, three thousand yards East of Aunay, with the 1st Royal Tanks, and just North of Hamars, from which the Mont Pinçon feature was clearly visible across a narrow valley, with the 5th Dragoon Guards. Early the next morning, under cover of mist, "A" Company of the 1/5th Queens moved down into the little village of Vallée at the foot of the road leading up through the pine and chestnut woods to the plateau of the Mont Pinçon feature. These advances, however, had

Aunay-sur-Odon

not been without difficulty. The leading squadron of the 11th Hussars had lost a troop on mines and from well-placed bazookas; the 1st Royal Tanks had had a sharp engagement with infantry supported by anti-tank guns to clear Bonnemaison; and the company of the Queens in Vallée had a difficult time with numerous mines, losing two carriers, and were virtually cut off by sustained and accurate shell and mortar fire on the village itself, and upon any movement thence up the road to the high ground to the North. The enemy was in possession of excellent observation, and as the road was extremely dusty owing to the dry weather, any movement brought down fire at once.

The 6th was spent mainly in reorganisation. The only practicable centre-line for the Division was through Aunay, a spectacle of desolation unequalled by anything except, possibly, the Rhineland towns. All roads, except the country lanes which had been taken by 22nd Armoured Brigade, and which were quite unsuited to the passage of the entire Division, led to Aunay, to end in a mass of rubble and craters. However, the enemy had by now withdrawn from the area, and the Royal Engineers were able to construct a by-pass unhindered except by shell-fire. But, until this was completed, the only practicable route for continuing the advance was through Vallée and on to the high ground beyond, upon which the enemy had concentrated some forty guns, mainly 88's and 75 mm self-propelled guns. Accordingly, the 1/7th Queens were ordered to carry out a night attack on the night of the 6/7th of August to clear as far as Les Trois Maries, a small hamlet around a cross-roads two thousand yards South of Vallée and on the plateau beyond the thick woods screening the slopes of Mont Pinçon.

The enemy, in addition to his guns on the plateau, was known to be holding the lower slopes, and the attack by the 1/7th Queens was almost a model of its kind. It was supported by a series of box barrages, open to the North, and sustained until called off by the Commanding Officer of the 1/7th Queens. The first stage, to advance half-way up the slope, went well, as the enemy was clearly surprised in his slit trenches, and after some hand-to-hand fighting in the woods, preferred surrender to withdrawing through the barrage. Indeed, some went so far as to fall in in formed bodies on the road and to double smartly down to the village under escort. The second phase went equally well, and white handkerchiefs began to appear until, at first light, the leading troops were held up just short of their objective, the cross-roads, where enemy with machine-guns were in position centred round a house. By this time, however, the road had been cleared of mines by the Royal Engineers and, after the house had been demolished by the self-propelled anti-tank guns of the Norfolk Yeomanry, the enemy withdrew. Thirty minutes later the inevitable counter-attack came in, which caused considerable casualties among one platoon until it was dispersed by small arms fire and the defensive fire of the artillery. Under cover of mist, the 1/7th Queens were able to consolidate to a certain extent before being heavily mortared as soon as the sun broke through. They remained in this position, with the 1st Royal Tanks in support, until withdrawn on the 10th. Their attack had been highly successful and, at a cost of four officers and forty other ranks killed and wounded, a hundred and forty-two prisoners had been taken, an unknown but considerable number of Germans killed, four guns, seventeen light machine-guns and three vehicles captured.

Meanwhile, the roads through Aunay had been cleared sufficiently to allow the Division through. 43rd Division were on the high ground around Ondefontaine, and 50th Division had advanced towards Le Plessis Grimoult to clear Mont Pinçon itself. The Division's task was finally to clear the wooded area between Mont Pinçon and Les Trois Maries. There were still considerable numbers of enemy on the ridge itself, well supported by 88 mms and anti-tank guns which had been unable to withdraw. As a result it was not until the 9th that the entire ridge between Aunay and La Vallée was completely cleared.

The Division, less 3rd and 5th Royal Horse Artillery and 5th Dragoon Guards, who remained in support of 43rd Division, was then withdrawn to concentrate and rest around Aunay, a rest much needed by all arms, particularly 131 Brigade, one of whose battalions, the 1/6th Queens, had been reduced in strength to such an extent that on

Major-General G. W. E. J. Erskine, CB, DSO

the 6th of August the rifle companies totalled only eight, fifteen, forty and fifty-five of all ranks respectively, the full strength of a company being approximately one hundred all ranks.

On the 4th of August, Major-General Erskine, who had commanded the Division with such success since Tripoli, left us, a loss which affected all ranks. He was replaced by Major-General Verney, and General Erskine's departure was followed shortly by that of Brigadier Hinde, the commander of 22nd Armoured Brigade, who was replaced by Brigadier Mackeson on the 10th of August, and that of Brigadier Mews, the CRA, whose command was taken over by Brigadier Lyon-Smith.

Our period of rest was cut short on the 14th of August, when orders were received to join 1st Corps East of Caen, at a time when a large proportion of the troops were enjoying the fine weather at a rest camp by the sea, and various senior staff officers, including the GSO I, were sampling delights farther afield in the comparatively unharmed areas through which the Americans had advanced, on the West coast of the Cotentin Peninsula. The former were recovered with some ease, and the latter, in spite of attempts by an enthusiastic Liaison Officer, sent to find them, to persuade the American Military Police that they were a particularly dangerous species of deserter, eventually rejoined the Division unmolested and in good time.

CHAPTER VI

THE BEGINNING OF THE BREAK-THROUGH
CAPTURE OF LISIEUX AND THE ADVANCE TO THE SEINE

The 14th of August—the 29th of August, 1944

By the 14th of August, the Germans were in full retreat on all fronts. They had repented too late of their disastrous attempts at counter-attack round Domfront and Mortain, and were now hastily withdrawing East to the Seine through Falaise, their other escape routes between Paris and Orleans having already been cut by the American Third Army, now near Argentan, South of Falaise. 30th Corps were going well towards Condé-sur-Noireau, and the Canadians had at last broken out from South of Caen, reaching a point just short of Falaise on the 15th.

Falaise

The task of the Division was, then, to exploit First Canadian Army's success to the Seine, a distance of sixty-five miles, advancing due East along the general axis of St. Pierre-sur-Dives, Livarot and Lisieux. As far as St. Pierre, the country was the same rolling cornfields that we knew so well, but beyond the river valley, it rose sharply into a series of well-wooded plateaux, intersected by the steep-sided valleys of the Rivers Vie, Touques, Orbec and Risle, apart from valleys cut by numerous smaller streams. It was primarily a country of small pastures, woods and orchards, closely resembling the "bocage", except for the handsome, half-timbered, thatched farmhouses. At no time was the enemy on our front in much greater strength than an infantry division, reinforced with tanks and self-propelled guns from several battle groups formed from the remnants of 12 SS and 21 Panzer Divisions, whose task, not unduly difficult in view of the nature of the country, was to hold open the right flank of the "Falaise Gap", while withdrawing steadily to the Seine. It was this factor that made our advance so much easier than it had been in the "bocage", and moreover, at no time was the enemy in sufficient strength to deny every approach, with the result that 11th Hussars, who once again formed part of the Division, were always able to find a way round.

By the evening of the 16th of August, the Division was concentrated in a crowded and dusty area, well littered with the debris of war, "brewed" tanks and vehicles, dead cattle, abandoned guns and a number of unburied corpses. The journey across had been long and slow, through clouds of dust and through some of the worst areas of the Normandy fighting. May-sur-Orne, where we crossed the river, was once a pleasant stone village, sheltered by the steep wooded banks of the Orne river, and surrounded by deep, rich pastures and meadows. It was now a mass of rubble, its trees broken and stripped of their leaves, its riches rotting among the bomb craters. That night and the following one were also made unpleasant, though not particularly dangerous, by the Luftwaffe.

Destruction, as an ever-present companion to war, was soon to be left behind. The next morning 131 Brigade led off through St. Pierre-sur-Dives which had already been taken practically intact by 51st Division. Shortly after St. Pierre, the road rises abruptly to eight hundred feet, winding all the way, to the plateau above the valley, and on the South side was overlooked by the feature of Quevrue, at the top of which was found a hunting lodge where Rommel was said to have spent much time. The villages in the valley, Boissey, Mittois and Ecots, were cleared without much opposition, other than spandaus and mortars, the enemy's main position being on the high ground. Here every bend concealed a Tiger, Panther or anti-tank gun, and every village had its quota of infantry. Mines were not numerous, but every bridge and culvert was blown and in places the roads were cratered. Movement off the roads was limited, and the enemy gunners were in the habit of letting the infantry through their positions and then firing at the tanks. But in the course of the next two days, the 1/6th and 1/7th Queens,

St Pierre-sur-Dives

admirably supported by the Cromwells of the 8th Hussars, had worked their way forward to the edge of the plateau overlooking Livarot and the valley of the River Vie. The enemy were still virtually immovable on the main road, but making use of bye-roads to the North, where opposition was weaker, by four o'clock in the afternoon, patrols of 8th Hussars had found a serviceable bridge intact and unguarded, which was crossed by 1/5th Queens and a squadron of 8th Hussars, followed shortly afterwards by part of the 1st Rifle Brigade. Opposition was mainly in the form of harassing fire from 88 mm's, which had good observation from the other side of the valley. During the night the enemy withdrew from the West bank of the river, except for some snipers and stragglers, a Panther with no petrol, and a Tiger with a broken track. Patrols of the Rifle Brigade into Livarot found the town clear, although the next morning it became a popular target for the enemy's 88 mms.

On the 20th, the Engineers completed a bridge at Livarot to replace the one that the enemy had blown, our original bridge by now also showing signs of strain. Meanwhile, the 1/5th Queens had secured a second bridgehead one and a half miles North-East of Livarot, on the Lisieux road; the Royal Engineers had built a bridge, and in the afternoon 22nd Armoured Brigade, with the 5th Royal Tank Regiment leading, passed through. 11th Hussars, who were protecting the East and Southern flanks, destroyed many anti-tank guns during the day, and also a Panther, no mean feat considering that their heaviest anti-tank gun was a two-pounder on the Daimler armoured car. At Fervaques, six and a half miles to the North-East, they discovered a bridge over the River Touques intact, but covered by fire, and they succeeded in preventing enemy infantry, who were on the far bank, from approaching in order to prepare it for demolition, until the arrival of the 5th Royal Tanks and part of the 1st Rifle Brigade, who were better equipped to establish a firm bridgehead. This they did against some opposition from shelling, spandaus and mortars, capturing a considerable quantity of transport, including that carrying the German breakfasts. The next day, the enemy twice counter-attacked, on one occasion supported by six Tigers, but, after some hard fighting, both attacks were driven off. At the same time, 1st Royal Tanks, with a company of the Rifle Brigade, were advancing up the main road from Livarot. After an uncomfortable night in pitch darkness and pouring rain, during which constant and confused small arms battles were being fought against numerous parties of enemy attempting to work through their positions, the 11th Hussars, who had come up into the lead, advanced to within three miles of Lisieux on the 21st, overrunning the guns of 272 Division on the way. Otherwise progress was slow, being hampered by two counter-attacks in the Livarot area from both West and East, which were repulsed, but which made it necessary for the bulk of the infantry to be left behind until other troops could come up. The day, in which two hundred prisoners had been taken, amongst them two optimistic military policemen who drove into Livarot with the intention of signing the axis of 21st Panzer Division, culminated in

Livarot

a spirited effort by twelve young SS, either drunk or drugged, who attempted very vocally to recapture Livarot with bayonets. One wounded man survived.

Livarot was our first real experience of "liberation". Tricolour flags were out before our troops arrived; the apothecary was arrested as a collaborator, and, for those who got in early, excellent wine, as a change from Calvados or watery cider, was produced by the proprietress of the principal local café. The welcome was restrained but sincere, and here for the first time we met the Resistance movement, which provided us with good information, and also handed over a number of allied airmen, some of whom had been with them for a considerable time. The battle for Livarot, however, had not been easy. It had taken three days to cover the nine miles from St. Pierre, and daily casualties were some forty to fifty men and three to four tanks. Against this, the daily average of prisoners was slightly greater. Prisoners, indeed, included one young man who was permanently handcuffed to a French girl, a touching example of fidelity perpetuated by inability to find the key, and a tenor from the Armenian opera, who, after one exhibition of his talent, was relegated to dishwashing as a task more becoming to his natural aptitudes.

Lisieux

The 22nd and 23rd were spent fighting for Lisieux, advances Eastwards from Fervaques proving impracticable. The town lies in the narrow valley of the Touques, overlooked on all sides by wooded hills. The 11th Hussars had found all approaches from the East and South-East held by road blocks covered with spandaus and bazookas. One armoured car, accompanied by infantry, succeeded in destroying two spandau posts, but the infantry, following up, were stopped by accurate shell fire. Attempts were also made to cross the River Orbec which runs South-East of the town, and to get on to the high ground to the East around St. Jacques. The bridge was blown, but the infantry succeeded in wading across to form a small bridgehead which was eventually withdrawn owing to heavy and accurate mortar fire. The next day the attempt was resumed and 1st Royal Tanks found a way round by the Basilica of St. Thérèse. A foothold was gained and St. Jacques occupied in spite of opposition from Tigers and Panthers of 1 SS Division, but the centre of the town was still held and two tanks were lost in trying to get through. Stubborn infantry fighting, assisted by 51st (Highland) Division, who had by now drawn level, cleared the town of the anti-tank guns and bazookas which constituted the bulk of the opposition, although snipers were still holding out in the cathedral, and by about four o'clock the town was virtually ours. The inevitable counter-attack on the 1st Royal Tanks and 1/7th Queens around St. Jacques could only muster seventeen men under a serjeant, of whom two were killed and the rest surrendered.

By this time the enemy had once more withdrawn to his next rearguard position, the line of the River Risle. On the 24th, 11th Hussars were practically out of contact, and after a twenty mile advance, no enemy were met until, early on the 25th, 11th Hussars met infantry and a few guns withdrawing North and North-East around St. Georges du Vièvre, together with mines and four Mark IVs to the South. St. Georges itself was soon found clear, but the enemy clearly intended holding a position around Montfort to the North-East, where there were one 88 mm, two 75 mm guns and a Tiger. Pont Authou, on the main road running East from St. Georges, was also held, the bridge being blown, but in the afternoon a bridge was found intact two thousand yards to the North and the village cleared by 5th Dragoon Guards and 1st Rifle Brigade.

The next day the Division was across the Risle in some strength, the enemy having withdrawn to the railway line running East and West, South of the Forêt de Montfort. By this time the Canadians were in Bernay, nine miles to the South-West, and 49th Division attacking Pont Audemer, five miles to the North. All that remained to be done was the clearance of such enemy rearguards and stragglers as remained South of the River Seine, whose escape route was by now virtually cut except over the ferries at the Seine mouth. This task occupied until the 28th. 1st Royal Tanks soon found a way through the Forêt de Montfort, and on the 25th the Engineers succeeded in building bridges at both Montfort and Pont Authou in spite of the difficulties caused by craters as a result of Royal Air Force bombing. Many infantry still remained in the area of Bourneville and Routot, five miles North of our crossings, but these were cleared on the 27th, though snipers were troublesome in the forest, which was not finally cleared until swept by the 1/7th Queens, 1st Rifle Brigade and the Free French Forces of the Interior on the 28th. Enormous execution was also caused to enemy transport columns wandering vainly in search of a way over the river. On the 28th of August the Division withdrew over the Risle for rest and maintenance, handing over the area to 49th Division, who by now were only left with the forests around the Seine to clear.

From Livarot onwards, although limited by a narrow frontage, the Division had at last operated as an armoured formation, if only to a small extent. Nothing particularly dramatic had occurred, and for most of the way, except for the twenty miles between Livarot and St. Georges, the advance had been continuously contested. Moreover, casualties had not been light, and the time had not yet come when we should be fighting against a completely beaten and demoralised enemy as was the case in the advance to Ghent. At the time it was hard to believe that the Battle for France was now virtually over, for the enemy still appeared to have plenty of fight left in him, but the final move to complete a decisive victory was now drawing near. On the 29th of August we were transferred to 12th Corps, a happy association which was to continue almost uninterrupted till we entered Hamburg eight months later.

Chapter VII

THE BREAK-THROUGH: CAPTURE OF GHENT
The 29th of August—the 7th of September, 1944

For the first time since the African campaign, the Division was once more to be used in its most successful role, the break-through, unhampered by pockets which could not be by-passed. Certain aspects of the campaign we had already glimpsed—the cheering crowds, the proffered drinks, the flowers, kisses, and energetic if sometimes rather trying partisans, but in front of us had always been enemy forces, usually comparatively well equipped, who were acting in obedience to an organised command. From now on, until Ghent, we had left behind the dust and stench of the bridgehead, the never-ending artillery fire and the overcrowded roads, for a war in which the tanks or armoured cars could get on or get round, through virtually undamaged towns and villages. True, there was much hard fighting to be done, but it was fighting for which we were equipped, and the opposition was such as we could either overcome with our own weapons or else outmanoeuvre by our superior mobility. Thus, within a week, the Division was in Ghent, having covered a distance on the direct route of a hundred miles and captured 9000 prisoners. In the light of the final battles for Germany, this may not appear so remarkable an achievement, but compared to the events of the preceding period, when advances were counted in thousands of yards and prisoners in tens or occasionally hundreds, it represented victory on a scale we had not experienced for over a year—a victory for which the credit must equally be shared between the fighting and administrative echelons, whose careful planning and extremely long hours of driving over roads, often incompletely cleared, were thus rewarded.

By the 29th of August the vital victories in the Battle of France had already been won. The armour of the German First Army and Fifth Panzer Army had been largely destroyed in the Falaise, Mortain and Avranches battles in the preceding weeks, and the remnants had withdrawn, it was believed, to the area North-East of Metz, with the exception of 9 and 10 SS Panzer Divisions, which had fruitlessly endeavoured to counter-attack the American bridgeheads over the Seine, West of Paris. It was estimated that of the ten Panzer and fourteen Infantry Divisions involved in the Battle of the Bridgehead not more than 115 tanks and 67,000 men had been extricated. The infantry remnants had been handed over to the Seventh Army to hold the line of the Seine, but, with the Americans up to the Meuse by the 30th of August, they were left with no alternative but to

River Seine at Les Andelys

withdraw as fast as possible to the more vital task of defending the frontiers of Germany itself. On the enemy's left were seven divisions withdrawing up the Rhône Valley, whose successful intervention in the main battle was already forestalled by the American occupation of Sedan and Verdun on the 30th of August. On his right, Fifteenth Army still remained largely intact, covering the Channel ports, but with the collapse of the centre, it was unlikely that this infantry army, consisting principally of second-rate divisions, completely horse-drawn, could do more than stand where it was until the garrisons were reduced, or endeavour to withdraw either across the front of the advancing Allied armour or northwards along the coast to the shelter of the Dutch river lines. The enemy's previous strategy had been to pivot on the fortresses of the channel coast, but, with the American break-through, he had been deprived of the power to do this, and could only leave the channel ports to their own devices, whilst withdrawing Fifth Panzer Army and Seventh Army before First United States and Second British Armies, executing what delays he might by demolitions and individual rearguard actions until he reached the security of his next natural defence line, namely, the Vosges and the Meuse, with behind them the fortifications of the Eifel and the Siegfried line. He was now carrying out in reverse the strategy of every successful invasion of France from the East.

In the light of this, it seemed likely that the Allies would not be faced in the West with opposition from more than isolated unmotorised infantry units, supported possibly by self-propelled guns but in no position to offer any co-ordinated defence and lacking the power to withdraw or to manœuvre. Moreover, since their transport was largely horse-drawn, they risked being overrun before they could even complete the necessary demolitions. By the 29th of August the Americans were streaming towards the Franco-Belgian frontier beyond Troyes and on the 30th had crossed the Meuse. West of Paris they had handed over to 30th British Corps their bridgehead at Mantes, and 30 Corps had also secured a second bridgehead of their own farther West at Vernon. At these places the Guards and 11th Armoured Divisions were being passed through and were reporting meeting only light opposition. In the centre 12th Corps had seized bridgeheads at Les Andelys, Muids and Aude with 53rd and 15th (Scottish) Divisions, while we were moving across from 1st Corps, in the Montfort area, to exploit them. On the left First Canadian Army had secured the line of the River Seine from Elboeuf to the mouth and were pushing across the river from Elboeuf to the Eastern suburbs of Rouen. Strategically, the battle for France had already been won; it only remained for the Second British Army to complete the tactical victory on the left and to win the battle for the Channel ports, the flying-bomb bases and Belgium.

Road to Les Andelys

To achieve this, 30th Corps on the right was to advance from their existing bridgehead on to Amiens, Arras, Brussels and Antwerp, with Guards Armoured Division on the right and 11th Armoured Division on the left. 12th Corps, in the centre, was to advance on Ghent, but excluding Amiens, in order to protect the left of 30th Corps; while, on the coast, First Canadian Army was to reduce the garrisons of the Channel ports and to clear the flying-bomb sites.

V1 launching site on the Somme

On the 29th of August, accordingly, the Division set off from the area of Montfort, first along the close hedges and orchards of the Risle Valley, then climbing up to the high rolling cornlands between the Risle and the Seine to concentrate in the area of Le Neubourg, some twelve miles South-East of the River Seine. This area had been cleared by the Americans some days before, and, apart from the wrecked and burnt-out tanks and vehicles, was practically untouched by war. A reminder of the enemy's difficulties was the discovery in the woods of the chateau at St. Aubin of two Royal Tigers destroyed by their owners, 12 SS, before their withdrawal. In spite of this, however, they were not deterred from inscribing on the châtelaine's tables their intention to return. The night of the 29th/30th of August, during which it poured with rain, was spent in the open, a discouraging start to the operation, but, although throughout the weather was by no means perfect, it never rained sufficiently to cause any real difficulties. The Division spent the 30th in maintenance, which, after two weeks of almost continuous action, was extremely necessary. That afternoon Major-General Verney held his final conference on Operation "Goodwood Meeting".

Abandoned equipment and dead horses litter the roadside as the Germans retreat through France

Here it was announced that the final objective of the Division was to be Ghent, and the immediate object of the operation the seizure of the Somme crossings between inclusive Abbéville and exclusive Amiens, which was reserved for 11th Armoured Division. In addition to the normal complement of the Division, we had under command 4th Armoured Brigade, commanded by Brigadier R. M. P. Carver, DSO, MC, and the Royals, an armoured car regiment under the command of Lieutenant-Colonel Lloyd. At the time, 4th Armoured Brigade and the Royals were already across the River Seine in 53rd Division's bridgehead. We were also given a Medium Regiment, much extra bridging equipment, and additional services to supply 4th Armoured Brigade. The Division was to advance on a two-brigade front, with 4th Armoured Brigade on the right and 22nd Armoured Brigade on the left, while the infantry, 131 Brigade, were to follow on, remaining concentrated as long as possible, in order to be in a position to force the River Somme should it prove necessary. The Royals and the 11th Hussars were to reconnoitre the right and left fronts respectively.

By the early morning of the 31st of August, when the advance of the Division started, the enemy's disintegration on our front was apparent. There was little organised enemy resistance, and much of the fighting consisted in capturing rearguards or fleeing columns of horse-drawn transport and infantry; indeed, the 11th Hussars succeeded in riding down and destroying a galloping battery of 150 mm guns. The country was, however, on the side of the enemy, well-wooded and with many hedged fields and orchards, enabling small parties of infantry to establish themselves on the lines of communication, with the result that, at one stage, the Brigade Headquarters of 4th Armoured Brigade in Bazancourt was surrounded by infantry, who were only cleared by the intervention of the 3rd/4th County of London Yeomanry, a company of the 2nd King's Royal Rifle Corps and the Maquis. The latter, in spite of what appeared to the casual onlooker to be somewhat aimless and indeed rather dangerous shooting, did excellent work, and it was no uncommon sight to see considerable numbers of prisoners emerging from by-roads under their guard. Such pockets as 4th Armoured could not annihilate with their own resources, as at Poix, where the enemy infantry was supported by a Tiger and an 88 mm, were by-passed, a step which the complicated net-work of secondary roads and the enemy's lack of co-ordination

Crossing the River Seine at St Pierre de Vauvray

made quite feasible. By mid-morning on the 1st of September, after halting for the night, 4th Armoured, who by now were ranging far and wide, were over the Somme with the Royals just West of Amiens and at Hangest, mid-way between Abbéville and Amiens, with a squadron of the Greys and a company of the 2nd King's Royal Rifle Corps. This latter bridge subsequently collapsed, and, in the absence of any other intact bridges on the Corps front, the only route available to the Division was over a bridge just West of Amiens. This bridge was in the area of 30th Corps, who agreed to allow the Division to use it, and 44th Royal Tanks crossed and got up to Vignacourt, some ten miles beyond. Even so, however, it was obvious that at least one more bridge was required, as the Amiens bridge was a comparatively flimsy structure at the end of a narrow winding road and unsuited to the passage and subsequent maintenance of a further Armoured Brigade and one infantry brigade.

Near St Pierre de Vauvray on the Seine

Meanwhile the remainder of the Division was faced with the task of getting over the Seine. 11th Hussars were fortunate in starting off first at 3 a.m. on the 31st, and by the evening of the 1st had pushed their patrols out as far as the Eastern outskirts of Abbéville. But with only two bridges over the Seine, of which only one would bear the weight of the tanks and heavier vehicles in the Division, progress was bound to be slow. For most of us the day was spent in an endless, often stationary, column, wondering whether there would be time to "brew up" or not, with the bridges sometimes closed either for repairs or for return traffic. However, eventually the columns got over bit by bit, in clouds of dust, and once across progress was good as far as Gournay. Here 22nd Armoured Brigade, with the 5th Dragoon Guards in the lead, turned North-West towards Aumâle, but found both their roads held by anti-tank guns in the villages of La Caille Fontaine and La Formerie. Their difficulties were further increased by the virtual impossibility of manœuvring off the roads. After some sharp fighting the opposition was overcome, only to be met with in similar form a few miles farther on at Abancourt, which was only cleared after being outflanked to the North by "C" Squadron and assaulted by "A" Company of the Rifle Brigade. The next morning thirty survivors of this garrison surrendered, but this action proved a foretaste of what we were to meet the whole way up on our left flank. That night the remainder of 1st Rifle Brigade, starting in moonlight at 2.15 a.m., outflanked Abancourt and made contact with 4th Armoured Brigade and the Canadians. However, these efforts were once more frustrated, as in the morning the main body of the Brigade were again held up by the sudden intrusion of Canadian troops on their centre line.

131 Brigade were the last to cross, and, in spite of traffic hold-ups, were successfully concentrated in the area North of Gournay. We also obtained 71st Brigade from 53rd Division to look after our left flank in the rear of the 11th Hussars, which relieved us of some of the anxieties with regard to our open left flank, such as beset us at a later stage of the campaign.

Thus, by the end of our second day, our first obstacle, the Somme, had been successfully crossed, but once more we were faced with the problem of getting the Division forward through the bottleneck of a single bridge. 22nd Armoured Brigade were still on the left, concentrated West of Molliens Vidames, having spent the day in reconnaissance towards the Somme at Condé, only to meet enemy at Airaines, which made operations to secure a bridgehead nearer Abbéville too costly in time to be worth while. Accordingly, the Divisional Commander decided to push on that night, the 1st/2nd of September, over the existing bridge with 131 Brigade, giving them 5th Royal Tanks as armour, while at the same time building a second bridge at Picquigny, some five miles farther West, for 22nd Armoured Brigade. 4th Armoured Brigade were to remain in position covering our left just North of the Somme. Through the night of the 1st/2nd of September the tanks, carriers and troop-carrying lorries of 131 Brigade rolled down the main road from Molliens Vidames to Amiens, lurched off down a field track, through the narrow streets of the suburbs of Amiens and across the bridge. Although the night was dark and for the most part pouring with rain, thus assisting in the break-up of the already inadequate roads, it is to the credit of the drivers that hold-ups were few. Moreover, the bridge itself had never been designed for this weight of traffic, and, as the last tanks of Main Division Headquarters passed over the next morning, its shaking structure finally had to be condemned. Meanwhile, at Picquigny, the

Picquigny on the River Somme

sappers, working through the night, were building their bridge in record time, although delayed by small-arms fire, which had to be suppressed by a company of the Queen's, and also by accurate artillery fire. By 11 p.m. on the 1st their bridge was completed and 22nd Armoured Brigade moved across to concentrate a few miles North-West of Amiens.

By now we had lost 4th Armoured Brigade, who remained behind North-West of Amiens, under the command of 12th Corps, and the task of protecting the left flank was given to 71st Infantry Brigade of 53rd Division, who crossed the Somme in the afternoon of the 2nd of September.

The crossing of the Somme marks a definite stage in the operations preceding the capture of Ghent. It was followed by a complicated series of manœuvres, which ended in the disengagement of the Division just South of Lille and our advance on Ghent itself via Audenarde. Certain general considerations, although they did not necessarily become apparent until after the start of operations, will serve to give continuity to what might otherwise appear to be a series of somewhat unco-ordinated manœuvres. Thus, as the farthest West and the last to start of the three British Armoured Divisions, we were the first to feel the effect of any reorganisation on the part of the enemy, and were continually liable to bump the troops watching the Eastern flank of the German 15th Army. The enemy were in occupation of defensive positions on a line South and North roughly from Auxi le Château, through St. Pôl and Bours, West of the road St. Pôl—Lillers, along the road Lillers to Béthune and both West and East of Béthune along the La Bassée canal. At the Southern end of this line the enemy contented himself with occupying the more important towns with infantry garrisons of about two hundred men, supported by a couple of anti-tank guns, as at Auxi and St. Pôl. Farther North, however, his forces thickened up until, on the La Bassée canal, he had in position two strong Grenadier Regiments of 59 Infantry Division, with an adequate complement of supporting arms and Engineers to arrange for the necessary demolitions. The second factor was the ground. Between the Somme and the valley of the Lille coalfield it was mainly open corn land, intersected by the steep and wooded valleys of the Rivers Calanches and Authies, which gave good scope for the speed of our tanks. But, here again, the Northern road net converged upon the towns of St. Pôl and Lillers, each set in a river valley, and each held in some strength by the enemy, whilst the North-Eastern net from St. Pôl led, after some eight miles, into the valley of the Lille coalfield, dropping abruptly into a maze of collieries, factories, villages, railway embankments, dykes and canals. In such an area one armoured division could easily be held by a comparatively small number of enemy. The third factor was our primary task, that of protecting the left flank of Second Army, which, with the Guards in Brussels on the 3rd of September, would not have been achieved by fighting a confused and inconclusive battle in the coalfields or in the strongly held towns to the South-West. Accordingly our operations from the 2nd to the 4th of September inclusive fall into four distinct groups: first, the

Slag heaps near Lens

advance to St. Pôl and operations in that area; secondly, an attempt by the 1st Royal Tanks and 1st Rifle Brigade to work round the North-Western edge of the coalfield through Lillers and Estaires; thirdly, an attempt by the remainder of 22nd Armoured Brigade to cross the La Bassée canal, using the road network running North-East of St. Pôl to La Bassée; and fourthly, the disengagement of the Division to the East and the continuation of the advance from an area just East of Lille.

We have already seen that the advance across the Somme was headed by 131 Infantry Brigade with the 5th Royal Tanks leading, directed on Bernaville, some twenty miles North-East of Amiens. No opposition was met with until Domart, fourteen miles along the route, when the leading squadron found itself being mortared and machine-

V1 launching site at Oeuf, near St Pôl

gunned. Assisted by a company of the 1/6th Queens, who immediately came up into position, the tanks, after engaging all likely targets in the area, were soon able to push on. At Berneuil, where a flying-bomb site was captured, some more enemy were located, but after a short fight, in which a Regiment from 4th Armoured Brigade assisted, these were soon cornered and four hundred made prisoner. Again, farther on at Bernaville, four 105 mm guns attempted a stand, firing over open sights, but a few shots sufficed to force the crews to abandon their guns and surrender.

After one or two similar engagements, the leading squadron finally crossed the river a few miles North-East of Doullens. Meanwhile the 8th Hussars and the 1/5th Queens, after a sharp fight at Frévent, had reached St. Pôl some eighteen miles to the North, where they were held by a small enemy battle group with three guns. Accordingly, at 3 p.m. it was decided to bring up 22nd Brigade, who were to pick up 8th Hussars and 1/7th Queens on the way, and by-pass St. Pôl to the East and West. 131 Brigade continued to mask St. Pôl with the 1/5th Queens and Auxi le Château with the 1/6th Queens, in order to protect the Western flank. By last light they were relieved by 71st Infantry Brigade and able to concentrate in the area of Frévent. Thus ended the first stage of the operations since the Somme, in which the Division had covered forty-eight miles and at one time had been spread over a front of some eighteen miles. It was a day of comparatively hard fighting, and it is interesting to note, bearing in mind our task of flank protection, that the Guards Armoured Division had passed on by four or five miles East of this area the day before with comparative ease.

The plan to by-pass St. Pôl fell into two stages: first, the 1st Royal Tanks and the 1st Rifle Brigade were to move North on to Lillers through Cauchy: and secondly, the 5th Dragoon Guards, followed by the 5th Royal Tanks and 1/7th Queens, were to move North-East through Diéval and subsequently up to the area of La Bassée.

1st Royal Tanks and 1st Rifle Brigade, after the minimum time for orders, set off from Fienvilliers, some twenty-five miles South of St. Pôl, at 5 p.m. on the afternoon of the 2nd of September. They thus had to work through the greater part of the Division in order to get out at all, and it says much for the traffic discipline of all that they succeeded in doing this without undue difficulty. Later that evening it came on to rain heavily, and the task of finding a way round to the East of St. Pôl, already difficult enough on account of the almost total absence of maps, was complicated by the difficulty of finding a way for wheels. After a number of skirmishes, which on one occasion necessitated the deployment of "CC" Battery of 5th Royal Horse Artillery, by 8 p.m. a way across the main Hesdin—St. Pôl road was found. The tanks went on full-out, leaving the slower half-tracks and carriers to follow on as best they could. By darkness the leading tanks were at Tangry, seven miles farther on, with their reconnaissance troop pushed out another six miles just short of Cauchy crossroads, the objective for the night. Fortunately, although dark, the night was not overcast, and the two regiments, reaching Cauchy by midnight, leaguered for the night. However, with guards, standing patrols, orders and replenishment, there was little rest for the majority, and in the course of the night a German patrol of twenty men approached the leaguer, to be destroyed by Besas, Brens, mortars and the guns of "CC" Battery as they withdrew. The next morning the advance continued as far as Lillers, some five miles beyond Cauchy, where the Rifle Brigade, less "C" Company, and one squadron of the tanks were left behind to protect the centre line. Lillers was found to be strongly held, but with the assistance of the Maquis, who made up in gallantry and dash for what they lacked in skill, a way was cleared for the armour, guns and part of the Motor Company to reach the La Bassée canal, only to find the two remaining bridges blown as they approached.

By this time this comparatively small force was beginning to feel the effects of its exposed position on the left flank. Its forward elements were committed to a more extensive reconnaissance of the canal; at Lillers the greater part of the Motor Company and a squadron of tanks were, with French assistance, only just holding their own in street fighting against continual enemy attempts to infiltrate from the East. As soon as one street was cleared another party of enemy would try to get in, and, but for the Maquis, the task would have been entirely beyond the Company. To the South of Cauchy the enemy were across the centre line, and to the North of Lillers there were still enemy with bazookas, machine guns and spandaus between Lillers and the canal. A gallant carrier patrol from Cauchy, under a serjeant, made contact with 5th Dragoon Guards advancing East from St. Pôl near Divion, and later, after organising a diversionary attack with the rifles of the Maquis, succeeded in overrunning a German 105 mm battery in this area. But the 5th Dragoon Guards were committed on a different task, and this contact made no difference to the general situation of the force.

Earlier in the morning, 11th Hussars had found a bridge over the La Bassée canal at Hinges, some distance East of Lillers. Accordingly, 1st Royal Tanks were ordered by wireless to move East from Lillers, rather than North, the Brigade axis having been altered to run North-Eastwards from St. Pôl. This meant abandoning Lillers, and it was with great regret that this was done. Fortunately, however, the French proved capable of holding their own in the centre of the town, although some civilians were killed on the outskirts. 1st Rifle Brigade was brought up from Cauchy to about one and a half miles East of Lillers to cover the withdrawal of 1st Royal Tanks, who were to lead the advance over the bridge on to Locon and Estaires. By darkness the leading tanks were about Locon and well on the way to Estaires, in contact with the enemy on both roads, as were the rearguards of the Rifle Brigade closing up nine miles away. Indeed, "CC" Battery in the middle of the column had their guns facing both ways. In the absence of maps further progress in the darkness was impossible, and the column closed up, with the Rifle Brigade making the bridge secure at Hinges. By midnight on the 3rd, "C"

Squadron, 1st Royal Tanks, reached, twenty miles beyond Lillers, the bridge at Estaires, which was blown, but on the way they succeeded in inflicting many casualties on the enemy and destroying two 88 mm guns. Meanwhile, the remainder of the regiment, with the gunners, spent the morning engaging enemy transport moving North-East out of Béthune, and 1st Rifle Brigade pushed out patrols to the East. A carrier patrol, directed on Béthune, after capturing considerable numbers of prisoners and horsed transport, received an urgent appeal from the Maquis, beleaguered by the Germans near the prison in the centre of the town. A further patrol was sent out, reinforced by two tanks, and by 2 p.m. had worked through the town, and, to their great relief, made contact with the 8th Hussars coming up from the South.

The time for the relief of this force had now come. Unable to reach a small bridgehead gained by the 5th Dragoon Guards between Béthune and La Bassée to the East, an attempt which cost four tanks, it was withdrawn to the area South-East of Béthune to go into reserve, the greater part spending one more night holding the bridge at Hinges and Béthune, until relieved at four o'clock the next morning by troops of 53rd Division. For three days and three nights, largely cut off and unable to evacuate wounded or prisoners, let alone replenish, the force had been continuously moving and fighting, often scarcely in touch by wireless within itself, and usually out of touch with Brigade Headquarters. Nevertheless it had captured far more than its own strength in prisoners, apart from inflicting much damage on the enemy. They were destined to remain in the area of Béthune for some time, fully benefiting from the hospitality of the grateful populace, until the traffic and administrative situation enabled them to return to the Division.

We must now return to the remainder of the Division on the night of the 2nd/3rd of September. While the 1st Royal Tanks group was by-passing St. Pôl to the West, the 5th Dragoon Guards were doing the same thing to the East, and by 11.15 p.m. had cut the road running North-East between St. Pôl and Divion. Next morning, after advancing along this axis, they found themselves held twelve to fifteen miles on in wooded country to the South-West of Divion. Here they remained until midday, patrolling the roads from St. Pôl to Lillers and Divion and taking seventy prisoners.

Meanwhile, at first light on the 3rd, the 11th Hussars had set out from their leaguer North of Frévent to reconnoitre on the right flank of the Division towards Béthune and the La Bassée canal. Using the network of minor roads, running North-East from the St. Pôl—Arras road, they had progressed between thirty and forty miles by about midday and their patrols were reporting Béthune and La Bassée held. However, midway between these two places, along the canal, they had found, in addition to the bridge at Hinges, a bridge at Cambrin, which, although partially destroyed, was thought to be capable of taking tanks. As a result of their discovery 22nd Brigade's centre line was changed to run through here. 5th Dragoon Guards were ordered to disengage and concentrate in the area of Diéval and at 4 p.m. to lead the Brigade up to Cambrin, where the 11th had spent the day shooting up all enemy who attempted to approach the bridge and complete its destruction. The advance went rapidly, without opposition, and Cambrin was soon reached. Covered by the fire of the remaining tanks of the squadron in the gardens on the canal bank, the leading troop of "C" Squadron passed down the narrow street to rush the bridge. All went well, but as the last tank got over the bridge collapsed, and a few hundred yards to the North two carriers of "A" Company the Rifle Brigade were knocked out by a 75 mm anti-tank gun. However, sufficient of the Riflemen were got across to form a tight bridgehead, and at 6.30 the next morning the Royal Engineers were able to bridge the gap with a scissors bridge. Meanwhile, the remainder of the Brigade, who had been joined by 5th Royal Tanks from Frévent, spent the night in the Mazingarbe area.

St Pôl

In the South, it had early been decided that St. Pôl was too stiff an obstacle for the 8th Hussars and 1/6th Queens to tackle, and the place had been handed over to 53rd Division. 131 Brigade moved up to concentrate on the high ground, four and a half miles short of the coalfield at Hersin, where Main Divisional Headquarters had been established, to be overwhelmed in the middle of the night by a horde of frightened men from Brouay who reported 2000 Germans between that place and our Headquarters. Frantic searches failed to find them, and Divisional Headquarters, heedless of earlier experience in Africa, retired to bed shortly before dawn.

The morning of the fourth was again spent in trying to force an adequate bridgehead over the La Bassée Canal, in order to continue the advance West of Lille. "C" Squadron 5th Dragoon Guards managed to work out on to the high ground North of the church at Cambrin, where it did considerable damage to the enemy in Givenchy, although losing one tank, and "A" Company of the Rifle Brigade enlarged their bridgehead slightly by clearing some houses in the Southern outskirts of Festubert. A squadron of 5th Dragoon Guards were pushed out East towards the road La Bassée—Estaires which was under enemy shellfire, and four enemy guns were destroyed by the fire of 5th Royal Horse Artillery directed by an OP tank with the squadron. Progress was slow and the enemy with machine guns, mortars and bazookas numerous. An attempt to reach La Bassée from the South found the bridge blown, 88 mm guns North of the canal and the enemy still holding out on the South bank. Moreover, as we have seen, the 1st Royal Tanks group had been equally unsuccessful in establishing a junction with the 5th Dragoon Guards from the North side of the canal.

By midday it was clear that the only hope of restoring mobility to the Division would be to disengage and move round behind the route already taken by 11th Armoured Division East of Lille; the only alternative would have been to have committed the infantry in a heavy and possibly prolonged battle in country which was in any case unsuitable for armour. Accordingly, the 11th Hussars had already been sent off that morning to reconnoitre suitable routes to the South and East of Lille. 131 Brigade with 8th Hussars, the 1/5th and 1/7th Queens were left to enlarge the Festubert bridgehead and clear the town, which they did that afternoon, while the armour, including the 1st Royal Tank Regiment and the 1st Battalion Rifle Brigade, was withdrawn South of the canal.

The next day 131 Brigade were relieved by 53rd Division and remained in reserve with 8th Hussars, 1st Royal Tanks, 1st Rifle Brigade and 3rd Royal Horse Artillery until the traffic and administrative situation permitted the two infantry battalions and the artillery to rejoin the Division on the 6th, followed later by the others on the 11th. Thus ended the second stage of the advance on Ghent. Fortunately we had not lost our power to manoeuvre, and the broad front on which 30th Corps had advanced enabled us to utilise their roads without interfering with their administrative arrangements.

At 3.30 p.m. on the 4th of September the advance on Ghent continued. The force initially taking part was small, consisting only of a squadron of the 11th Hussars in the lead, followed by the 5th Royal Tank Regiment, with under command a company of the 1/6th Queens, the remainder of the 1/6th Queens and the 5th Dragoon Guards. In addition to their own echelons, they also took with them the petrol lorries of the 8th Hussars, 1st Royal Tank Regiment and the 1st Rifle Brigade.

The route was through the almost continuous small towns and villages to the South and South-East of Lille, and then followed the

Audenarde

main road through Audenarde running along the West bank of the River Scheldt, on which river stands the city of Ghent. It was flat going all the way along the poplar-lined roads, through the intensely cultivated, dyked fields of Flanders, the rich farms with their orchards, and the numerous ugly villages and hamlets, the horizon bounded on every side by roofs and the inevitable lines of willows and poplars. As if to compensate for the drabness of the landscape, the houses were decorated with enormous Belgian flags, and cheering, excited civilians lined the streets across which were draped suitable expressions of

82

greeting, including one which announced somewhat equivocally, "You are quite welcome".

Of the enemy, little was known except that he was likely to be in strength to the West and North-West of our axis, many of them trying to work their way East, in ignorance of the true situation, and in Ghent itself we found a garrison of some 1000 men well supported with 88 mm guns. In general, however, once seriously threatened, particularly by tanks, the enemy showed considerable readiness to surrender, and within two days the barracks at Audenarde was crammed with over 2000 weary and hungry Germans.

By last light on the 4th, the leading tanks had reached Kerkhoven, some forty-six miles from the start, without having met opposition, although, as they passed through to the South of Lille, some German guns were shelling an outpost of 50th Division just off the road.

The next morning, 5th Royal Tank Regiment, after securing Cruysanthem, five miles to the North-West of Audenarde, without difficulty, continued on towards Ghent. The first enemy were met at Nazareth, in the form of some infantry supported by an 88 mm gun, which was destroyed by "C" Squadron after it had been outflanked by "A". The accompanying infantry then withdrew. Meanwhile, civilians were reporting numerous enemy South and South-West of Ghent; an expedition to Laethem-St-Martin, six miles to the South-West, secured 300 prisoners, and the regiment disposed itself to cut all the roads leading out of the city between the Rivers Lys and Scheldt. "C" Squadron, who were working up to the city itself, found a road block held by infantry about one and a half miles to the South, and it was decided to carry out a co-ordinated attack with the company of the 1/6th Queens at 6 p.m. This was just about to start when a civilian approached the Squadron Leader to say that the garrison was prepared to surrender.

There followed a series of remarkable episodes. The Squadron Leader and the Regimental Commander went forward to the road block, commanded by an officer, who said that he and his Major would both like to surrender. Shortly afterwards, the Major himself appeared, dramatically draped in a white sheet, and said that, while he did not care for such a drastic step without the permission of his General, he thought that the latter would be prepared to surrender the entire garrison of 1000 men, if a British officer could accompany him to his Divisional Headquarters. Accordingly, the Squadron Leader was blindfolded and taken to see the German General. The General, however, was all for rank and refused to discuss anything with anybody less than another General. But he condescended to send a message through two of his officers to say that he was having difficulty in getting through to his Corps Commander, whose permission was required, and that he would accompany the Squadron Leader to the barrier with an answer at 8 p.m. By that time, however, the German communication system was showing no signs of improvement, which also appeared to be indicated by the continuance of their shelling and demolitions. To reinforce the demand for rank, the Brigadier then came up, as the German Intelligence Staff had apparently detected a flaw in an attempted imposture by the Commanding Officer of 5th Royal Tank Regiment. At a quarter to one in the morning the German General and his staff at last appeared, immaculately booted, spurred and uniformed, to parley with their opponents, dressed with that disregard for convention known only to this Division. Perhaps encouraged by this, General Daser stepped into the room, clicked his heels and gave the Nazi salute, after which he demanded that all junior officers leave the room. The only result of this theatrical entry was that he was immediately asked for a definite answer about the surrender of the town, which only elicited more clicking of spurs and another Nazi salute. The hopeless nature of his position was then explained to him, and he was told that any damage to the town and its inhabitants by air and artillery support would be his fault and his alone, and that continued fighting would have no influence on the final outcome, but would only reduce the numbers of Germans in the next generation. But "honour" asserted itself, and, after a private talk with the Brigadier had produced no result, General Daser returned to his own lines, after apologising for his failure to stop the fire of his guns during the negotiations. None the less, that night, on arriving back at his own Headquarters, he did order the withdrawal of his troops to the North of the town, which spared the beautiful old city the destruction that street fighting would have entailed. Subsequent German shelling fortunately did no serious

Chateau Carpontier—German Headquarters in Ghent

damage to any of the many architectural monuments, although it succeeded somewhat in quietening the orgy of "liberation" which followed the clearance of the area South of the canal the next morning.

During and after the liberation of Ghent the 5th Dragoon Guards were also active to the East. Following the 5th Royal Tank Regiment, they had been ordered up to the area of the bridges over the Scheldt at Melle and Wetteren, some five miles South-East of Ghent, as a result of a report from 11th Hussars that the bridge at Wetteren was undamaged. On the afternoon of the 5th of September they found the bridge at Melle blown, but that at Wetteren only slightly damaged, although under small arms fire from houses on the North bank. With the help of Belgian patriots the bridge was lowered, "B" Squadron got across and cleared the houses with the help of some infantry of 50th Division who happened to be near. Little opposition was met and the regiment soon succeeded in cutting the roads running from Ghent between the canal and the river. An attempt by the enemy to break out in this direction was defeated by a company of the 1/6th Queens and "B" Squadron, resulting in the capture of twenty-five prisoners. Considerable casualties to the enemy, including the destruction of four 105 mm field guns, were also caused on the Lokeren road during the night. The next day, however, was more lively. 4th Field Squadron of the Royal Engineers, who had been detailed to look after the Wetteren bridge, found themselves attacked by an SS Company supported by mortars and anti-tank guns. Fierce fighting took place in the houses and gardens to the North of the bridge, but the field squadron held their own and the enemy lost

Wetteren lock

twenty-five killed and ten prisoners, including their commander. A company of the 1/6th Queens arrived later to take over but there was no further trouble. Finally, on the 7th, the 5th Dragoon Guards succeeded in linking up with the forces in Ghent, although an attempt to force a crossing of the canal was beaten back by heavy fire.

An equally serious menace, during the two days of the 5th and 6th of September, were the constant attempts by the enemy to cut our lines of communication between Ghent and Audenarde. 4th Armoured Brigade had been ordered up to prevent this, but owing to the distance, they did not arrive until the 7th of September, and in the meantime, one military policeman had been killed on a point in the Northern outskirts of Audenarde, and the petrol point attacked to the South. Although the enemy's strength was considerable, in few cases were his attacks pressed home with sufficient determination to constitute a real danger, but they were sufficient to cause anxiety, and more important, traffic hold-ups owing to the general uncertainty as to the situation. Meanwhile, on the 6th, to discourage the Germans in their belief that a road still remained open to the fatherland from Western Flanders, the bridges over the Lys, West of Ghent, were blown. None the less, that night, the 1/7th Queens coming up from the South were forced to fight a heavy action in the Audenarde area, killing and wounding over a hundred of the enemy. Subsequently there was little further trouble. Eventually a Brigade of the 15th (Scottish) Division arrived to take over this area, and was able to report with triumph, over the wireless, the capture of over "one zer-r-ro, zer-r-ro, zer-r-ro" prisoners in the barracks of the town. They were not disillusioned, and later this Brigade gave much valuable assistance in clearing the Northern part of Ghent.

So far, in this narrative, little has been said of the activities of the Services within the Division, and, in an operation of this nature, proportionately greater strain probably fell on them than on the fighting components.

Before the start of operations, careful planning by the administrative staff ensured that every vehicle was used in its most economical capacity, For instance, within Brigades, the ratio of petrol to ammunition was increased above the normal, with the result that at no time was there any shortage of petrol, and the reduced holdings of ammunition in 2nd Line transport proved quite adequate for all requirements. But perhaps the hardest worked of all were the Royal Army Service Corps drivers. The operations started from the bases of the Normandy bridgehead, and, since no ports were captured in the course of the fighting, the bases had to remain where they were. Lack of transport at Corps and Army, together with the speed of the advance, made it impossible for Corps and Army supply points to be moved up in conformity with the movement of the Armoured Divisions. The Royal Army Service Corps drivers found themselves with an ever-increasing journey to the rear, and to the Divisional echelons forward, not to mention the traffic difficulties inevitable in the earlier part of the campaign when all traffic had to go through the bottle-necks of the Seine and Somme bridges. Three to four hours in every twenty-four for rest, food and maintenance was nothing uncommon throughout the campaign to Ghent. Moreover, with the enemy always active on our left flank, many of the journeys had to pass through areas that were incompletely cleared, and practically every administrative unit in the Division had skirmishes, real or imaginary, with parties of enemy left behind by the forward troops. In the same way, considerable care had to be taken by replenishment columns in the early morning, going down roads which were liable to visitation during the previous night. The dangers to which the supply services were subjected were equally those of Provost, who, apart from their normal quota of long hours in all weathers on traffic control, were peculiarly vulnerable on exposed, lonely points or when travelling unescorted, and, as we have seen, two casualties were suffered by them. Fortunately, in general, casualties and sickness were light during these battles, but the medical staffs had the same problems over the evacuation of casualties as had the Service Corps over supplies, as rear medical installations were equally tied to the bases of the Normandy bridgehead. Ordnance had to confine its activities to carrying what stocks it could, having first taken steps to ensure that all units had stocked themselves to capacity before starting, and no serious difficulties were found later in the way of providing spare parts. The workshops, again, could only send forward their recovery sections, but they did much invaluable work in clearing roads and forming dumps of "crocks" for later repair, when the workshops could move forward. Finally, there was the vital problem of communications. Signallers at all levels were constantly being asked to force wireless-sets to do more than that for which they were designed, and, remembering that there was no time to lay telephone lines, it was only by their skill and high standard of operating that communications were as good as they were.

A tribute must also be paid to the civilian population of France and Belgium. The presence of a large and friendly population in the battle area was to some extent a mixed blessing. On the credit side, it provided us with considerable auxiliary forces from the Resistance movements. Their quality depended greatly upon that of the local leaders, being best organised as we progressed farther North, but, in general, they made up in dash and reckless courage for what they lacked in skill. Not only were they extremely useful in mopping-up operations in towns, villages and woods, but they also did excellent work guarding prisoners. Moreover, in some instances, Regiments recruited small, semi-permanent "commandos" who remained with them. Secondly, they were invaluable as guides, owing to the extreme shortage of maps, as, throughout this operation, an allotment of three large-scale maps for a squadron or company was not unusual. Thirdly, they provided hospital facilities, and first-rate treatment for those of our own and enemy wounded whom it was not practicable to evacuate. From the intelligence aspect, their value varied greatly. Undoubtedly they provided a great deal of information, which often was grossly exaggerated, since, to many civilians, anything on tracks and much on wheels was a tank, and German forces were rarely numbered in less than thousands. But when, assisted by the acquisition of French and Belgian Liaison officers, trained and careful observers were distinguished, their information was usually extremely accurate and saved many lives. Lastly, no one will ever forget the enormous moral stimulus of the "liberation" atmosphere, even though at times the knowledge that, later, advanced troops and patrols would have to withdraw, as at Lillers, caused much concern. Civilians in these friendly areas, as was inevitable, never learnt that three armoured cars did not constitute permanent liberation, and in some cases, the enemy, assisted by collaborators, followed up our withdrawing patrols, to punish the over-enthusiastic. Each vehicle was covered with flowers, resembling rather a hearse at a rich funeral than a fighting vehicle, and on their sides was a maze of chalked inscriptions, ranging from pious hopes for an early death of Hitler, to the addresses of the more attractive young women. When the troops did come out of the line, the welcome of the civilians did, perhaps more than anything else, to make rest periods a reality, particularly at Béthune, Ghent and St. Nicholas, and few members of the Division failed to get their "feet under the table" and enjoy the best that the people had to offer.

Thus ended our part in the great advance of the British Second Army to Brussels, Antwerp and Ghent. Between these three places and the sea there still remained large elements of at least two German Corps, not to mention numerous Flak and administrative units, in whose reduction the Division was soon to take a part. To reach Ghent, including all the various diversions, the Division covered close on 300 miles. Exact figures of the total amount of guns and vehicles destroyed and prisoners taken are not, unfortunately, available. Although the total of prisoners through the Divisional cage during the week was 6000, at least half that number again were handed over to the Maquis, and were never seen by the Divisional staff. The cost to us was less than a dozen tanks destroyed, and under a hundred casualties in killed, wounded and missing.

CHAPTER VIII

MOPPING UP OPERATIONS IN BELGIUM AND HOLLAND—
THE ADVANCE INTO WESTERN BRABANT

The 7th of September—10th of November, 1944

By the 7th of September the period of dramatic advances was, for the moment, ended. After a period of natural indecision, particularly in Western Holland and along the valley of the Meuse, the enemy succeeded in reorganising his broken Armies with surprising speed, and by the end of the month Fifteenth Army had succeeded in withdrawing ninety thousand men over the Scheldt ferries. He had insufficient forces available to garrison his entire line, by now stretching from the mouth of the Scheldt to the Swiss frontier, in equal strength, and therefore decided to concentrate on holding the two flanks, first, the Western Netherlands in order to deny to the Allies the use of Antwerp, which had been captured intact, and to provide bases for the "V" weapons, upon which propaganda at home was increasingly reliant, and, secondly, the Alsace-Lorraine front, which, if only for reasons of prestige, required to be maintained intact. The centre, based upon the obstacles of the Meuse, and the fortifications of the German frontier behind, was left comparatively lightly held.

The operations of the Division during this period consisted, then, of a short period immediately following the capture of the Southern portion of Ghent, during which the enemy's disorganisation and weakness was exploited to expand the area under our control both North and East, and a far longer period from the 10th of September to the 20th of October during which we were employed containing and probing the enemy in the South-Western Netherlands. These latter operations were at first subsidiary to the airborne attack from Eindhoven to Arnhem, and later developed into an advance Eastwards, which, combined with the attacks of First Canadian Army on Beveland and the area North of the Scheldt, was designed to open the port of Antwerp.

The 7th of September brought the last attempt on the part of Fifteenth Army to break out. From then onwards, the enemy concentrated upon maintaining a line from North of Ghent, along the Canal de Stekene, which runs North and then East, to the river Scheldt near Zwyndrecht, due West of Antwerp. Until this line was consolidated, the 11th Hussars and the Royals had excellent days rounding up stragglers—six hundred prisoners were taken on the 8th alone—although occasionally handicapped by attempts on the part of the enemy to return in strength, as he did at Lokeren, ten miles East of Ghent on the 8th. The following day, St. Nicholas, a further six miles East, was occupied by the 1st Rifle Brigade at slight cost, and patrols from thence to the River Scheldt opposite Antwerp cleared the area, capturing a Heavy Anti-Aircraft Battery and several anti-tank guns in the process. Thereafter, activity was limited to keeping the enemy at a suitable distance by patrolling, since an advance to the coast across the dyke-ridden polders would have been a major infantry operation for which no forces were yet available.

Canal and factory area—Ghent

In Ghent itself, during this period, enemy activity was limited mainly to random artillery and mortar fire, which did surprisingly little damage, and on the 10th, 131 Brigade, assisted by a brigade from 15th (Scottish) Division, successfully cleared the factory area North of the river, hampered mainly by snipers and artillery fire. By now, First Canadian Army were coming up from the South, and the following morning the town was handed over to the Infantry Brigade of the Polish Armoured Division, their Armoured Brigade taking over the commitments of 4th Armoured Brigade to the East on the following day.

The Division then withdrew out of the line around Mâlines for a short rest period, taking under command 71st Infantry Brigade who were holding Antwerp. The 11th Hussars remained in position watching the line of the Canal de Jonction, between Antwerp and Lierre. On the 16th, the Infantry Brigade were once more in the line, on the Canal de Jonction, around Herenthals, some twenty miles East of Antwerp, which by now had been handed over to 2nd Canadian Infantry Division. The enemy, although determined to hold a small bridgehead South of the Canal, which led to a number of patrol clashes, was not particularly aggressive, except for shelling and mortaring, there being no dearth of guns to the North, and the snipers of 1/7th Queens had some excellent days from a commanding position in a well-built factory overlooking the Canal.

On the 17th occurred the great airborne operation, designed to capture the bridges from North of the Albert Canal just East of Lommel, over which the Guards Armoured Division was attacking, to the Waal at Arnhem, and thus to open a way into the heart of Germany, North of the Siegfried line. At first the Division took no part, except to offer hospitality to the crews of the odd glider or Dakota which crashed in our area, but on the 24th we moved across to just South of Eindhoven, in order to protect the long flank of the Guards and 43rd Divisions who so nearly succeeded in relieving the 1st Airborne Division at Arnhem, after the initial hard battles to get through the forests and moorlands on the Belgian-Dutch frontier.

The enemy had, by now, organised the best part of two infantry divisions, of whom a number were parachutists, between Eindhoven and the River Maas to the North, and had succeeded in cutting the centre line of 30th Corps between the Airborne troops garrisoning Eindhoven and those around the bridge over the Zuid Willemsvaart at Veghel, some twenty miles beyond. This, the Division was given to clear.

The road was not a good one, narrow and embanked most of the way, and running through flat, sandy fields, interspersed by considerable stretches of birch and pine-forests, which, in addition to the inevitable dykes, afforded ample cover for small parties of enemy infantry with bazookas and offered little scope for manoeuvre. The population was confined mainly to the neat modern villages, with small isolated farms in the cultivated areas. Moreover, with the road cut for twenty-four hours, the traffic congestion just North of Eindhoven was appalling, long queues of the echelon vehicles of the Guards Armoured Division waiting to get forward. On the 25th, 5th Dragoon Guards reached St. Oedenrode, three and three-quarter miles South of Veghel, against considerable opposition from enemy bazookas, who were still across the road, supported by a Panther, and in the woods to the East of it, but patrols of the 101st United States Airborne Division were contacted coming down from Veghel. The following afternoon the centre line was once more cut by a small raiding party supported by a Panther. This was eventually driven off, although the enemy still remained in some strength within a few thousand yards of the road, around Olland and North-West of Veghel, and the centre line was subjected to a considerable amount of harassing fire between Veghel and St. Oedenrode. Armoured patrols had, however, reached five thousand yards to the North-West to the railway line at Schijndel. The next day 131 Brigade came up to take over the protection of the centre line between Veghel and St. Oedenrode, and the armour continued to enlarge the salient, West towards Dinther and Heeswijk with the 5th

Royal Tanks, and North towards Nistelrode with the 1st Royal Tanks. After a short engagement at Heesch, two miles beyond Nistelrode, 11th Hussars pushed on to Oss. On the 29th, 131 Brigade, less one battalion, and the 8th Hussars were relieved South of the Zuid Willemsvaart by 158th Brigade from 53rd (Welsh) Division, and the line was stabilised as it was to remain for the next three weeks. 131 Brigade held a front of approximately four thousand yards from the canal near Middlerode, running North-East, with 22nd Brigade to the North as far as the main road from Oss to s'Hertogenbosch, patrolling South-Eastwards among the woods and farms. 11th Hussars were responsible for Oss itself and patrolled over the maze of dykes and polders, East and North to the Maas, on the Southern banks of which the enemy still maintained small garrisons.

North of the Canal, the enemy was nowhere in great strength, though mortars and artillery to the South were inclined to be active over 131 Brigade's area. He concentrated on holding the more vital approaches to s'Hertogenbosch with small strong points, well equipped with bazookas and supported by anti-tank guns and mines, a task which, in view of the restrictions upon armoured movement imposed by dykes and woods, was not particularly difficult, and he changed position frequently in order to surprise our armoured patrols. On one occasion the 1st Royal Tanks patrolling around Nulands Vinkel lost two Honeys and a Cromwell to bazookas in a very few minutes. On two occasions he indulged in counter-attacks, in battalion strength against Heesch on the 26th, which cost the enemy two hundred and fifty prisoners, and a small one against Geffen on the 11th which cost him twenty casualties. Both of these were dispersed by artillery and small arms fire without undue difficulty. Later in the period, reinforced by more determined parachutists, his patrolling became considerably more active. Indeed, once, on a particularly dark and foggy night, a standing patrol of the Queens heard movement close by, and waited for a target to appear. The success of their ambush was, however, to a certain extent, mitigated by an enemy soldier tripping over the patrol's Bren gun at the crucial moment when it was about to fire, although casualties were inflicted upon the enemy patrol by Stens and grenades. On another occasion, the enemy carried out a comparatively well executed raid on one of our standing patrols, covered by a mortar barrage, and succeeded in taking some prisoners.

Before the line was firmly stabilised, prisoners amounted to some two hundred, of whom many were little more than deserters, fed up with the perpetual marching, counter-marching, lack of food and rest, and the wet and depressing surroundings. These included an interesting gentleman dressed in civilian trousers and a snipers' jacket, who had been sent to report on unit signs in the area, and who, but for his imperfect command of the English language, might well have got away with it as an officer out for an evening's sport. Thereafter, we obtained a steady trickle of deserters.

Our own activities were very similar to those of the enemy. Harassing fire was put down on targets located by patrols or civilians; and day patrolling continued by the tanks and armoured cars, in the course of which many small parties of enemy infantry and mortars were shot up. At night time, the infantry and motor battalion kept up a vigorous patrolling policy, with standing and reconnaissance patrols, which, as time wore on, became increasingly more hazardous owing to the poor variety available in the choice of routes, and as a result a number of casualties were suffered. An excellent picture of the enemy's habits and dispositions was, none the less, obtained.

In general, it was a monotonous and depressing period of routine activity. Opportunities for recreation were limited, since Eindhoven, the only town available, was a considerable distance away, down a road always thronged with traffic, and when once reached was crowded with troops. Moreover, in contrast to Belgium, the civilian population, inevitably poor, owing to the extent of their families and the naturally inhospitable nature of the country, had suffered much from the German occupation, and were not in a position to give the same welcome and hospitality to the troops as had been the case in Belgium and was later experienced at Tilburg.

On the 2nd of October, Brigadier Pepper left to take over command of the School of Infantry at Barnard Castle and was replaced by Brigadier Cox. The only other event of any interest during this period was a vigorous competition, originally instituted by the enemy, in the destruction of church towers, which the enemy falsely believed were used by us as observation posts. He began by firing eighty shells at Dinther tower, but it was solidly constructed and remained standing. 158th Brigade retaliated by making an effective job of the church towers of Olland and Weibosch. The enemy's answer was the attack on Geffen, previously mentioned, which was designed to blow the tower, and on being foiled, he attempted, but without complete success, to achieve his aim by the use of a self-propelled gun brought up specially for the purpose. In order to achieve priority, we then attempted the destruction of Nuland, but the enemy drew level by destroying it himself. The tower at Oss was frequently mentioned as being a likely objective for a raid, and on one occasion the enemy did make a half-hearted approach to the town, but were driven off by the 11th Hussars. By the 20th of October, honours remained roughly even, and fortunately we never had occasion to attack the cathedral at s'Hertogenbosch, containing the only tower in the area of any considerable architectural importance.

The enemy's policy by now was simply to gain time until the winter should make operations over the rivers, guarding the frontiers of Germany, virtually impossible. On the West, he was endeavouring to hold on to Walcheren, Beveland and Southern Zeeland until forcibly expelled. In the centre, if pressed, he was prepared to withdraw over the Maas, to economise troops, but was not prepared to abandon Western Holland, owing to the advantages it held in providing "V" weapon sites for operations against Antwerp and London, and in providing bases for "E" boats and midget submarines directed on allied shipping attempting to use Antwerp. The British salient at Nijmegen was by now contained, after a sharp counter-attack, and could be neutralised as much by flooding and the weather as by troops on the ground. South-East of Nijmegen, to Maesyck, an armoured counter-attack in the middle of October, across the marshes from Venlo, had done its work in hampering any preparations that the enemy considered we might have made for crossing the Maas before the winter set in. The armour had withdrawn by now, and the function of the infantry was to withdraw, when pressed, over the Maas. To the South-East Aachen was captured at the end of October, but the German frontier, although breached, was protected by the river lines of the Roer and Erft, of which the former could easily be flooded from the dams. On the remainder of the long front opposite the Americans, the German line was already based on a series of natural mountain barriers, the Eifel, the Ardennes, the hills of Alsace and the Vosges, which, as the weather deteriorated, became increasingly easy to hold. To hold the line, the Reich and all non-fighting fronts had been combed to provide the infantry for the Volksgrenadiers and the parachutists, by now mostly parachutists in name only, but held together by a cadre of hard-bitten survivors, officers and NCOs from the more glorious days. For the most part, the German infantryman was a dispirited creature, short of food, rest and supporting weapons, elderly or very young, recently discharged from hospital and often only half-trained. German commanders threatened or appealed to decency in order to check the flow of desertions, but nevertheless this motley collection was still capable of fighting, and fighting well, held together by the leadership of a very small number of officers and NCOs, and driven on by the momentum of Wehrmacht and party discipline which was to take a long time to run down. Meanwhile, behind the infantry, the higher command were attempting to build up an armoured force for a decisive counter-offensive in the West.

Twenty-First Army Group's next task, after the airborne operations had been halted at Arnhem, was to free the port of Antwerp, use of which was still denied to us by the enemy occupation of Beveland and Walcheren. Moreover, the enemy bridgehead South of the Scheldt at Breskens was not eliminated, although the Canadians advancing Northwards from Antwerp had succeeded in cutting the neck of the Beveland Peninsula, and Walcheren had been largely flooded by the cutting of the sea-wall. Until First Canadian Army should be in a position to assault Walcheren and Beveland, Second Army was to advance Westwards from the Nijmegen corridor, with 12th Corps, and North-Eastwards from the Antwerp bridgehead with 1st Corps on to Breda, thus cutting the enemy's land line of communications over the Moerdijk bridge near the mouth of the Maas.

12th Corps plan was for 15th (Scottish) Division to attack North-West from Best towards Tilburg. 51st (Highland) Division, who had come up on our left, were to break through the enemy positions immediately South of the Zuid Willemsvaart as far as the river lines running South and North through s'Hertogenbosch, after which 7th Armoured was to pass through to clear the wooded country between the railway line Tilburg—s'Hertogenbosch and the Aftwateringskanaal, from thence exploiting West between the Maas and the Wilhelmina

s'Hertogenbosch

Canal. Meanwhile, 53rd (Welsh) Division was to attack s'Hertogenbosch from the line of our present positions, clear the town and establish themselves between the River Maas and the Aftwateringskanaal.

The country was typical of Brabant. From the Dommel Westwards, the Northern part consisted mainly of thick woods, alternating with large stretches of pine-covered sand dunes. To the South it was slightly more cultivated but again interspersed with thick woods. Westward of the road from Loon-op-Zand to Tilburg, the woods and fields dropped imperceptibly into polder, heavily cultivated fields of silt on clay, each surrounded by a dyke, and often lined with trees. The roads over the whole area were few and poor, for the most part embanked and very liable to collapse under the weight of armoured vehicles. Moreover, operations were to a certain extent hampered by the lengthening nights, and were extended for a considerably longer period, aided by the wet, than would in summer have been necessary. In general the fighting tended to be monotonous and hard, but not particularly bitter, as the enemy was always prepared to withdraw if pressed, being in no position to reinforce his troops.

The first three days of the battle which opened the Tilburg campaign were devoted to infantry fighting to secure bridgeheads over the rivers Dommel and Aa by 51st (Highland) Division, and to seize s'Hertogenbosch by 53rd (Welsh) Division, who had under command the 5th Dragoon Guards and 5th Royal Tanks. The Division's part was an attack by 131 Brigade to clear the area of

Middelrode, Doornhoek and Berlicum to within four thousand yards of s'Hertogenbosch. The attack was supported by the Divisional Artillery and 131 Brigade had under command the 8th Hussars, 1st Royal Tanks and detachments of Flails* and Crocodiles†.

The people of Berlicum, near s'Hertogenbosch, honour a soldier of 1/7th Queens Royal Regiment

The attack was entirely successful, due largely to the very accurate knowledge of the enemy's strength and dispositions built up by patrolling; for example, it was appreciated that the enemy had 712 Division, somewhat under strength, in the line, together with battle groups formed from 59 Division, an appreciation which proved quite correct; successful also due to careful planning and study. All troops to be engaged, except one company of 1/5th Queens, were withdrawn from the line to practise street fighting in Dinther in co-operation with 8th Hussars, and were personally briefed by their commanding officers.

* Tanks designed to clear minefields
† Flame-throwing tanks

The attack began at five past ten in the morning of the 22nd of October, but from four o'clock onwards the artillery had fired a series of terrific concentrations on all known or suspected enemy gun areas to the South of the Zuid Willemsvaart, where the bulk of the enemy artillery was positioned. 1/7th Queens then led off along sandy tracks to capture Middelrode, making slow progress against spandaus and numerous mines, which involved delays for the tanks and Crocodiles. Meanwhile, 1/5th Queens moved forward from their positions, to form up one thousand yards farther on, in order to take Doornhoek by working across country. The arrival of the armour was once more delayed by mines. Within three hundred yards of crossing the start line an enemy strong-point was met, covered by yet more mines. Two tanks were knocked out on the minefield, and a Flail hit by a captured six-pounder as it attempted to clear a way for other tanks. Two tank commanders were also shot by riflemen as they were looking out of their turrets. Meanwhile, the mines were cleared, and once through, the infantry were able to outflank the enemy positions. Doornhoek was rapidly cleared in half-an-hour, the Crocodiles proving too much for enemy morale. But Middelrode still held out, casualties being caused to the 1/7th Queens by mortar and shell fire, and was not cleared until seven o'clock the next morning. Berlicum, however, offered little resistance to the 1/5th Queens, as the enemy had few reserves in his rear areas.

Meanwhile, 51st (Highland) Division's attack had gone well, and on the evening of the 24th they had reached the line of the River Aa, but were unable to make much progress with a bridge at Esch owing to heavy shell and mortar fire. On the 25th, the Division moved across from North of the Zuid Willemsvaart over a bridge built by the Royal Engineers at Dinther, in order to exploit North-East. The next day was spent trying to find a way out over the Aa. The obvious route was over the bridge at Esch but this had been destroyed by shell fire, so 8th Hussars, a company of the 1/7th Queens and 1st Rifle Brigade went to find a way out farther South, where 11th Hussars had already been held up. By the time the force was assembled it was already dark, and patrols of the Rifle Brigade reported that the bridges in any case were blown and that there was no suitable crossing place.

The next morning, 51st (Highland) Division had made the Esch bridgehead firm, and 22nd Armoured Brigade, with 5th Royal Tanks leading, set out to block the roads leading North and North-East out of Tilburg. 5th Royal Tanks had some difficulty at first with self-propelled guns, but by evening had worked down through difficult country and against small pockets of infantry with the inevitable self-propelled guns, to the North of Oisterwijk. 1st Royal Tanks, taking the Northerly route, made excellent progress and by four o'clock in the afternoon were in the outskirts of Udenhout, ten miles from Esch. By dark they had captured Udenhout, and for the loss of two tanks to bazookas had destroyed an anti-tank gun and taken eighty prisoners. Meanwhile their rear was secured by 131 Brigade and two squadrons of 11th Hussars protecting the right flank.

The enemy had, by now, established a second line, with its left resting on Waaspijk, thence running South-East to Loon-op-Zand and

Udenhout—Loon-op-Zand road

the surrounding woods and sandhills. Its right was well dug-in in the woods covering Dongen, three miles North-East of Tilburg. South of this, resistance below the Wilhelmina Canal had virtually collapsed; Tilburg was entered by 15th (Scottish) Division on the evening of the 27th, and patrols of the 11th Hussars had no great difficulty in working down to the canal opposite Tilburg. But the reduction of the enemy line North of Tilburg was a different matter and was not completed until the 29th. The plan was for 8th Hussars and 1/7th Queens, later reinforced by 1/5th Queens, to attack Loon-op-Zand from the South and East, while 5th Dragoon Guards, with two companies of the 1st Rifle Brigade, were directed on Dongen.

The attacks on Loon-op-Zand made, at first, little progress. The woods to the South-East and East were heavily mined and contained plenty of bazooka-men in good positions, and neither 8th Hussars nor a squadron of the 11th Hussars were able to make much progress. To the South was a road-block and plenty of infantry, who held up the 1/7th Queens all day. By the following morning 51st Division, on the North, directed on Geertruidenberg, had come up, and 1/5th Queens were able to clear the town from the West. 1st Royal Tanks were then passed through Loon-op-Zand, directed on Oosterhout, and also with orders to assist 5th Dragoon Guards by an attack on the enemy's rear should it prove necessary.

The battle for the woods East of Dongen followed much the same course as the battle for Loon-op-Zand. On the 27th, advancing West

Geertruidenberg

of the road from Tilburg to Loon-op-Zand, 5th Dragoon Guards had met fire from 75 mms in the woods, and attempts to destroy them by fire were prevented by infantrymen with bazookas. The key to the enemy position was in a belt of woodland some seven thousand yards beyond the road, fronted by a completely bare stretch of open ground. A patrol on the night of the 27th/28th found the woods still strongly held, and next morning the carriers of "I" Company of the Rifle Brigade worked down to the Tilburg road, taking some prisoners in the copses which held the enemy's outposts. On the 29th the assault on the enemy's main position, supported by four Medium Regiments, went in, three platoons of the Rifle Brigade being carried on twelve tanks of the 5th Dragoon Guards, whose flanks were covered by a smoke screen. The attack was a failure. The leading tanks ran on to boggy ground three hundred yards short of the objective, two being inextricably bogged. An attempt by the remainder to choose firmer ground met a minefield, upon which two tanks were knocked out by mines and a third by a 75 mm. The riflemen then withdrew to re-organise under cover of the fire of the remaining tanks and their own Light Machine Guns, returning to the attack three-quarters of an hour later, this time on foot, by a different approach. Supported by Besa fire from the tanks, they reached their objective with only minor losses, and took forty prisoners. The remainder of the woods was then cleared by "A" Company of the Rifle Brigade on tanks, and a few more prisoners were taken. The force then advanced, without opposition except from mines, to occupy Dongen.

Meanwhile, on the morning of the 29th, the 1st Royal Tanks had passed through 1/5th Queens as planned and, although delayed for a time by a tank which broke down, blocking the road at a point where it was impossible to manoeuvre off it, and at which the enemy had decided to bring down a concentration of artillery fire, causing some casualties, by last light had reached Vaart, five miles on. The next morning they again pushed on towards Oosterhout. A blown bridge caused some delay, but was bridged by a "scissors". On the outskirts of Oosterhout three tanks were knocked out by an anti-tank gun, but by two o'clock the place was clear, and patrols of the Rifle Brigade pushed North towards Ramsdoncksveer, which 51st Division had yet to clear.

By now, the Polish Armoured Division, advancing North from Breda, had occupied the area West of Oosterhout, but were held up a few thousand yards farther North. 51st Division were also making slow progress on our right. Eventually, however, Ramsdoncksveer was taken by them and handed over to 1st Rifle Brigade during the night. The position of the Rifle Brigade was not ideal, as they were overlooked from the taller buildings of the old fortress town of Geertruidenberg, across the Wilhelmina Canal, and for the next two days, until the Polish Armoured Division reached the Maas, they were active with mortars and patrolling although, fortunately, the enemy never succeeded in locating their positions in spite of many attempts.

On 2nd November the Division took over entirely from 51st Division, holding a broad front of some twenty thousand yards, well back from the river. The enemy were not aggressive, and our standard routine was for dawn and dusk patrols to the river-line, which the enemy varied with a little shelling. Meanwhile, the final object of the operation was achieved when Beveland and Walcheren were cleared on the 1st, and, on the 3rd, 53rd Division cleared the "island" between the Aftwateringskanaal and the Maas, capturing a number of disillusioned prisoners, who complained bitterly that they had intended to evacuate the place in any case that night. On the 28th the first Allied convoy entered Antwerp.

From our own point of view these operations, once the destruction of the Schijndel area had been left behind, brought us once more into a "liberation" area, particularly Tilburg, but also in the large and prosperous villages around. Tilburg itself was rather unfairly entered by Divisional Headquarters the day following its capture by 15th (Scottish) Division, who then had to leave, while we enjoyed the very generous hospitality of the townspeople.

In the course of these operations, lasting roughly ten days, the Division destroyed or captured eight self-propelled guns, twelve anti-tank guns of various calibres, and inflicted some eight hundred casualties on the enemy. To achieve this we lost twenty-two tanks and a considerable number in killed and wounded. These figures explain the comparative slowness of the advance. Cromwell tanks are at their best in country over which they can manoeuvre and use their speed. In Western Brabant, with its dykes, embanked roads and frequent woods, swift armoured movement was only possible when virtually unopposed and opposition, though comparatively weak, involved an infantry battle at an infantry pace. On the 10th of November, with sad hearts, particularly among those who felt that Tilburg would be an excellent place in which to spend Christmas, the Division moved across to the opposite extremity of the front, to concentrate in the Bree area, although 22nd Armoured Brigade remained behind temporarily until suitable accommodation could be found for them.

CHAPTER IX

HOLDING THE LINE IN EAST BRABANT AND LIMBURG: THE CAPTURE OF PANHEEL LOCK: OPERATION "BLACKCOCK"

The 10th of November, 1944—21st of February, 1945

November, December, and the first half of January were spent holding the line on the right-hand flank of Second Army's sector, first on the West and later on the East bank of the River Maas. The big events, 8th Corps' attack to the North of us to clear the German bridgehead over the Maas at Venlo, 9th United States Army's attacks to bring their line up to the River Roer around Geilenkirchen, Julich and Linnich, and the German counter-offensive in the Ardennes to the South for the most part passed us by. Our role was almost entirely static, patrolling against a motley collection of parachutists and Volksgrenadiers, and enduring a certain amount of shelling, either in the flooded pastures of the valley of the Maas, or the equally sodden cornlands North of Sittard until, on the 16th, we carried out a limited attack to bring the line up to the line of the Roer valley. Throughout this period the only real change in our existence was brought about by the weather, which at Christmas time suddenly turned bitterly cold, freezing the floods and covering the country with up to two and a half feet of snow.

In November the Division was reorganised. On the 22nd Major-General L. O. Lyne, DSO, came to command us from 50th Division, and shortly afterwards 131 Infantry Brigade lost 1/6th and 1/7th Queens in exchange for 2nd Battalion The Devonshire Regiment and 9th Battalion The Durham Light Infantry, both from 50th Division. Shortly after the arrival of Major-General Lyne, two new additions were also made to the permanent establishment of the Division, a Divisional School at Brussels, and a concert party. The former, both for its instructors and equipment, was found entirely from within the Division, and provided a wide range of courses to meet the needs of both the Armoured Regiments and the Infantry Battalions. Much valuable work was done, not only in ensuring a uniform standard of knowledge and training throughout the Division, and in providing refresher courses on weapons and vehicles, to which subjects, vital though they are, the necessary attention cannot possibly be given in the field, but also, by bringing together junior leaders of all arms to discuss and study each other's individual problems. Moreover, its proximity to Brussels gave the students adequate recreational facilities. The Concert Party, again, relied entirely upon their own resources, writing their own music and plays and designing and making their own costumes and scenery. Wherever operations have permitted, they have always come forward with first-rate productions, and their Christmas pantomime at Sittard had a run of which any West End manager might have been envious.

At first 131 Brigade, who relieved 71st Brigade of 53rd (Welsh) Division, were in position on the line of the Wessem Canal, facing both North and West. Patrolling was difficult owing to the enemy's use of searchlights and the good observation he had from the canal banks. Moreover, his artillery was active, and on one occasion Brigade Headquarters in Neeritter was hit by approximately twenty shells, which destroyed a number of amenities in an otherwise handsome "Kasteel".

On the 13th of November the Division was ordered to help 53rd Division in their forthcoming attack across the Wessem Canal to the North, by making a diversionary attack on the Panheel lock near Wessem. Aerial photographs showed that the lock gates were not yet destroyed, and that, by securing these, a good depth of water would be kept in the canal for boat crossings farther North. In addition, the threat of a crossing at Panheel would hold the enemy's attention from the main attack. 131 Brigade held Thorn, and it was finally decided

Panheel lock

that 1/7th Queens, supported by 8th Hussars and both artillery regiments, should assault the lock on the following day, before the main night attack went in farther North. There was an undulating plateau of high ground in between Thorn and the canal, although the right flank from the lock to the South was flat and marshy. The enemy was dug in along both sides of the raised canal bank and had a good field of fire to his front. One sunken track running through a copse provided the only approach and forming-up place. The battle started at four o'clock in the afternoon when sufficient light remained to gain the objective and to hold it during the night. An accurate and heavy barrage pounded the lock area and snipers were out in position protecting the forming-up place. The tanks of 8th Hussars went out on the left across the rolling country, and were able to shoot direct at the near bank of the canal. The assaulting company worked with them, but as soon as it left the cover of the sunken track it came under heavy shell and machine-gun fire. Two successive Company Commanders became casualties, then the reserve Company Commander was wounded at the forming-up place, which was now being heavily shelled. Despite this, a high standard of bravery and initiative was shown by the remaining junior commanders. On the left one platoon was pinned down, but another one rallied and made a wide left-hand sweep to reach the canal bank father North and work down towards the lock. Supported by tanks, which had been able to close up, this movement was successful and the Northern lock gate was captured intact. On the right, a reserve platoon was ordered to go forward and seize the Southern end of the lock. This platoon lost its Commander just as it started, but carried on, gallantly led by the Platoon Serjeant. It was unsupported by tanks because of the ground, but it used the copse and sunken track. It was heavily mortared whilst approaching the embankment, and then had to cross an anti-personnel minefield, but by magnificent dash and determination it arrived on the embankment, although very weak in numbers. By now, only three-quarters of an hour after the start, Panheel lock was secure and intact, the enemy having fled to the far bank, and the object of the attack was fully achieved. 53rd Division, working down from the North bank of the Canal, cleared up to Wessem and the banks of the Maas beyond during the following days. 131 Brigade accordingly moved slightly North and West, occupying the villages on the river bank and patrolling forward by night, the enemy still maintaining a small bridgehead in the island formed by the loop of the Maas, and occasionally sending boating-patrols, usually disastrous, on to our side of the river. Meanwhile the armour remained concentrated to the rear, and a squadron of the 11th Hussars watched the Maas between Ophoven and Maesyck, towards which the enemy occasionally patrolled.

The only other important event was a visit by Field-Marshal Sir Bernard Montgomery to present medal ribbons.

On the 7th December, 22nd Armoured Brigade moved over the Maas and took over from the Irish Guards between Roosteren and Nieuwstadt, followed by 131 Brigade the next day, who took over from 32nd Guards Brigade on their right, holding the reverse slope of a low ridge North-East of Sittard, overlooking the Maas valley. The Division was thereafter disposed as follows: 11th Hussars garrisoned Roosteren, between the Juliana Canal and the river, maintaining a troop as an outpost on the East side of the canal at Gebroek, and 1st Rifle Brigade, whose companies were periodically relieved by dismounted squadrons from the armoured regiments, occupied the deserted villages of Holtum and Nieuwstadt. This was 22nd Armoured Brigade's area of responsibility, and their task consisted in watching in the North, while maintaining constant foot patrols across the waterlogged fields, with their many streams and ditches, towards the Vloed Beek, a small stream running roughly parallel with the line, along which were the enemy's principal defences. This line had been held by both sides since September, and was liberally covered with mines, which various generations of our predecessors had in some cases omitted to mark, and further additions were also regularly made by both Brigades. To the right of 22nd Armoured Brigade, 131 Infantry Brigade had a Battalion in Millen, a Battalion in Tuddern and a Battalion, relieved when 52nd (Lowland) Division took over on our right, in the woods to the East. Their task was equally patrolling towards the villages of Isenbruch, Hongen and Havert, through which the enemy continued his line from the Vloed Beek. Two armoured regiments remained in reserve behind 22nd Armoured Brigade, a third was in Sittard, and the fourth in reserve behind 131 Brigade. The Division's frontage was some twelve thousand yards long, held very weakly by one squadron and two companies over half its length, and three battalions covering the rest. Main Divisional Headquarters was, until

Geleen

shortly before Christmas, at Limbricht, gallantly facing an enemy three thousand yards to the North-East, with nothing in between except an exiguous minefield. Eventually they exchanged positions with the 5th Royal Tanks, and withdrew to the greater safety of Geleen.

Originally it was planned that the Division should take part in an attack to extend the line to the Roer, but this operation, largely owing to the sodden character of the ground, was put off, until finally it reappeared under a different name and a different form on the 16th of January. The enemy and the cold, however, kept forward troops well occupied. First, with some heavy railway guns behind, and owing to his proximity to the Fatherland, he had more artillery and ammunition available than had been our experience since Normandy days, and shelling both on the forward villages, whose cellars gave good protection, and on Sittard itself, tended at times to be heavy. Secondly, patrolling by both sides was vigorous and active. The enemy's reconnaissance was on a more ambitious scale than that to which we had previously been accustomed. It was distinguished by the lavish use of patrol dogs, but on several occasions this did not prevent our own standing patrols from having the satisfactory experience of listening in to clashes between enemy patrols. Early on Boxing Day a strong fighting patrol captured Gebroek, causing us to lose several armoured cars and an Observation Post Tank; however, the place was re-taken the same day by two Troops each of the 8th and 11th Hussars, the enemy withdrawing at their approach. On our own side, on the left, the Rifle Brigade paid almost nightly visits to the streams South of the Vloed Beek, to inspect the sites of the various blown bridges and to look for new enemy minefields or patrols. Clashes were frequent, the enemy's standing patrols on the banks of the streams usually being alert. On the high ground to the right both sides maintained a chain of standing patrols occupying tactical features such as track junctions, forward of their main positions, and our own reconnaissance patrols, who brought back much valuable information as to the location of new enemy posts or minefields, were frequently involved in close actions with Sten guns and grenades against Spandaus. When the snow fell patrolling was carried out in white camouflage suits which, provided weapons were camouflaged as well, gave a very high degree of concealment. On the other hand, the snow made it extremely hard to detect the enemy's minefields, one of which caused heavy casualties to a raiding party of the 9th Durham Light Infantry, directed upon Isenbruch on the night of the 9th of January. A great increase in air activity was noticeable, carried out in conjunction with the Ardennes counter-offensive on the 16th of December, when a number of bombs were dropped on Sittard, and on the 1st of January, when the great assault on the Allied airfields was undertaken. For the first time we came into contact with his fast, silent, jet-propelled aircraft, and the Light Anti-Aircraft did well to shoot down two on the first occasion, and a further seven, of which only four were picked up, on the second. About the time of the opening of the counter-offensive in the Ardennes, a great increase in tracked activity and movement was heard behind the enemy lines, which at first caused some alarm, until a deserter appeared who dispelled our fears, saying he had seen nothing, although air reports also seemed to indicate bridging activity. With the introduction of some galloping horses to the nightly programme, these interesting noises were put down to a gramophone, and we were a little surprised to be told by two Allied airmen, picked up in the course of the January offensive, that, in fact, during this period the enemy had brought up considerable numbers of tanks and was openly boasting of an attack down to Maastricht and Liège. These reinforcements eventually moved off about Christmas time, so they said, doubtless because the enemy's air reconnaissance had revealed plenty of armour behind our thinly held line—8th Armoured Brigade were also in reserve behind us—and because the growing lack of success of the Ardennes counter-offensive necessitated their employment down there. A further result of the Ardennes offensive, in view of the prominent part played by German wolves disguised as American sheep, was to make all ranks highly suspicious, resulting in the incarceration of a number of innocent American officers and soldiers who had decided that Christmas was as good a time as any for visits to their girl friends in our area.

The Division spent Christmas in Germany and Holland, with some rear elements in Belgium. The 1/5th Queens, who were holding the line in front of the village of Wehr, just inside Germany, spent Christmas

Troops produce home comforts for a slit trench

in the traditional manner. Two Companies were in reserve and were able to celebrate in glorious style. They took over the local "Gasthof", where the Christmas morning service was held, and in the afternoon dined and made merry. Mr. Frank Gillard, correspondent of the BBC, spent Christmas with this Battalion and introduced Corporal Pass of "D" Company, who spoke on the wireless just before the King's speech. It was a signal honour for the Battalion—Christmas in Germany, after Africa, Italy and Normandy. The enemy activity on Christmas night was confined to the singing of "Heilige Nacht", which floated across the frost-bound no-man's land. This was countered by the Division, whose choir took part in the carol singing, broadcast on the BBC, at 21st Army Group.

On the 13th of January we undertook the first stage of Operation "Blackcock", designed to bring the Allied line up to the line of the River Roer on a front of approximately twelve miles, against two German Infantry Divisions, 176 and 183, supported by a number of self-propelled guns and likely to be reinforced by the parachutists holding the Maas to their North. Unlike the operation planned for December, but abandoned on account of the weather, the Division was now to play the leading part, and had under its command for the first phase the 8th Armoured Brigade and 155 Brigade from the 52nd Division. It was decided to make use of our advanced left flank to break into the enemy position across the Vloed Beek and open the main road from Sittard to Schilberg from the rear, thus avoiding the extensive minefields and elaborate defences which would have confronted any frontal attack. 8th Armoured Brigade and 155 Brigade were to be passed down the Sittard—Schilberg road as soon as it could be opened and then to turn South-East and, by a rapid night move, to seize the dominating high ground in the Waldfeucht, Bocket, Koningsbosch triangle. This would outflank and render largely untenable the whole enemy position on the Corps front. 52nd Division and, later, 43rd Division were then to roll up the main enemy defensive area. Subsequently, all enemy forces on the west of the Roer were to be destroyed by a series of co-ordinated thrusts in a North-Easterly direction, with the 7th Armoured Division setting the pace. Plenty of time was available, and the plan was worked out in great detail. The troops who were to take part in the initial break-in rehearsed the part which they were to play. Extensive precautions were undertaken to preserve secrecy, and when this was no longer possible, to mislead the enemy as to how and where the main attack would be delivered.

The Divisional plan was to open the offensive by the capture of the small village of Bakenhoven, some one thousand yards beyond our forward positions, to be followed up three days later by a two-pronged attack to get us on to the main Sittard—Roermond road. The left-hand force, 9th Durham Light Infantry, advancing along roads which were little more than banked up tracks, liable to collapse completely at the slightest thaw, was to bridge the Vloed Beek at Bakenhoven and to capture Dieteren, two thousand yards beyond. From thence 1st Royal Tanks, less one squadron, and 2nd Devons in Kangaroos*, were to

---

* Armoured Personnel Carriers

Troops in camouflage clothing near Nieuwstadt

exploit on to Echt, Schilberg and Hingen. Meanwhile, covered by "I" Company of the 1st Rifle Brigade, the two streams South of the Vloed Beek on the main road were to be bridged, after which 1/5th Queens, supported by "B" Squadron of the 1st Royal Tanks, were to capture Susteren. 8th Armoured Brigade would then follow through, turning off East in order to loosen the opposition on 52nd (Lowland) Division's front, who were on our right on the high ground North-East of Sittard, and were to attack North towards Waldfeucht and join up with 8th Armoured Brigade. Finally, 43rd Division, on the right of 52nd, were to close up on to the valley of the Worm which, after running North-East from Geilenkirchen, turns North-West to join the River Roer. To return to the Division, having captured Echt, we were to exploit North-West in the triangle between the Maas and the Roer, the left flank being cleared by First Commando Brigade, who came under our command for this operation.

Throughout the operation, in spite of occasional slight thaws, the ground was frost-bound and snow-covered.

On the morning of the 13th, three days before "D" Day, and after a considerable artillery barrage, Bakenhoven was captured by 1/5th Queens, after the Flail tanks had cleared a way through the minefield. No prisoners were taken, as after a little firing in the streets, the enemy made off under cover of fog, leaving twenty-five dead behind. The only enemy response was some slight shelling and mortaring. Until "D" Day, nothing untoward occurred except a small enemy counter-attack against Bakenhoven, which was driven off without difficulty and with heavy enemy loss.

The next stage was postponed for twelve hours because of a thick fog which had settled over the area, but luckily the enemy were quiet except for some shelling of Gebroek and Bakenhoven, and final marshalling for the advance was completed on the 15th of January. The ground and weather were vital factors in the opening stages of operation "Blackcock"; the decision to strike for Echt and Schilberg with tanks could only be made if the frost held and the going was firm. Early on the 16th all was ready, and at 7.30 a.m.

AFVs are painted white for snow warfare

Crossing a dyke near Dieteren

9th Durham Light Infantry assaulted the Vloed Beek opposite Bakenhoven. They carried carefully made ladders to cross the twenty-foot stream and were, in fact, a purely infantry force carrying all that was necessary for their maintenance until vehicles could be got across the dykes. The assault was successful despite heavy enemy shelling and some small arms fire. A bridge was captured intact over the second dyke just in front of Dieteren, and by 10.30 a.m. all companies were on their objectives in the village. Many prisoners were taken, and a company of 1/5th Queens under command of 9th Durham Light Infantry branched off to the South to occupy a concrete works which was thought to contain a strong point and might have been a source of trouble later. The salient feature of this first battle was the outstanding determination of the Durhams, who faced the enemy and the bitter weather undaunted, and by their example inspired all others to make the operation a success. The next problem was to bridge the Vloed Beek in order that vehicles could cross to the support of 9th Durham Light Infantry and carry out the next phases of the operation. During the 16th of January and on into the early hours of the 17th, 621st Field Squadron Royal Engineers fought to bull-doze a causeway over the obstacle. They were hampered by the thick fog, which, mixed with smoke fired from the 25-pounders, reduced vision to a few yards. Their stores lorries bogged in the mud and they worked under constant and accurate shelling of the crossing site. The tenacity and bravery of the Sappers was beyond all praise. Meanwhile, owing to a light thaw, which was rapidly making the Gebroek road on the West impassable even to tracks, it was decided to proceed straight away with what was originally planned as the third preliminary stage of the operation, the capture of Susteren from the West. During the night of the 16th/17th of January, Churchill bridgelayers were successfully put in position over the two streams to the South of the Vloed Beek, although the Rifle Brigade had trouble with an enemy patrol encountered on the way, who made off, losing their dog, and, later, had to blast a small standing patrol out of a house covering the second bridging site.

1/5th Queens, having moved up during the 16th of January to Gebroek, started their approach march to cross the Vloed Beek at two o'clock in the morning of the 17th. Conditions were extremely bad; a slight thaw had produced thick mud, and the fog still persisted.

Blown bridge over the Vloed Beek, near Susteren

Susteren

The night was pitch dark. Each Company and Battalion Headquarters could only take a Jeep and a carrier for essential stores and ammunition, and it was impossible even to manhandle the six-pounder anti-tank guns across the dykes in the dark. The crowning trial was a counter-attack by Spandau teams South down the Vloed Beek from the direction of Susteren. This took place as the leading Company and Battalion Headquarters were making the crossing. A very dangerous situation was saved by the column dropping off Bren gun teams to return the fire, and, above all, by the heavy defensive fire which 3rd Royal Horse Artillery put down on the flank of the leading Company. This was so accurate that prisoners said later that almost all the counter-attacking force were killed or wounded. The Queens escaped without a single casualty from this affair and their approach march continued. By eight o'clock a Company had secured a foothold in the Northern part of the village, to be counter-attacked an hour later by approximately a battalion of infantry supported by four tanks and self-propelled guns before the 1st Royal Tanks were able to cross the Vloed Beek to their support. Two of the enemy tanks were knocked out, one by a Piat, after which the remaining two withdrew, and the enemy infantry, having suffered casualties from artillery and small arms fire, withdrew into the houses on the approach of "B" Squadron, 1st Royal Tanks. Hard fighting still continued, and by three o'clock, the whole place was clear except the South-West corner, from which the enemy was ejected by last light. The attack on Susteren, however, so distracted the enemy that during the day, the Sappers, covered by 1st Rifle Brigade, had been able to make good progress in bridging the Vloed Beek to the South. Oud Roosteren, which earlier patrols of the 11th Hussars had found held, was also captured by the 6th Kings Own Scottish Borderers, under our command from 52nd (Lowland) Division, and twenty-five prisoners taken. "C" Squadron, 1st Royal Tanks, with the 2nd Devons and some Crocodiles, then pushed farther up the appalling tracks beyond Oud Roosteren to capture Ophoven and the Western part of Echt. Altogether, over a hundred prisoners had been taken, for comparatively small losses. By this time the Gebroek road was almost impassable, and, although, in spite of shell fire, the Sappers had completed the two remaining bridges South of Susteren, an attempt by the 1st Royal Tanks to push on up the main road to Schilberg that night was halted at a road block fifteen hundred yards beyond Susteren, where a crater left the road unusable throughout the next day.

5.5 gun howitzers lay down a barrage before the attack on Susteren

Tank passes over one of the bridges into Susteren

The next morning, the 18th, 1st Royal Tanks and 2nd Devons, continued their advance Eastwards in Echt and by a quarter past seven had captured the centre of the town and knocked out a 75 mm anti-tank gun, although losing one Crocodile. They then advanced to take Hingen, two thousands yards to the North-East. Meanwhile, the remainder of 1st Royal Tanks advancing up the main road from the South, although held up by four anti-tank guns at the road block of the night before, and losing two tanks, had managed to work round, against two self-propelled guns, to join up with the Squadron in Schilberg. 8th Armoured Brigade then came up the main road from Sittard and, owing to the crater in the road, were forced to turn off towards Heide. Here they met a minefield, and also considerable numbers of enemy, but by last light had advanced three thousand yards to the marshes and woods South of Kloster Lilbosch. By first light the next morning, they were established on the high ground threatening Waldfeucht and were engaged in heavy fighting with infantry and self-propelled guns in country which offered little scope for manoeuvre. Their rapid and bold advance turned a considerable portion of the enemy's main defensive line and enabled 52nd Division to join up with them that evening. The enemy were still not cleared from the woods South-East of Susteren, a task which occupied the 1/5th Queens the best part of the 19th.

By the 20th, our original roads through Bakenhoven and Gebroek, aided by a sudden thaw, had collapsed, but the centre line was now clear, and 22nd Armoured Brigade was able to begin its task of exploiting towards Montfort, four and a half miles beyond Schilberg. The first obstacle was the village of St. Joost, two thousand yards beyond Schilberg, and garrisoned by three companies of parachutists. Meanwhile, 11th Hussars moved up towards the enemy positions on the banks of the Maas and by the evening, after capturing a section of parachutists in Berkelaar, had advanced five miles to enter Maasbracht unopposed. Maasbracht was then taken over by 1st Commando Brigade on the following day.

The battle for St. Joost, however, occupied the whole of the 20th and 21st. Originally, the assault was carried out by "I" Company, 1st Rifle Brigade, supported by 8th Hussars and a troop of "Crocodiles". The attack started well with the capture of seventeen

Echt

Schilberg

prisoners, but, thereafter, the two platoons originally committed had to grind a way from house to house with hand-grenades and Sten guns. After an hour and a half of bitter hand-to-hand fighting, by which time the third remaining platoon of "I" Company had been put in, about five hundred yards had been gained, twenty enemy killed and a further forty prisoners captured, at the cost of three men killed, including one platoon sergeant, and twenty-three wounded, including the remaining platoon sergeants. The Durham Light Infantry were then put in, but three attacks made little further progress, largely owing to technical difficulties with the Crocodiles. Finally, in the afternoon of the 21st, as a result of the very close co-operation of 8th Hussars and the satisfactory functioning of the Crocodiles, the Durhams succeeded in clearing all but the final two hundred yards of the village. This was completed by two platoons of "C" Company of the Rifle Brigade, who succeeded in capturing a self-propelled gun intact. The final score was sixty prisoners and three self-propelled guns, but according to Hübner, the regimental commander of the parachutists, one company had been annihilated and another received very heavy casualties indeed.

On the right, operations by 52nd Division had been going well. Waldfeucht had been captured, and the patrols of the 11th Hussars had pushed on five thousand yards down the road from Schilberg to Waldfeucht. On the 22nd, once St. Joost was cleared, operations started for the capture of Montfort, which was completed by the afternoon of the 23rd. Originally, the task was given to 5th Dragoon Guards and "C" Company, 1st Rifle Brigade, advancing on two routes. They relieved the reconnaissance troop of 8th Hussars on the stream, some five hundred yards West of Montfort, over which the bridges were blown, and the Northern force, consisting of a troop of 5th Dragoon Guards and two platoons of the Rifle Brigade, crossed over a bridge rapidly built by 4th Field Squadron Royal Engineers, and captured the village of Aandenberg, just North of Montfort. Here they were continually counter-attacked by infantry and spandaus, and suffered some casualties until 1/5th Queens moved up to make the area more secure in the course of the night. Meanwhile, the Southern column had had difficulty in crossing on their route, owing to mines and anti-tank guns firing over open ground, although the position was finally secured by "I" Company, 1st Rifle Brigade. The situation to the North was not entirely clear until the next afternoon

St Joost

Crocodiles in operation at St Joost

when 2nd Devons came up on the tanks of 5th Royal Tanks and cleared the road from St. Joost and the woods East of Aandenberg, from which the enemy had been engaging 1/5th Queens with close-range small arms fire. Montfort, by this time, had been reported clear, and was occupied by 1/5th Queens without opposition, other than mountains of rubble and crowds of refugees, the result of a Royal Air Force attack on the preceding afternoon.

The Division's attack was now continued on three axes. On the right, 131 Brigade advanced with 1st Royal Tanks and 1/5th Queens, who had been relieved in Montfort by 1st Rifle Brigade, to capture the area around Posterholt, five miles East of Montfort, from the road running East from Schilberg. In the centre, 22nd Armoured Brigade with 2nd Devons and 5th Dragoon Guards were to clear St. Odilienberg, on the high ground West of the River Roer, and on the left 1st Commando Brigade with the 8th Hussars, had on the evening of the 24th, already entered Linne, later to withdraw to a better position slightly to the West, and were patrolling vigorously to the South. The enemy was, by now, falling back behind the Roer, except opposite the Commandos, leaving in his trail a sea of mines, occasional small spandau and bazooka posts, and relying upon blown bridges over the stream East of Montfort to hold us up. By the 27th, Posterholt and St. Odilienberg had both been secured, delays being due more to the close nature of the country and enemy mining than to any great opposition, and the Commandos were firm in Linne, small numbers of prisoners continuing to come in from all these operations. On the 29th, the 1/5th Queens occupied Paarlo, to the South of Posterholt.

At the beginning of February the Division was regrouped with 11th Hussars in contact with 52nd Division on the right, who had by now gained all their objectives, 131 Brigade holding the centre from Paarlo to St. Odilienberg, each battalion maintaining a company in reserve in Echt, and 1st Commando Brigade from South of Linne to the river bank. Each brigade had an armoured regiment under command and 22nd Armoured Brigade remained in reserve, with the Rifle Brigade in Montfort. The enemy remained quiet, except for a counter-attack on Paarlo on the night of the 29th-30th, which cost him ten prisoners and many other casualties from mortar and

Attack on St Joost

Montfort

small arms fire, and contented himself with harassing our forward positions with fire from his guns in the Siegfried Line. The Commandos, as the only Brigade in close contact with the enemy during the closing days of January, patrolled actively and fiercely, flushing "Bell" Island on the River Maas on the night of the 28th, and the heavily mined woods to the South-East of Linne on the 30th, suffering and inflicting casualties on both occasions. On the 31st the enemy blew up his last remaining bridge over the Roer, South of Roermund, at Vlodrop, an act which may be regarded as the finale to operation "Blackcock". The extreme cold had made conditions, particularly for the infantry, as hard and exacting as any experienced in this war. No praise can be too high for the fine qualities of endurance and the dogged determination and fighting spirit of all ranks.

Operation "Blackcock" was remarkable in two particulars, first, for the successful employment of an Armoured Division in mid-winter, over snow, and secondly, as the first occasion that the Division had ever operated with Commando troops. The success of the first was due, to some extent, to the very careful system of traffic control instituted, since, without this, Brigades and units would not have been able to get out and defeat the enemy by their fighting qualities and by having the right people at the right place. It must be remembered that throughout the operation the Division was using a single one-way road; at first, the miserable track running North of Buchten through Gebroek and Oud Roosteren, and later, when that collapsed, the main road from Sittard, which could only be used one-way through Susteren and over the bridges. Accordingly, Liaison Officers with wireless sets were posted at all important junctions, and worked tirelessly for four days and nights, largely without sleep, in conditions of the greatest misery and cold, to ensure that all movement proceeded in accordance with pre-arranged priorities with the minimum of friction. On the second aspect, some further study of the Commando operations is worth while, in view of the close friendship so rapidly established between them and the armoured regiments with whom they worked. On the 24th they carried out a raid on Linne and the station to the South, for his part in which Lance-Corporal Harden, of the Royal Army Medical Corps, was awarded a posthumous Victoria Cross. Later, although forced to withdraw against a counter-attack by Mark IVs, twenty-three enemy dead were counted when they re-entered the place three days afterwards. On the 28th, they raided "Bell" Island, on the opposite bank of the Maas. They reached the West end of the island, after landing without casualties, and a violent battle with grenades took place, reinforced on the enemy's part by accurate shell fire. Five of the enemy were killed and one prisoner taken, but

St Odilienberg

the evacuation of the wounded was made particularly difficult by the strong current which necessitated eight men paddling to each boat, together with swimmers alongside, in a temperature well below zero. In the afternoon of the 25th, a successful raid on the Heide wood was carried out, in conjunction with the 5th Royal Tanks, in which the

Linne

Commandos, although co-operating with tanks for almost the first time, fell into the drill at once. Thereafter, they contented themselves with local patrolling and propaganda broadcasts, reinforced by artillery concentrations, against the island which brought about the surrender of twelve men; an enemy patrol which was rash enough to approach their positions was very roughly handled, three enemy being killed and one taken prisoner, at the cost of three men wounded to the Commandos.

We remained in our positions overlooking the Maas until the 21st of February, when the Division moved to concentrate and rest North of Bree, after having maintained a battalion resting in Maesyck barracks for most of this time. It was a period of little activity, except for the artillery, occasional patrol clashes and a spirited appearance of the Luftwaffe which inflicted no damage. But for the first and only occasion in our history, we came under direct American command, in this case that of Lieutenant-General Anderson of XVIth

United States Corps. (We had already long ago achieved the record of having served under every Corps in First Canadian and Second British Armies.) On the 2nd of February the great frost finally

Brew up

ended and three weeks later we made our way over the Maas, the relief of the Division having been delayed twenty-four hours, in a final sea of mud, admiring, as we left, the peace-time precision with which 8th United States Armoured Division motored up the road to our relief.

Chapter X

A BRIEF PERIOD OF REST. THE BATTLE OF GERMANY

The 21st of February—9th of May, 1945

As a rest area, the country round Weert and Bree, to which we moved, was not ideal, being for the most part overcrowded with troops and civilians, distant from Brussels and set in depressing surroundings, in the North verging into marsh and in the South flat, bare fields. Moreover, prolonged experience of numerous troops, added to the fact that Lent was now upon us, had made the local priesthood somewhat suspicious of "Tommy's" intentions to the girls, and in most areas dances were difficult to organise. However, in Weert, football pitches and a gymnasium were available, so that the Division was able to run two highly successful football competitions, one a unit tournament, the other a knock-out between Brigades and the Royal Artillery, and also a knock-out boxing competition between Brigades. The inter-unit football league was won by 65th Anti-tank Regiment against 131 Brigade Field Ambulance, on a replay after a draw, by three goals to two; the inter-Brigade football was won by 22nd Brigade against the Royal Artillery, two goals to one, and the boxing by the Royal Artillery in a triangular contest.

Equally, training and re-equipment played an important part in view of our next operation, the great advance into Germany. 131 Brigade carried out a series of exercises over the River Maas on assault landings in co-operation with amphibious vehicles, and a street-fighting exercise without troops to study the co-operation of tanks and infantry, to which much thought and discussion were devoted, culminating in a series of lectures at Divisional Headquarters. 22nd Armoured Brigade received twenty-five new tanks, straight from England, as replacements for tanks with a high mileage. We were also visited on the 5th March by the Commander-in-Chief, Field-Marshal Sir Bernard Montgomery, who presented medal ribbons earned during Operation "Blackcock".

The period culminated with the planning of Operation "Plunder" for the crossing of the Rhine and the invasion of Germany, with all the familiar trappings of "Overlord" present, locked doors, blacked-out windows, and harassed senior staff officers. Before approaching the story of the operation itself, we must look back slightly over the preceding period, for the events of late February and March were, if anything, even more decisive than "Plunder" itself, as it was during these battles that the German organisation was broken as a co-ordinated system of command and planning.

In mid-February, the Canadian First Army, consisting largely of British formations, began the attack through the Reichswald Forest, an attack which not only attracted to itself all the available German reserves of infantry, parachutists and armour, but was carried out through country which was entirely on the side of the defender, a country of few roads and these all indifferent, of sodden fields and forests heavily mined, while on the Rhine valley flank it became simply deep floods. This attack inevitably made slow progress. It was followed at the end of February by the attack of the United States Ninth Army across the Roer, designed to split the German forces West of the Rhine in two and then to swing North from opposite Cologne to join up with the Canadian First Army. After the initial brilliant crossing of the flooded Roer, Ninth Army's attack broke through, and at the same time General Patton's Third Army drove South of the Eifel and on to the Rhine thirty miles South of Cologne. By the 12th of March, Ninth Army's and First Canadian Army's attacks had joined up, and between them had captured forty-five thousand prisoners and inflicted a further twenty thousand long term casualties. On this front the enemy had in position two Armies, 1st Parachute Army opposite the Canadians, and Fifteenth Army opposite the Ninth. Between them they consisted of ten infantry divisions, four parachute divisions and six Panzer or Panzer Grenadier Divisions, all of whose infantry component had been reduced by a half, and the armour by something less as a result of First Canadian and Ninth United States Armies' attacks. But Fifteenth Army had only barely succeeded in getting out of the Cologne Plain without a complete rout, and it was severely disorganised. Only First Parachute Army had succeeded in preserving its organisation more or less intact, and had withdrawn across the Rhine at Wesel through a small bridgehead which had resisted all efforts to secure its elimination. Meanwhile, in the South, General Patton's advance had been decisive. Seventh Army had been broken on the Moselle, uncovering the flank of Fifth Panzer Army in the Eifel, who attempted, too late, to join the scramble to the Rhine. Briefly, the result was that the enemy out of these two armies lost in two weeks one hundred and twenty thousand prisoners, a bridge intact over the Rhine at Remagen and never again succeeded in reorganising his Southern front, which little more than a month later finally collapsed in the mountains of Bavaria and the Czecho-Slovak frontier, hemmed in between the Russians and Americans. To complete the picture of imminent disaster, by the end of March the Russians were on the Oder. The only available striking force, Sixth SS Panzer Army, was irrevocably committed to a losing battle in the Plains of Hungary, and the remainder of the enemy's Armies in Italy and Norway were, through the collapse of the enemy's land and sea transport system under the pressure of Allied air attack, powerless to intervene to save the Fatherland except to the extent of providing one infantry division each a month.

The Second British Army's part in Operation "Plunder" was to cross the Rhine at three main points, at Rees with 30th Corps, and at Xanten and Wesel with 12th Corps. The landings were to be covered by airborne landings on 12th Corps' front to seize intact the bridges behind the Rhine. On our right, some seven miles upstream, Ninth

United States Army was to cross at Dinslaken. 12th Corps' plan was for 15th (Scottish) Division to undertake the Xanten crossings, and to complete the construction of a number of ferries and three bridges, one fit for tanks, as soon as possible. Meanwhile, the Commandos were to land at Wesel. The landings were to be carried out in darkness on the night of the 23rd/24th of March, and the next morning the 6th British Airborne and 17th United States Airborne Divisions were to land on a front of some five miles wide, two miles East of Wesel, and to seize the river crossings over the Ijssel and Lippe. As soon as the ferries had got into position, 4th Armoured Brigade, less one regiment which crossed with the assault craft, was to cross in support of 15th (Scottish) Division, and 7th Armoured Division was to cross over the bridge at Xanten to exploit East and parallel with the Lippe, while 53rd (Welsh) Division crossed on the lighter bridges, to come up on our left, taking under its wing 4th Armoured Brigade.

On the evening of the 23rd, everything was in readiness. On our own side of the river, 52nd (Lowland) Division, who had finally eliminated the pocket West of Wesel, were holding the line, with 15th (Scottish) Division, 53rd (Welsh) Division, 4th Armoured Brigade and a mass of bridging equipment concentrated behind them, while opposite the Corps front was a part of 2 Parachute Division, holding the river North of Bislich, and the Grenadiers of 84 Infantry Division in the woods, and along the river from thence to Wesel. The Division itself, except for 3rd and 5th Royal Horse Artillery, who were supporting the Commandos, still remained around Heeze, a hundred miles from the Rhine, and did not move across until the 25th, when they concentrated North of Geldern.

The assault went in successfully, opposition being strongest on the front held by the parachutists. By the end of the day, the Commandos had secured the greater part of Wesel, capturing two hundred prisoners; 15th Scottish had got a good foothold at Bislich and had pushed on some three miles to the edge of the woods to the North and nearly half way to Wesel. On the North, however, towards 51st (Highland) Division, who had not yet captured Rees, opposition across open fields was still severe. 6th Airborne's landings had suffered heavy casualties, but they had captured their bridges, in particular the bridge we were to use at Hamminkeln, two miles beyond Wesel, and had a firm foothold in the area, although they had not yet joined up with the land forces. By the evening of the 26th, opposition against 15th (Scottish) was still heavy, though they now controlled twelve thousand yards of the East bank of the Rhine, and had a bridgehead some seven or eight thousand yards in depth. The Americans from Dinslaken had gone well, and by now had linked up with the airborne troops on the Lippe bridges. In spite of heavy shelling and night bombing, the bridging on 12th Corps front had progressed well, and by the morning of the 27th a tank bridge, although damaged during the night by a near miss, was in position between Xanten and Bislich, together with a lighter bridge farther downstream.

On the morning of the 27th, the Division started to move across, headed by the 11th Hussars. The pace was inevitably slow, as beyond

ACV5 crossing the Rhine

the river all traffic had only a narrow secondary road to serve its needs, and on to this road was coming traffic from two bridges, meeting at right angles half-way along its length. Moreover, there was an inevitable small amount of traffic, such as ambulances, coming against the stream. However, bit by bit, the Division fought its way across, and 11th Hussars got out along a narrow road running parallel with the Rhine towards the main road from Wesel. Here they met the 6th Airborne, who had a Parachute Brigade in the woods to the North-East of Wesel, and drove along forest tracks to Hamminkeln, held by 6th Air Landing Brigade, who had by now advanced through the orchards and fields of the valley to a low sandy ridge, covered with pine trees, overlooking Brunen, four and a half miles beyond. The bridge at Brunen was blocked by rubble, and patrols operating to the flanks had a busy time with spandaus, bazookas and an occasional self-propelled gun, apart from great difficulty in moving along the soft, sandy tracks. By the late afternoon, 5th Dragoon Guards had come up, but were halted at a blown bridge on the main road half-way between Brunen and Raesfeld, three and a half miles from Brunen. Here, although an 88 mm was abandoned, after the tanks appeared, the blow was covered by fire from mortars and two self-propelled guns. 11th Hussars then endeavoured to find a way round to the North, but were at every point held up by anti-tank guns.

From the 29th to the 30th, 22nd Armoured Brigade led the advance on a three regimental front. On the left, 5th Royal Tanks were directed on Borken across the wooded plateau to the North of the main road from Brunen to Raesfeld. In the centre, 5th Dragoon Guards and 9th Durham Light Infantry continued to advance along the main road, with the intention of turning North at Raesfeld and coming up on Borken from the South. On the right, 1st Royal Tanks went East to Heiden, and the next day were directed North to Ramsdorf. Opposition was heaviest, at first, on the left. Good roads or tracks were hard to find, and a number of tanks became bogged in the soft, sandy soil. The woods gave ample cover to the parachutists, plentifully armed with bazookas, and supported by self-propelled guns, who were holding the left flank of 2 Parachute Corps. After much fighting, in the course of which some fifty enemy were killed and ninety prisoners taken, 5th Royal Tanks reached Borken on the night of the 28th, after the place had already been occupied by 5th Dragoon Guards and 9th Durham Light Infantry. For, along the centre route, opposition had been much easier. During the night of the 27th/28th, the self-propelled guns, covering the blown bridge between Brunen and Raesfeld, had withdrawn. In the morning the gap was bridged. Raesfeld was lightly held, and was captured without difficulty by "A" Company, 1st Rifle

The breakout from the Rhine bridgehead. Tanks pass through Brunen

Stadtlohn

Brigade, who took thirty prisoners. 9th Durham Light Infantry were, accordingly, brought up behind 5th Dragoon Guards, and the group advanced on Borken, meeting slight opposition from bazookas and self-propelled guns. Borken was impassable, owing to the many craters caused by bombing, but a way round was found, and the force leagured for the night South of Gemen, having advanced ten miles during the day. During the night, Gemen was cleared by the 9th Durham Light Infantry, and at six o'clock on the 29th, the advance was resumed. Progress off the roads was difficult, as tanks became easily bogged, and the advance was temporarily held up, after four miles, by a platoon of enemy infantry, supported by four self-propelled guns, in the outskirts of Weseke. This was overcome by a company of the Durhams, supported by the tanks, and four self-propelled guns were destroyed or captured, of which two became bogged as they left the road. The group was now directed on Stadtlohn, six and a half miles beyond, and by seven o'clock in the evening had got half-way, to the outskirts of Südlohn, having destroyed a further four self-propelled guns and much transport on the way. Südlohn, again, was hopelessly blocked by the craters caused by bombing, and, while the rest of the group looked for a way round the desolation, "A" Company of the Rifle Brigade, eventually joined by a troop of tanks, were dismounted and, during the night, fought their way into the outskirts of Stadtlohn, where they held on in spite of continual enemy counter-attacks. Meanwhile, 4th Field Squadron, Royal Engineers, worked hard to improve the roads, and at 4 a.m. on the 30th 5th Dragoon Guards and 9th

Durham Light Infantry came up to join the riflemen. Stadtlohn was garrisoned by two Battalions of 857 Grenadier Regiment, who had hastily come up from Holland, and before recounting its reduction, we must return to events on the right and left flanks.

1st Royal Tanks with their Motor Company, "C" Company of the 1st Rifle Brigade, formed the right-hand column. On the evening of the 28th, they had been ordered to capture Heiden, three miles East of Raesfeld, and thence to advance North-East to Gescher. By the evening, after being slightly shelled, they had reached Heiden, which, burning fiercely and containing an ammunition dump, could not be entered in strength. The enemy were withdrawing as we came up. The next morning they were ordered North towards Ramsdorf, four and three-quarter miles from Raesfeld. Rain was falling and going off the roads over the soft fields very bad. Just South of Ramsdorf, "B" Squadron lost a tank to a bazooka, and in attempting to cross the river over a flimsy wooden bridge, this collapsed. However, the reconnaissance troop, on the main road, entered the town past a road block which was not held, but met enemy with bazookas in the centre, who knocked out two tanks and killed or wounded several men. After every

Stadtlohn, showing common road block

other house had been "brewed" by the tanks, the town was cleared by two platoons of the Rifle Brigade and a Squadron brought in over a fascine built with German labour. Further progress on this flank was stopped, as 11th Armoured Division were coming up on our right to exploit beyond Coesfeld, which had already been captured by 6th Airborne Division and 6th Guards Tank Brigade. The Regiment accordingly returned to Südlohn, preparatory to passing through the 5th Dragoon Guards on the centre route.

Meanwhile, on the left 5th Royal Tanks were relieved on the morning of the 29th by 8th Hussars, and remained temporarily West of Borken, under command of 131 Brigade. 8th Hussars' orders were to protect the main axis, namely that of 5th Dragoon Guards, by advancing on Oding, seven thousand yards South-West of Stadtlohn. The 29th was spent dealing with opposition, chiefly self-propelled guns and small parties of infantry, to the North-West of Borken, and enemy in strength were not met until the woods just short of the Regiment's objective. Here was a good natural position, extending across both sides of the road, secured from outflanking by the difficult going over the fields on either side. After four tanks had been lost in probing the enemy's defences, it soon became clear that only a methodical clearing of the woods by infantry would open the way to Oding. The only infantry available, "I" Company, 1st Rifle Brigade, successfully cleared the Western half of the woods, but the enemy still remained strongly entrenched on the opposite side of the road. At five o'clock in the afternoon, a company of the 2nd Devons arrived, but by this time a Squadron had worked round the Eastern flank of the woods, capturing fifty prisoners, and had reached the bridge on the Southern outskirts of Oding, where the charges were removed. This had the effect of loosening enemy opposition in the Eastern half of the woods, which was cleared by the 2nd Devons without difficulty. On the 31st the Regiment moved into Oding, only to find that the bridge to the East was blown. By now, 4th Armoured Brigade had come up and, that afternoon, the Regiment returned to the area of Südlohn.

Early in the afternoon on the 29th, as 131 Brigade and 5th Royal Tanks were coming up, fighting had again broken out in the woods North of Borken, where the remainder of 33 Panzer Grenadier Ersatz Battalion were established with a self-propelled gun and two 88's. This was cleared by 5th Royal Tanks and 1/5th Queens and the two 88's knocked out. 131 Brigade leaguered for the night between Weseke and Südlohn, and 155th Brigade, who had come under our command from 52nd Division, moved up to protect the centre line around Borken and Raesfeld.

In the centre the main obstacle to further progress on the 30th proved to be the town of Stadtlohn. The town itself had been bombed into a mass of rubble, except for part of the church tower, which alone remained standing. By mid-day, after hard fighting, 9th Durham Light Infantry had secured the town but found the main bridge blown and the streets blocked with rubble. 5th Dragoon Guards, however, found a second bridge to the North-East which, although the Royal Engineers

The bridge at Stadtlohn

expressed considerable misgivings as to its ability to take tanks, survived long enough for the 1st Royal Tanks and 1/5th Queens to get over, while the Royal Engineers built a Bailey over the stream. Opposition in the woods to the North was largely by-passed by taking side roads, some of which were mined, and, after a short battle at Wullen, where 1/5th Queens overran a small party supported by mortars and a self-propelled gun, 1st Royal Tanks pushed on eleven miles in the dark, towards the outskirts of Ahaus, all entrances to which were held at road blocks. During the night, after a prearranged artillery programme, Ahaus was entered, and found to contain many mines and booby traps in addition to the numerous bomb craters. After spending the morning in replenishment, 1st Royal Tanks turned North-East towards the River Ems. The road and the ground on either side were open and covered by a number of anti-tank guns, self-propelled 75 mms and towed 50 mms. Advance down the main road was at first impossible, and a Honey tank was knocked out by a self-propelled gun. Accordingly, "C" Squadron with "C" Company, 1st Rifle Brigade, went off across country to outflank the enemy positions to the South. This achieved its object and, although two tanks were lost in the process, the enemy guns eventually withdrew, enabling the remainder of the Regiment and a Company of the 1/5th Queens in "Kangaroos" to motor down the main road for six miles, as far as the outskirts of Heek, the garrison of which was overcome in a night attack by the 1/5th Queens. The next day, the 1st of April, the first real "swan" began. 1st Royal

Tanks Group remained guarding the centre line and 5th Dragoon Guards, 11th Hussars and 9th Durham Light Infantry came into the lead, directed on Rheine, under command of 131 Brigade. Although held up for a short time by some infantry around a mined road-block at Metelen, by early afternoon the force had pushed on twenty miles to the outskirts of Rheine, had captured a hospital intact, and destroyed a few incautious enemy motorists on the way. That evening, the 9th Durham Light Infantry fought their way in against a garrison from our old opponents, 857 Grenadier Regiment, capturing and killing many, to find the bridges over the Ems blown. Later, they were withdrawn, as patrols to the river reported many enemy holding the far bank, which would have required a full-scale infantry attack in order to overcome them, and would have lost much valuable time. Accordingly, on the following day, Rheine was handed over to 157 Brigade, and 131 Brigade, less 1/5th Queens, concentrated to the South-West in an area already cleared by 11th Armoured Division, who by now had drawn ahead.

While the operations round Stadtlohn were in progress on the 30th, a patrol of the 11th Hussars, operating on the left, had reached to within a thousand yards of Vreden, and reported meeting little opposition. The capture of Vreden, with its bridge over the River Berkel, would cut the line of retreat of the parachutists operating on our left. 5th Royal Tanks and 2nd Devons were therefore sent off that night to secure it, going over bad tracks until they reached the main road, where a road-block caused some delay to the column until it was removed. Although enemy were present in the woods, no serious opposition was met until the outskirts of Vreden, where the leading tank was hit by a bazooka and the following one became ditched and surrounded by enemy infantry. The infantry on these two tanks managed to fight their way back to the main body, although they suffered casualties. But, while a plan was being made to deal with this strong-point, the enemy withdrew. 5th Royal Tanks then succeeded in entering the town, but as the leading tank approached the bridge the enemy blew it. However, they destroyed a self-propelled gun which showed itself on the far side. The column then returned to Stadtlohn to refuel, and was redirected once more on to the left flank, on to Ottenstein and Wessum, two and a half miles West of Ahaus. Ottenstein was reached at last light on the 31st, after a short infantry battle in which thirty prisoners were taken, and after much difficulty with craters on the road. A few more prisoners were taken and a self-propelled gun, which had been troublesome, destroyed to the North. Beyond Ottenstein more enemy were met, well dug in and still prepared to fight. The company of the 2nd Devons with 5th Royal Tanks succeeded in penetrating the enemy positions, but opposition was too great and they were forced to withdraw. The force therefore remained watching the flank in that area, patrolling towards Wessum. Meanwhile, as we have seen, 131 Brigade were continuing the advance up the main road towards Rheine and 22nd Armoured Brigade was now directed as left flank protection on the road from Nienburg to Ochtrupp, two or three miles to the North, from where considerable enemy activity, shelling and mortaring had been experienced, and from where it was suspected a counter-attack might develop. To replace the company of the Devons, 5th Royal Tanks were given "I" Company of the 1st Rifle Brigade, and the advance, 5th Royal Tanks having had very little rest after their continuous movement for forty-eight hours, began at three o'clock in the afternoon of the 1st. Two miles beyond Nienburg, their leading vehicle, a scout car, was hit by a bazooka and the crew killed. The enemy were in some strength in a wood astride the road, which was also plentifully sown with mines. Although the tanks succeeded in working right round it, the riflemen were unable to clear more than half, and it was decided to remain firm in position and not to press on towards Ochtrupp. In any case, the anticipated enemy counter-attack never developed into anything more serious than shelling and mortaring on 12th Corps Headquarters in the wooded country North-East of Metelen, although the Air OP Squadron was attacked by bazookas on the night of the 2nd of April and four out of seven of their aircraft destroyed. There were by now many isolated enemy at large. Armoured cars of the 11th Hussars had shot up considerable numbers just off

Tac HQ 22 Armoured Brigade. Brigadier Wingfield and his staff

the centre line before 22nd Armoured Brigade came up, and at any stop a few smiling prisoners would usually appear.

As we advanced farther and faster, the enemy's disorganisation was to become increasingly more apparent, since German units tended to have less and less conception as to the general position. The supply system, except behind the parachutists on our left, was disintegrating equally with the chain of command. Reinforcements were no longer sent to units within an organised formation, but were handed over as an independent command to any suitable—and often to any unsuitable—officer to take to the front. Having arrived at what the commander considered a good place to stop, the next step was to organise a supply system from civilian houses and any abandoned ammunition dumps that might be found. In the meantime, the commander often lost either his command to a more senior officer or his men to somebody else equally in search of reinforcements. Depending on the quality of their leaders, whose morale was assisted by entire ignorance of the situation or refusal to accept the facts, these "ad hoc" units at times organised themselves for defence and resisted. More often than not, on the approach of our tanks, they either fired their last bazooka and then surrendered or, having no bazookas, withdrew into the comparative safety of the forest, there either to continue the battle against less well-equipped troops than the tanks, or else simply and frankly to find civilian clothes and desert before an opportunity arose for them once more to be impressed into a battle group by some irate and still bellicose Major. Indeed, their dilemma was very similar to that raised by Hilaire Belloc in his immortal poem on "Bears" and their fate very much the same. If for any reason, usually the presence of an organised Regiment or Division on a river line, the momentum of our advance was slowed, these battle groups were taken under command and often fought surprisingly well. On the other hand, in addition to these groups of stragglers or drafts, there were a certain number of units such as the Panzerjagdkommandos, consisting of selected officers and men, who had a definite offensive mission, often behind our lines, and these were infinitely more dangerous.

We must now return to the situation around Rheine on the main centre line. On the 2nd, 157 Brigade attacked over the Ems, and by evening, against heavy opposition from spandaus, mortars and shellfire, had established two and a half companies on the far bank. The remainder of the Division regrouped and was joined by 22nd Armoured Brigade, preparatory to advancing East from Rheine through the steep wooded hills of the Tecklenburg Range, using a bridge over the Ems that had been built the previous day by 11th Armoured Division, and a further bridge over the Dortmund-Ems Canal at Riesenbeck that they had captured intact. The enemy appeared to be in some strength in the Tecklenburg Hills, from which he had excellent observation, with isolated parties between the Ems and the canal East of Rheine, who were engaged by patrols of the 11th Hussars, protecting our left flank. Shelling on the bridge by a battery of 75 mms and on the low ground beyond by an 88 mm was considerable and accurate, and during the afternoon seventy men attempted to rush the bridge from the wooded slopes three hundred yards to the North, but were driven off by the concentrated rapid fire of a troop of Bofors on anti-aircraft protection of the bridge.

The 2nd of April marks the end of the first stage in the battle for Germany. In a week we had advanced a hundred and twenty miles, almost continuously opposed. Many casualties had been inflicted on the enemy in killed and prisoners, as well as on his vehicles. However, we were now once more faced with a natural obstacle, the River Ems, backed by the Teutoburger Wald. This obstacle had already been outflanked by 11th Armoured Division on our right, who were going well towards Osnabrück, having broken through the hills at Tecklenburg itself some eight miles to the East. They still, however, had two depleted battalions of 159th Brigade, supported by an armoured regiment, holding a bridgehead East of the Dortmund-Ems Canal. 11th Armoured's plan was to move due East in the general direction of Hanover, and we were to advance slightly North of them. We had indeed been unable to get out at Rheine, but at the time there seemed a good chance of breaking through at Ibbenbüren, then turning East along the excellent roads running through the undulating foothills to the North of the Tecklenburg Range, crossing the Ems-Weser Canal North of Osnabrück, and from there using the roads running North-East and North towards the Weser crossings South of Bremen. Thus we would avoid the hold-ups and traffic difficulties which would arise from using the bad road which was 11th Armoured Division's centre line to the South of the Tecklenburg Hills.

On the early morning of the 3rd the Division was disposed as follows:—131 Brigade, still in the lead, were concentrated in the Riesenbeck area, preparatory to carrying out an attack through the existing bridgehead of 159th Brigade. 155th Brigade from 52nd Division were coming up to take over the defence of the centre line behind them. 22nd Armoured Brigade were moving up into reserve South of Rheine. The first task of the Division then was the capture of Ibbenbüren.

In the previous twenty-four hours the Monmouths and Herefords of 159th Brigade had fought off fanatical counter-attacks. They had originally pushed up the ridge opposite their bridgehead and had secured positions on the right overlooking the main road cutting through the hills towards Ibbenbüren. It was difficult to support these positions, and the enemy, who had assembled strong forces in the surrounding woods, succeeded in pushing them back to the lowest open slopes of the ridge. On the 3rd of April 159th Brigade were holding the canal bridgehead with approximately one Battalion, closely supported by tanks. 131 Brigade's task was to pass through and attack Ibbenbüren, a road centre which lay in a valley North of the escarpment of the Teutoburger Wald and which was backed by another ridge of hills. There were two ways into Ibbenbüren which passed through the hills from South to North, one from the bridgehead area and one farther East.

Ibbenbüren. The ridge which was stubbornly defended

The original plan was for 2nd Devons to attack and clear the wooded ridge from the left flank (opposite the canal bridge), working East along its crest, while 9th Durham Light Infantry and 5th Dragoon Guards pushed through the Eastern road to the town. The Devons attack went well and they captured over a hundred prisoners. By the afternoon they were firm on the ridge, and 9th Durham Light Infantry and 5th Dragoon Guards had contacted the enemy in their advance up the gorge. Then began a grim battle against the fanatical Officer Cadets and NCO instructors who were charged with the defence of Ibbenbüren. They sniped from the thick woods and had roaming machine-gun parties but little heavy support. Also, because of the nature of the country, artillery support was difficult for 9th Durham Light Infantry, and the battle developed into an infantry duel with close-range tank support. Accurate sniping, heavy machine-gun fire and German bazooka teams brought the advance to a standstill in the evening, and it was decided to make firm for the night. At last light 2nd Devons were relieved in their positions by 7th/9th Royal Scots of 155th Brigade and passed to under command 22nd Armoured Brigade.

The next day, the 4th of April, 9th Durham Light Infantry and 5th Dragoon Guards continued their attack and soon had one platoon across the stream which runs in front of Ibbenbüren. While their attack was going in 155th Brigade put in an attack from the high ground taken over from 2nd Devons and advanced South-East to secure both sides of the Westerly or main road leading into the town. Opposition to the 9th Durham Light Infantry and 5th Dragoon Guards group stiffened, however, and until dusk the battle was continued, with deadly enemy sniping and fanatical resistance from well concealed positions. Tanks who spotted the enemy in houses burnt them down immediately—but the enemy remained in the blazing ruins, firing to the last, before themselves being burnt in the holocaust. The cooler efforts of the snipers resulted in several tank commanders being shot through the tank slits. But, despite this resistance, the Durhams took about thirty prisoners and killed many more. 5th Dragoon Guards had succeeded, ultimately, in knocking down a road block which barred their way towards the town, but at nightfall a converging attack up the left-hand road by a Brigade of 53rd Division following up was unsuccessful. The Durhams were ordered to withdraw two platoons from across the stream and to hold firm the ground won until the next day, when the Brigade would be relieved of the task of attacking Ibbenbüren.

By the evening of the 3rd it had become clear that the capture of Ibbenbüren would be a slow business, and 11th Armoured, having captured a bridge intact over the Osnabrück Canal at Halen, it was decided to pass 22nd Armoured Brigade along their centre line and over their bridge to capture the bridges to the North and North-East on the Ems-Weser Canal. This movement was carried out throughout the 4th and the following night, along indifferent roads blocked with the echelons of 11th Armoured, with burning Ibbenbüren lighting up the Northern sky. Once out, however, opposition was practically non-existent, and by last light on the 4th, after a non-stop run of fifty miles, 5th Royal Tanks had seized a bridge intact over the Ems-Weser Canal, eighteen miles North-East of Osnabrück, 1st Royal Tanks and 2nd Devons guarding the bridges and the flank behind them. The next day their advance continued, against slight opposition, another twenty miles to Wagenfeld and Diepholz. Occasional road blocks were met, but these were quickly dealt with, and it was not until Lembruch, seven miles South of Diepholz, that there was any serious opposition. As the leading tank approached, two 88 mms opened fire. The first gun was immediately knocked out, and the second, joined shortly afterwards by two more, were dealt with by "G" Battery, 5th Royal Horse Artillery. The village was entered by the leading troop, closely followed by a platoon of "I" Company of the Rifle Brigade, who mopped up the remaining stragglers. In the afternoon, the Luftwaffe put in one of its rare appearances with a dozen or so Focke Wulfs and jet-propelled aircraft, who strafed the road continuously, appearing without warning from the low clouds. They inflicted surprisingly little damage, although General Lyne had a narrow escape, and three were claimed as shot down. By the evening the Regiment was in Wagenfeld, having killed some thirty enemy and taken fifty prisoners, and knocked out or captured four 88 mm, one 75 mm and two 20 mm guns, all at a cost of two men wounded. On the morning of the 6th, Diepholz was entered without opposition, although many mines were found, and the Regiment turned East towards Sulingen, having warned the Burgomaster over the civil telephone system, which was quite intact, that resistance would be the worse for him and his village. The Burgomaster replied that he was all for surrender, but that he was at the moment hampered in carrying out his plans by the presence of a tank, whose location he was obliging enough to give us. The tank was accordingly "brewed", as was a 75 mm which attempted to hold up the advance, after firing five shots, all of which missed. By this time 1st Royal Tanks had come up to Sulingen from the South after an uneventful run. All told, in the course of two days four hundred and fifty prisoners had been taken.

Fortunately, the centre line was protected on the left by a series of natural obstacles, the loop of the Ems-Weser Canal North of Osnabrück, the Dümmer See and the vast expanse of marsh around it. Although a small composite force had to be left to guard the vital points, namely, the bridges and places from which the enemy might have attempted to infiltrate from his positions to the North of the Canal, we were not involved in the ceaseless expeditions to cover the left flank that had been such a feature of the advance to Rheine, with the result that those Regiments and Battalions left behind, 8th Hussars, 3rd Royal Horse Artillery, a dismounted battery of the Norfolk Yeomanry, and 1/5th Queens could get a certain amount of rest. Meanwhile, 131 Brigade, consisting of 5th Dragoon Guards and 9th Durham Light Infantry, remained almost inaccessible fifty miles behind still fighting desperately for Ibbenbüren, though relieved on the night of the 5th by 71st Brigade from 53rd (Welsh) Division.

Hoya bridge

On the 6th of April, the Divisional centre-line was altered to run North-East, directed on the crossings of the Weser at Hoya and Verden. During the night of the 5th/6th of April, 1st Royal Tanks and 2nd Devons kept up their advance, and before dawn on the 6th, without meeting opposition in the road centres, had covered forty miles to reach Hoya, when the bridge was blown as the leading tank approached. Small parties of enemy with bazookas, one of which was captured by the Protection Troop of Main Divisional Headquarters, still remained near the centre line, but except on the river, where the enemy had prepared his demolitions, opposition was purely local and spasmodic. On the next day, the 7th, 8th Hussars, who had been following up 1st Royal Tanks, approached the bridge West of Verden, only to discover it strongly protected by infantry and self-propelled guns, which made a quick dash for the bridge out of the question.

By this time, both 131st and 155th Infantry Brigades were catching up, and on the 7th, as it was apparent that the Germans meant to fight hard for all crossings, the Division turned to face West in order to cut off First Parachute Army, retreating before 30th Corps to Bremen. The infantry brigades were disposed on the Southern flank of the salient towards Bremen, 131 Brigade being concentrated around Barven, between Diepholz and Sulingen, through which the Divisional axis ran from Wagenfeld, and 155th Brigade still protecting the flank around Diepholz. 131 Brigade were accordingly moved North to secure Bassum and Twistringen, twenty and fifteen miles North-East of Diepholz respectively on the main road to Bremen, while 155th Brigade attacked from Diepholz itself. 22nd Armoured Brigade were to advance West from the area East of Verden towards the Southern approaches of Bremen, leaving behind 1st Royal Tanks and 2nd Devons to screen the line of the river.

By the evening of the 7th, 131 Brigade had reached, against moderate opposition from small parties of infantry with bazookas, the outskirts of Bassum and Twistringen, which were entered on the following day. On the 8th, 155th Brigade attacked North-East to capture Barnstorf in spite of a blown bridge covered by 88 mms, linking up with 131 Brigade at Bassum on the 9th. Meanwhile, 8th Hussars, after "brewing up" every house, had captured Riede, eleven and a half miles South-East of Bremen, and Syke, some three miles farther South, also on the main road, was captured by 5th Royal Tanks and 11th Hussars. In the North, however, the river crossings were still held.

The nearer we got to Bremen, the stronger the opposition became, and as we advanced West we ran into the flank guards of 15th Panzer Grenadier Division retreating North, flank guards consisting mainly of self-propelled guns protected by small parties of Panzer Grenadiers. At one time, 11th Hussars, operating between Bassum and Syke, were in contact simultaneously with fourteen self-propelled guns. These flank guards on occasions produced small but vigorous counter-attacks, as when on the 8th three companies of infantry, supported by two Tigers, attempted to recapture Syke, but were driven off by the Support Company of the 1st Rifle Brigade and a self-propelled battery of the Norfolk

Yeomanry, who knocked out a Tiger. The accompanying infantry was dispersed by artillery fire. Again, on the evening of the 10th, after 131 Brigade had advanced a further fifteen miles from Bassum and Twistringen to take Wildeshausen and Harpstedt, three enemy self-propelled guns followed one of our own withdrawing into the town to take up a position for the night. A confused close range fight followed in the gathering darkness in which we lost several tanks, a number of soft vehicles and some prisoners, before the attack was finally beaten off. Farther North, we succeeded in expanding the area under our control, the 8th Hussars getting within seven thousand yards of Bremen, against bazookas and self-propelled guns, and 5th Royal Horse Artillery shelling the city.

By the evening of the 10th, it was clear that the battle for Bremen was going to be a slow business, as First Parachute Army were determined to keep the way open, and our principal opponents, 15 Panzer Grenadier Division and 18 SS Ersatz Battalion, a battalion whose strength was nearer to that of a regiment than a battalion, were determined and skilful fighters. In four days of fighting we had taken seventeen hundred prisoners and knocked out a considerable number of guns, both self-propelled and dual-purpose 88's, but, from the success of 11th Armoured Division, who, after a hard fight had secured a bridgehead some twenty-five miles to the South, with the 6th Airborne Division going faster still beyond Munster, it was clear that the decisive direction was East, and that, with the Division stretched out on a

Nienburg bridge

front of forty miles, the chances of cutting off Bremen, without a prolonged battle and considerably greater forces were small. Until we could move East, we remained probing and holding this salient, having under command three additional infantry Brigades, one from 53rd Division, holding the Eastern flank on the Weser, South of Hoya, one from 52nd Division in the centre, and one from 3rd British Division around Wildeshausen and Harpstedt. On the 11th and 12th, we handed over our sector to 3rd British Infantry Division from 30th Corps, and two days later moved South to concentrate East of Nienburg, where the Weser had been crossed by 53rd Division unopposed, as the Burgomaster of the town was one of the few responsible Germans who appreciated the real nature of the situation and was not prepared to shovel his town into the Wagnerian furnace of defeated Germany. Before we left, opposition South of the Weser and East of Bremen had been increasing daily and, just before we handed over, a squadron of the 11th Hussars opposite Bremen had been sharply counter-attacked from across the river.

53rd Division, although they had crossed the Weser successfully, were meeting heavy opposition, some ten miles farther on, at the outskirts of Rethem, covering the crossings over the River Aller, which were held by 2 Marine Division from Hamburg, who, if not particularly skilful, were nevertheless brave and determined fighters. 5th Royal Tanks went forward to help 53rd Division who were having a very tough battle for Rethem. During the fighting they succeeded in destroying eight 88 mms and a few 125 mm Flak guns defending the railway line, and the following day worked their way into the town itself.

One of the heavy AA guns knocked out by five tanks at Rethem

After two counter-attacks on Rethem had been repulsed, 53rd Division secured a crossing on the night of the 13th, and the next day 4th Armoured Brigade went across. 11th Armoured Division, fifteen miles to the South-East, at the same time also secured a crossing after meeting equalled bitter resistance.

On the 14th, 4th Armoured Brigade continued to expand their bridgehead, until by the morning of the 15th, they had reached, after meeting much opposition from self-propelled guns, Kirchboizen, seven miles along the main road to Soltau. The Division, led by 8th Hussars, followed but progress was slow, owing to the many craters in Rethem, and to the fact that the road beyond had to be improvised by the Royal Engineers across country, the main road being unusuable owing to craters. Moreover, at Kirchboizen, the main road had been very successfully blown, and 8th Hussars had to find a way across country through the sandy tracks in the woods to the South. However, by last light they had worked round to beyond Walsrode, a total distance of twenty-two miles, having dispersed a company of Marines with bazookas holding the Southern outskirts of the town. At the same time, the Royal Engineers had bridged the crater at Kirchboizen, and 1st Royal Tanks had advanced to four and a half miles North of Walsrode through steep and difficult wooded country. Walsrode was occupied in the evening by the 1/5th Queens. Many infantry still remained in the woods between the main road and the river, which were cleared during the following day by 155th Brigade.

Owing to the traffic hold-ups caused around Rethem by the bad roads and shelling on the bridge, 131 Brigade had not been able to cross on the 15th, and that night the bridge was bombed by some half-dozen aircraft, who damaged it temporarily. The bridge was not repaired for heavy wheeled traffic until midday, and the remainder of the armour, 5th Dragoon Guards and 5th Royal Tanks, were unable to start crossing until six o'clock in the evening.

The Division was now directed through Soltau and then once more North on to Hamburg. Accordingly, 22nd Armoured Brigade operated in two columns, one consisting of 8th Hussars going East along the main road towards Soltau, and the other consisting of the 1st Royal Tanks working North from Walsrode. On both routes the country was difficult, well-wooded and in the North steep. 1st Royal Tanks had much difficulty with road blocks, booby-trapped trees felled across the road and blown bridges, but working their way round through Ebbingen, reached Jarlingen, nine miles North of Walsrode, when a tank was knocked out by a bazooka. For a time movement was impossible; in front was a blown bridge and numerous enemy in the woods made manoeuvring very difficult. However, they constructed a causeway over the river and continued East, moving across country through woods and fields until they reached the road running North from Fallingbostel at Kroge. Here they turned North again through more open country to leaguer two miles West of Soltau. 8th Hussars on the easterly route also found the going difficult. Fallingbostel was held by infantry with mortars and an anti-tank gun. This was cleared by 1/5th Queens house by house, only to find that the bridge at the

Fallingbostel

end of the main street, which by now was burning well, was blown. This obstacle was by-passed over the ploughland to the South and the leading troops reached the Autobahn, where once more infantry and bazookas were encountered. By evening they had reached Fischendorf, seven and a half miles beyond Walsrode, and that night "I" Company of 1st Rifle Brigade pushed foot patrols across the river into Dorfmark.

Perhaps the greatest achievement of the operations of the 16th of April was the liberation of the great prison camp in the woods South-West of Fallingbostel. 8th Hussars sent a squadron down there to find, on their arrival, that the British had already taken over and that the main gate was guarded by sentries from the 1st Airborne Division, immaculate in scrubbed belts and gaiters and well-creased battle-dress. Inside were ten thousand British and American prisoners, commanded by Regimental Serjeant-Major Lord of the 1st Airborne Division, who was busily engaged in his office giving peace-time orders to his Orderly Warrant Officers. The administrative staff of the Division immediately arranged for rations, cigarettes and newspapers to be sent up, and the Camp was left under the command of Regimental Serjeant-Major Lord,

Released Prisoners of War at Fallingbostel

whose magnificent leadership prevented many difficulties that might otherwise have arisen, with the sudden transition from captivity to freedom of such large numbers of men, especially since many of the prisoners had been there since the fall of France, had suffered appalling hardships, and were, in some cases, in a very bad way. Amongst the prisoners, were a number who had been captured from 4th County of London Yeomanry and "A" Company, 1st Rifle Brigade, at Villers Bocage, nearly a year previously, thin but in good spirits, and a leave party from the Norfolk Yeomanry whose truck had taken a wrong turning a fortnight before and had fallen into the hands of the cadets at Ibbenbüren. In addition to the British and American prisoners, were some twelve thousand of other Allied Nationalities, whose condition was in some cases very bad, and whose control was by no means easy.

The situation on the evening of the 16th was as follows. 1st Royal Tanks were some two miles West of Soltau, which they reported strongly held by infantry and 88's, and they had already lost a tank

British section of the Prison Camp at Fallingbostel

to an 88 as they approached from the West. 8th Hussars were around Dorfmark, four miles to the South-West of Soltau, and 131 Brigade, less 1/5th Queens and with 5th Dragoon Guards, had come up to Walsrode, where they were relieved the next morning by 155th Brigade. 4th Armoured Brigade were North-West of Soltau on our left rear and 11th Armoured were level with us twelve miles to the East, with patrols of the Inns of Court Regiment in contact with the 11th Hussars on the Aller River.

In view of the delay which would be imposed by waiting for the reduction of Soltau, requiring at least an Infantry Brigade and suitable reconnaissance and artillery preparation, the Divisional Commander decided to by-pass Soltau to the West with 22nd Brigade and to reduce Soltau on the night of the 17th with 155th Brigade who would, by then, be in a position to take it on. 8th Hussars and a squadron of 11th Hussars, meanwhile, were to continue to attempt to find a way round to the East.

Opposition on the West was only moderate, but the going over tracks, whose foundation was a peat-bog, was appalling. However, by the evening, 1st Royal Tanks had almost reached the cross-roads at Welle, twelve miles North of Soltau on the main road to Harburg. Welle was held, and was not reduced until the next morning. 8th and 11th Hussars had a more difficult time. The country was very close, beech woods and thick pine trees, but after a sharp fight North of Soltau with self-propelled guns and Panthers, in the course of which at least one of each was destroyed, and in spite of spandau and bazooka

Soltau

teams, the 8th Hussars succeeded in reaching the main road at Heber five miles North of Soltau.

That night, 155th Brigade's attack, supported by 5th Dragoon Guards and "Crocodiles", went in and was entirely successful. By dawn, the entire town, of which a great part was in flames, had been captured, and patrols had pushed on to meet 8th Hussars to the North. With the clearance of Soltau, the final phase of operations had begun. The first task was to push on North in the hope of capturing the Elbe bridges at Harburg. The second was to clear an alternative route to the East of the main Soltau—Harburg road by advancing from Soltau and down from the North around Heber, in order to protect the centre line which, North of Soltau, ran for the greater part of its length through the forest and moors of the Lüneburg Heath. The forests East and South-East of Soltau were known to be full of enemy, mainly scratch units from the training centres of the Lüneburg Heath, and the situation to the West was far from clear. Bremen had by now been captured, but the last remnants of First Parachute Army were still trying to get out via Bremervörde to the Elbe crossings and ferries. On both flanks the 11th Hussars had been unable to get far, meeting numerous scattered parties of infantry in the forest North-East of Soltau, where they destroyed a 75 mm anti-tank gun, and strong opposition in the direction of Visselhovede, eight miles West of Soltau.

The advance on Harburg occupied until the 21st, with the Division operating on a front of some twenty-five thousand yards. Harburg lies at the head of a series of low ridges, running North and South

Mass graves of slave workers were found in the woods near Soltau. Local civilians were made to disinter the bodies and give them proper burial

from Welle, extending some seventeen miles from North to South, and ten from East to West. The greater part of these ridges were covered in forests, of which the most extensive were the Forest of Langeloh, through which ran the main road from Soltau, some three miles North of Welle, and to its North was the Harburg Forest. There were three main roads into Harburg; first, the Autobahn from Bremen, running East and West, and then turning North at Hittfeld; second, the main road from Soltau, running through the forest and then turning North-East leaving the Harburg forest on the left; and third, a road running up the Eastern flank of the ridge from Jesterburg. Between these were a considerable number of secondary roads. On the 18th, 1st Royal Tanks led off, captured Welle, but soon ran into bazookas on the Southern edge of the Forest of Langeloh. 8th Hussars and 1/5th Queens were then brought up to bypass the forest to the West, through Tostedt, in order to open a route for 5th Guards Armoured Brigade who were having trouble in their frontal attacks against Rotenburg; 8th Hussars were also ordered to exploit to the Autobahn at Hollenstedt on the West edge of the ridge. They were unable to take the main road from Welle to Tostedt, but after a prolonged battle with self-propelled and anti-tank guns and difficulties with the going, Tostedt was occupied. Next day, 1/5th Queens remained to hold Tostedt, and 8th Hussars pushed on five and a half miles to the Autobahn at Hollenstedt, where the crossing was covered by 88 mms. However, the Autobahn offered good cover and 1/5th Queens were brought up to assault Hollenstedt, which was taken after a Typhoon attack. 8th Hussars then turned East with two squadrons to Rade, five miles distant, after knocking out eight 88's along the Autobahn. Finally, on the 20th, still working up the West side of the ridge, they completed the remaining six miles to the edge of the Elbe valley, after a hard battle in Daerstorf against anti-tank guns and infantry, in which "A" Company of the 1st Rifle Brigade were involved in close hand-to-hand fighting. Here they remained, with OP's watching the port and approaches to Hamburg. At the same time, 1st Royal Tanks and 2nd Devons and, later 5th Dragoon Guards and 2nd Devons, were operating in the centre. An attempt on the 18th to outflank the forest of Langeloh to the North, that is East of Tostedt, ran into a Tiger, which caused a long hold-up until it was knocked out, although "C" Company, of the 1st Rifle Brigade, did much execution in the outskirts of the forest with flame-throwers. The next morning, the 19th, the enemy withdrew from the forest, and, although the Regiment was held up for a time by doubts as to whether 5th Royal Tanks were operating in their area, by last light they had advanced seven miles to reach the Autobahn at Dibbersen, on the East side of the Harburg Forest. From here 5th Dragoon Guards took over, and by early morning on the 20th, after some fairly stiff fighting, had reached the outer defences of the perimeter of Harburg around Vahrendorf and to the East, two and a half miles from Harburg. During the evening they were heavily shelled and it was clear that the enemy were in considerable strength. In addition to the reinforcement Battalion of 12 SS the garrison consisted of a motley collections of ships' crews and police, reinforced by many 88's from the Flak defences of Hamburg.

A last attempt to reach Harburg was made on the 21st by 5th Royal Tanks, under command of 131 Brigade, from the Eastern side of the ridge. Up till then, 131 Brigade, who had passed through Soltau on the 18th, had been doing protection on the right flank of 22nd Armoured Brigade, having detached a squadron of the 5th Royal Tanks to clear the woods to the East of the main road from Soltau to Harburg. This squadron got as far as Bispingen, eight miles North-East of Soltau, but there it was held up, and turned back to join the main body, advancing North on Buchholz, which was reached by last light on the 20th, after overcoming a number of road-blocks. Jesterburg, to the East of Buchholz, was also cleared. The next morning 5th Royal Tanks, led by "I" Company of the Rifle Brigade, started off North from Jesterburg for Harburg, via the Autobahn at Hittfeld, with the 9th Durham Light Infantry advancing on the parallel route to the East side of the Aue valley. Hittfeld, five miles on, was reached without undue difficulty, but when the leading tanks started off along the Autobahn for Harburg, the bridge, three thousand yards East of Hittfeld, was blown as they approached it. Advances North from Hittfeld again only ran up against the defences of Harburg, and it was clear that there was no possibility of rushing the bridges. Meanwhile, the right-hand column, after a sharp fight with an anti-tank gun and some infantry, entered Maschen and Stelle on the Southern extremity of the Elbe valley. This was practically the limit of our advance, until the surrender of Hamburg. In general, although the attempt for the bridges had to be abandoned, the fighting had been highly successful. Prisoners averaged over a thousand a day, including the greater part of a battalion from the Hamburg Police; some two hundred enemy had been killed, and many guns destroyed or captured for very small losses on our part. In any case, our object was achieved a fortnight later when Hamburg surrendered.

From now until the capitulation, the Division was occupied in clearing up the vast salient pointing towards Hamburg, that had been overrun during the preceding days. The salient originally had a frontage of some sixty miles, and, twenty-five miles apart, two entirely unrelated battles were being fought, in the North to mop up the area round the Autobahn, and to cover with patrols the area East and West, and in the South to clear up the obstinate enemy pocket East of Soltau.

First, for the relatively simpler task to the North, the Division, on the 21st, was reorganised to watch the enemy's defensive perimeter around Harburg, a task which naturally fell principally to the Infantry Brigade. They occupied a front of some seven thousand yards with their right flank resting on the village of Hittfeld, North of the Autobahn, and their left in the forest to the North-West around Vahrendorf. To the East, 5th Royal Tanks maintained a squadron in Maschen and patrolled East towards Winsen, which by now was occupied by the Inns of Court Regiment from 11th Armoured. No attempt was made to hold the Harburg forest, but the 1st Royal Tanks were kept in reserve around the Autobahn North of Buchholz in case any trouble should develop. The left-hand sector was held by 22nd Armoured

Brigade, with 8th Hussars and "I" Company of the Rifle Brigade patrolling from Elstorf, 5th Dragoon Guards in Moisburg, and 11th Hussars to the South-West of them, both regiments patrolling West. On the 22nd, Buxtehude, whose approaches had been reported held by the 11th Hussars on the previous day, was entered by an enterprising troop-leader of the 11th, who, after dispersing the crew of a 37 mm at the outskirts of the town, forced his way in to secure the surrender of a Rear-Admiral, five hundred officers and seamen, and five hundred Wrens in the Barracks, which on the following day were taken over by 1st Rifle Brigade, less the company with 8th Hussars.

Otherwise, apart from routine patrols and shelling, there was little other activity. On the 22nd a squadron of the 11th Hussars re-occupied Stelle, linking up with 11th Armoured Division. On the 23rd a standing patrol in the Harburg forest was overrun but later escaped. On the 24th, 2nd Devons carried out a highly successful attack with flame-throwers on an enemy post on the edge of the forest, killing thirty-six of the enemy, and on the 26th the enemy, 12 SS Reinforcement Battalion, staged an early morning attack on the 1/5th Queens East of Vahrendorf, and on the 2nd Devons to their left in the village itself. The position around the 1/5th Queens was restored without any difficulty, but the 2nd Devons for a time were engaged in heavy fighting until the enemy finally withdrew having lost sixty killed and seventy prisoners. On the left, 8th Hussars liberated one thousand seven hundred Belgian and Dutch officers on the 22nd. Following the capture of Buxtehude, patrols were able to get as far as Horneburg and Harsfelt. The approaches to both were mined and covered by fire, as well as the bridges blown, but, although Harsfelt surrendered, the garrison of Horneburg, after opening negotiations, unwisely changed their mind and received a hundred shells as a lesson. By the 25th, the Guards Armoured Division had also got patrols into this area, having advanced earlier up our centre line through Tostedt to outflank the enemy holding them around Rotenburg, and this area was eventually handed over to them. 5th Dragoon Guards maintained patrols from Buxtehude across the polders to the Elbe, which on one occasion led to an encounter with some Hitler Youths armed with bazookas, who withdrew to a marsh where they were heavily shelled. Field-Marshal Sir Bernard Montgomery also paid us another visit to present medal ribbons, unfortunately in pouring rain.

Between the positions facing Harburg, and Soltau, twenty-five miles as the crow flies, there was nobody, except for a daily patrol of the Inns of Court Regiment from 11th Armoured Division along the minor roads through the woods which, apparently, succeeded in convincing any wandering German soldiers that continued resistance was not worth while. On the left, the woods were equally not really cleared, but apart from an encounter with a small group of German marines by a Serjeant of the Light Anti-Aircraft Regiment, who was shooting within sight of Divisional Headquarters, nothing untoward occurred. In the ensuing struggle, one of the Marines was wounded, and several thousand rounds of Besa discouraged the remainder from continuing the operations projected against Divisional Headquarters.

In the Soltau pocket, however, matters were very different. The country in that area consists mainly of thick forest alternating with patches of open heath, and housed the barracks of many of the training establishments of the German Army. In addition, the forest also contained numerous dumps of both supplies and ammunition, which facilitated resistance. Until Soltau was captured, little attempt was made to clear the forest by either ourselves or 11th Armoured Division, as the roads through it were not required. It was known to be occupied, but, at first, we were slightly incredulous when a prisoner estimated the strength of the occupants at four thousand men. These men, comparatively well organised both from the command and supply aspects, took four days to reduce.

The first task was to clear the routes running North-East through the forests towards Lüneburg against a number of Hungarian SS and a Tank-hunting battalion. Progress at first was slow, being hampered by accurate mortar and spandau fire. Moreover, artillery support could only be used on a very limited scale for fear of setting off the numerous dumps of gas-shells known to be in the area. On the 21st, 160th Brigade, from 53rd Division, took over from 155th and were given the support of one squadron of 1st Royal Tanks. Two hundred and fifty prisoners were captured and the road opened as far as Bispingen, some ten miles North-East of Soltau. Isolated snipers, however, still remained at large, and progress South was limited. The next day, 1st Household Cavalry Regiment came under command, and succeeded in working down to Wietzendorf, twelve miles to the South-East where the bridge was blown and defended by an anti-tank gun. Farther to the North, 160th Brigade reported that opposition was loosening slightly and a further five hundred prisoners, two 75 mm guns and three Nebelwerfers captured. On the 23rd, the remainder of 1st Royal Tanks were sent down to their assistance, and although they did not fire a shot, their presence was sufficient to convince the enemy that surrender or self-demobilisation was the more prudent course. By the evening, 160th Brigade working from South to North and 1st Household Cavalry in the opposite direction had joined hands and seventeen hundred prisoners had been taken.

Although the resistance on the Harburg front towards the end of April did not seem to indicate that the military and political leaders of Germany were prepared to abandon their policy, declaimed so loudly and so often, of fighting to the last, in fact the end, as we now know, was very near. The Russians had completely broken through on the Berlin front and were driving a disorganised rabble in front of them to Mecklenburg. On the night of the 29th, 8th Corps and the Americans on their right crossed the Elbe, and although resistance at first was stiff, and the Luftwaffe and swimmers active against the bridges, by the 2nd of May it had virtually ceased. 6th Airborne Division and 11th Armoured Division were on the Baltic at Wismar and Lübeck, without opposition, and the last two German formations on 8th Corps front, commanded by Corps Witthoeft, with whom they were later to deal during the occupation, surrendered. The German front opposite the Americans in Bavaria and Czechoslovakia was

Meilsen. The small hamlet where negotiations for the surrender of Hamburg took place

disintegrating, and Italy surrendered to Field-Marshal Alexander the same day.

The Division was not called upon to cross the Elbe. Instead a new excitement arose, the possibility of the surrender of Hamburg, and eventually, what our neighbours secured by force, we secured by negotiation, a negotiation which began with a hospital in Harburg and ended with the final surrender of Germany, Denmark, Holland and Norway. On the 29th of April a deputation approached our lines, consisting of two staff officers and a civilian. They had come, they explained, to discuss the possibility of securing immunity from our artillery fire for the hospital at Harburg. We replied that, if hospitals insisted on positioning themselves within the zone of active operations, the staff and patients must accept the consequences, and that, as far as we were concerned, the alternative was either to evacuate the hospital, which the Germans alleged was impossible, or else to surrender Harburg. Honour began to assert itself among the military members but at this point the civilian member of the delegation, engaged in private conversation with the Divisional Intelligence Officer, introduced first, the question of securing immunity for his own concern, the Phoenix Rubber Works, and secondly, the question of surrendering Hamburg itself. He explained that, at a meeting of the Hamburg Chamber of Commerce, attended by the Gauleiter, Herr Kaufmann, the issue had been raised and favourably received, but it was felt that the Head of the Police and SS, a Graf von Bassewitz, was opposed to the plan, although the majority of the business interests in Hamburg were increasingly favourable. It was therefore decided, on our part, to try for the surrender of the city. The military representatives had, by this time, already returned, only to blow themselves up on a German minefield, prudently laid by 12 SS Ersatz Battalion before leaving the sector—in fact they survived unscathed—but the Manager of the Phoenix Rubber Works still remained as our last hope. A carefully composed letter was handed to him to convey to General Wolz, the commander of the garrison, which ran as follows:

"To: Major-General Wolz,
   Kampfkommandant, Hamburg.

Herr General !

1. The Reichsführer SS has already made an offer of unconditional surrender to the Western Powers. This offer was made through Count Bernadotte in Stockholm.

2. Before attacking Bremen we demanded the surrender of the City. As this offer was refused, we had no alternative but to attack with artillery and air support. Bremen fell in twenty-four hours, but not without much unnecessary bloodshed.

3. In the name of humanity, Herr General, we demand the surrender of Hamburg. For you as a soldier there can be no dishonour in following the example of famous Generals such as Gen d Pz Tr Josef Harpe, GOC Fifth Panzer Army, Genlt Fritz Bayerlein, GOC LIII Corps, and many others who have surrendered themselves and their commands. From the political point of view, there can surely be no reflection on you if you follow the example of the Reichsführer SS.

4. We therefore ask you, Herr General, to send into our lines an officer empowered to negotiate the surrender. Our forward troops have been warned to expect his arrival and not to shoot at him. He will be treated according to the Geneva Convention, and returned after the parley to his own lines.

5. The population of Hamburg will not easily forget its first large-scale raid by over one thousand heavy bombers. We now dispose of a bomber force five to ten times greater numerically, and operating from nearby airfields. After the war, the German people must be fed: the more Hamburg's dock installations are damaged, the greater are the chances of famine in Germany.

6. If this offer is refused, we shall have no alternative but to attack Hamburg with all the forces at our disposal."

Before leaving, the two military representatives, an Army Doctor and a Staff Officer who rejoiced in the title of Herr Doktor Oberleutnant Ritter von Laun, had held a short conversation, within ear-shot of their escort, who spoke fluent German. The Herr Professor Doktor

Stabsarzt remarked to his colleague: "Herr Leutnant—this is what we are fighting against—these fine young officers who have such a high level of culture that they might almost be Germans."

The night of the 1st May General Wolz sent his reply:

"Major-General L. O. Lyne,
    Commander of the Allied Troops.   Hamburg,
                                          1 May, 1945.
        Herr General:

The thoughts for which you have found so lucid an expression in your letter of 29th of April, 1945, have been considered by myself and by countless other responsible Commanders; not unnaturally, considering the present military and political situation.

The eventual surrender of Hamburg would have far-reaching military and political consequences for the whole of that part of Northern Germany that is not yet occupied and for Denmark. For this reason, the orders given to me to hold Hamburg to the last man can be seen to have a clear justification. But in spite of this I am prepared, together with an authorised representative of Reichsstatthalter and Gauleiter Kaufmann, to discuss with a representative empowered by GOC Second British Army to make decisions on military and political matters, the eventual surrender of Hamburg and the far-reaching consequences arising therefrom.

May I ask you to inform the GOC Second British Army of these proposals and to request that a time and place for discussion be fixed.

                                          Wolz,
                                          Major-General."

It was understood that General Wolz was negotiating on his own authority and indeed contrary to direct orders to defend the town. His staff officer was returned to him with a message that the General Officer Commanding 7th British Armoured Division would see General Wolz the following night if General Wolz came to offer unconditional surrender. On the way back to his own lines the staff officer asked if he might speak to our Brigadier alone. "As soldier to soldier," he said, "I ask your advice whether I and the staff ought to commit suicide on our return." The Brigadier replied: "That's entirely up to you." A Colonel pointed to the scarf covering the interpreter's eyes: "Isn't that a Brasenose scarf?" "No, Christ Church," replied the captain, "I was there studying the House of Lords." Late in the night of the 2nd of May General Wolz arrived in person. His opening words were:

"The principal point is the actual time General Lyne wishes to enter Hamburg."

During the day General Wolz had been ordered by General Keitel on the telephone to surrender, on the orders of Admiral Doenitz.

Further he was informed that a delegation of Generals and Admirals from the German High Command would be arriving early next morning to see the Army Group Commander. General Wolz showed himself most anxious to make our take-over of Hamburg as easy as possible. All officials would remain at their posts until replaced. There would be no demolitions; all SS troops had already marched away. It was agreed that we should cross the Forward Defended Localities at one o'clock in the afternoon of the 3rd of May. At eight o'clock in the morning of the 3rd of May General Wolz brought into our lines, to Divisional Headquarters, General Admiral von Friedeburg, General der Infanterie Kinsel and other high-ranking officers of the German Higher Command.

Tanks cross the first bridge into Hamburg

By now, bigger negotiations were in motion, but at a quarter past four on the 3rd of May the Division moved over the river to occupy Hamburg. The occupation itself was easy. No difficulties were incurred, other than the embarrassment of numberless German staff officers who eagerly awaited orders in every department from the Town Commandant's office, which gratefully emerged from its bunker, to the Rathaus, which was filled with a galaxy of splendidly dressed German officers.

On the 4th, 11th Hussars moved out to Pinneberg, twelve miles North-West of Hamburg. By now the surrender of Germany, although

Mass surrender of the Wehrmacht North of Hamburg

not officially declared, was a reality. Down every road a stream of German soldiers was met by their patrols, who only asked to be relieved of their arms. There was nobody between them and Hamburg except thousands of German soldiers and sailors, mostly on foot, but some packed in big ten-ton Diesel lorries and their trailers or in horse-drawn transport, making their way West to surrender. In the afternoon, a delegation, consisting once more of General-Admiral von Friedeburg and General Kinsel, was met by the 11th Hussars on the Quickborn road, and that evening we received the great news of the surrender of Germany, Denmark, Holland and Norway, and the news that hostilities were to cease at eight o'clock the next morning.

In the next few days the disarming of the German Army continued until VE Day was declared on the 8th, the Division having advanced to the Kiel Canal the day before. Our efforts as a fighting formation were over, and we were now concerned in securing an orderly disarmament and concentration of the German Army in the Western half of Schleswig, and in the innumerable problems of a military administration, and of the adjustment from war to peace.

Tanks in the centre of Hamburg

The campaign for the conquest of Germany had not been easy. To the very last the enemy had found troops to resist, and the last two weeks had seen the German Air Force re-appearing in an offensive role, strafing the GOC and his escort and others near Diepholz, and later Divisional Headquarters and the lines of communication towards the end of April. On the other hand, the civilian population, far from consisting of those fanatical guerillas which Himmler had led us to expect, were docile and often helpful. On only one occasion was any trouble experienced. This was towards the very end in Daerstorf, and the experiment was not repeated. Moreover, the enormous number of foreign workers and prisoners of war, all of whom supplied themselves with their national flags in a very short time, contributed the cheers and enthusiasm of earlier campaigns, if not the comforts. But now all was over. The Division had been in action when its first enemies, the Italians, had asked for an armistice and had been in action on the soil of Italy; it was now in action again on the soil of Germany, whose soldiers it had first met in the winter of 1940 on the desert frontier of Egypt, and whose surrender it now accepted on their own soil. The final act in this history was the entry of the Division into Berlin on the 4th of July, 1945, almost exactly five years after our first patrols had moved out from Mersa Matruh to the Egyptian frontier. Few remained who had passed through that long period, the first three years fighting against overwhelming odds, the last two of continual success. Many had left us to fight in Burma or elsewhere, but the graves of many also lie alongside the long road from Alexandria to Tunis, in the desert beyond, in Southern Italy, in Normandy, France, Belgium, Holland and Germany, whose sacrifice brought us to final victory.

BERLIN

The Division was settling down to its normal Occupational Duties in the area North of Hamburg and had been told that they would remain in this area for at least three months, when on the 14th of June a warning order was received from 21 Army Group that the Division must stand by to move to Berlin.

The news was at first received with some consternation by all those who had "dug themselves well in" in the Itzehoe area, but on further reflection everyone realised what an honour it was to be the first British Troops to enter the German capital, and immediately consternation changed to a thrill of excitement, and an orgy of vehicle painting began, Regiments vying with one another to see who could succeed in getting most paint on their vehicles before the great day of the entry.

Little definite information was available regarding the state of the accommodation in Berlin, but such scanty reports as were received showed clearly that the prospects were none too bright, and it was decided that it would be impossible to take the whole Division into the city, at least until detailed reconnaissance could be carried out. As permission to send representatives forward to carry out this reconnaissance was not granted by our Allies, a decision had to be taken based on the only reports available, and there was bound to be general disappointment amongst those Regiments who had to be left behind. And so, on the 16th of July, orders were issued that the following force would stand by at 48 hours notice to move to Berlin:

    Tac Div Headquarters
    Headquarters 131 Infantry Brigade
    3rd Royal Horse Artillery
    8th Hussars
    11th Hussars
    1/5 Queens
    2 Devons
    4 Field Squadron
    621 Field Squadron
    143 Field Park Squadron.

In addition to these, 21 Army Group, in order to make the force as representative as possible, placed under command 7th Armoured Division 1st Bn Grenadier Guards from the Guards Armoured Division and a composite Canadian Battalion from the First Canadian Army. All these Battalions and Regiments were, for the initial entry, placed under command 131 Infantry Brigade, while 22nd Armoured Brigade and Headquarters Royal Artillery remained behind in the Itzehoe area under command of the CRA.

From the 14th to the 20th of June the GOC and Staff of the Division were occupied in attending numerous conferences at 21 Army Group, which necessitated on every occasion a journey of 250 miles by road or 150 miles by air, and many uncomfortable and sick-making journeys were entailed by all concerned in Austers, admirably piloted by officers from "B" Flight, 653 AOP Squadron.

As a result of these conferences the organisation for the occupational troops became clearer. The Divisional Commander was to perform a dual role; firstly, he was to continue commanding this Division, and secondly he was to command all British Troops in Berlin. In addition to his own troops detailed for this task, Berlin Area, commanded by Brigadier Ravenhill, was placed under command to act as "Housekeepers", and little was it realised at that time what an apt title that was and how much "Housekeeping" would be required.

On the 16th of June, undaunted by the enormous task with which he was confronted, the Divisional Commander was ordered to stand by to fly from Lüneburg to Berlin to discuss with the Russians all details for the occupation, such as boundaries, dates of move, etc. However, it was found impossible to obtain clearance of the aircraft for this date and as a Dakota presents an easy target, even to our Allies, it was agreed that "discretion was the better part of valour" and the journey was postponed until clearance could be obtained. In fact, this clearance was not received until the 29th of June, and the Divisional Commander wisely decided that he would move his Tac Headquarters to Lüneburg to avoid excessively long journeys from his own Headquarters to the airfield and also to be closer to 21 Army Group, where he was required on most days to settle up the final details.

On the 19th of June, 131 Infantry Brigade and the troops under its command commenced the move to the concentration area which, it had been decided, should be in the Brunswick area. The troops stayed one night on the way down and sent forward reconnaissance parties to select accommodation. The prospects were particularly grim in the town itself, but eventually adequate facilities were found in the surrounding villages, and by the evening of the 20th of June the force was concentrated, with the exception of the 1st Battalion Grenadier Guards, who joined the group five days later. On the 24th of June, Tac Divisional Headquarters was increased in size and moved from Lüneburg to Flechtorf, eight miles North-East of Brunswick.

The next few days were spent in collecting small additional units which were to form part of Berlin Area, and in putting another coating or two of paint on all the vehicles! Meanwhile, the Divisional Commander was still standing by to fly to Berlin. At last, it was with great relief that clearance was received for a plane to land at Berlin on the 29th of June, and the Commander set off with Lieutenant-General Sir Ronald Weekes to make the necessary arrangements. A general air of expectancy came over the Division, and it was felt that the long-awaited moment of the triumphal entry could not now be long delayed.

After a lengthy conference in Berlin, at which much caviare and Vodka were consumed, the Divisional Commander returned on the evening of the 29th of June with the final details. A reconnaissance party to consist of the GOC, Brigadier Spurling, Brigadier Ravenhill and a small staff was to move by road on the 1st of July. The advance parties were to follow on the 2nd and the main body on the 4th of July.

The stage was now set and all final details were tied up. At least it was hoped they were, but the journey into Berlin was to prove as tricky an operation as many in which the Division had taken part during their long campaigns.

The reconnaissance party set off at first light on the 1st of July, and all went well until crossing the Elbe by the Autobahn bridge which the Russians had constructed alongside the main one which was blown. The GOC was leading the column and after the first few vehicles had crossed, a Russian sentry appeared on the far side and stated that his orders were to allow no vehicles of any type or nationality across the bridge, and that all traffic should use the temporary bridge in Magdeburg known as Friendship Bridge. Arguments and persuasion by the GOC proved of no avail, and it was eventually decided that if the Magdeburg Bridge lived up to its name, things might prove easier on that route. The column was turned round, and the remainder of the journey passed without incident, except for lengthy halts at each Russian Barrier, when it seemed necessary for the sentry to obtain permission from Moscow before allowing the column to pass.

On arrival in Berlin, the rest of the day was spent in hurried reconnaissance and the allocation of accommodation to Headquarters and Regiments, preparatory to the reception of advance parties the following day. The move of the latter passed without incident, and although the areas were bad and in many cases badly damaged, the layout was complete for the reception of the main body on the 4th of July.

The Great Day broke with a deluge of rain, which fortunately cleared as the day advanced. The move, headed by "C" Squadron 11th Hussars and followed by 1st Battalion Grenadier Guards, went according to plan until arrival at Friendship Bridge, which on this occasion belied its name. After a two hours halt, during which all efforts to persuade the Russian sentries that we were authorised to use this route were of no avail, eventually permission was granted to continue the journey. However, after the three leading units were safely across, the bridge was again closed, and the sentries stated that the Autobahn Bridge must be used for the remainder of the column. This switch was successfully accomplished, and the remainder of the move passed without incident.

The division enters Berlin. Major-General Lyne taking the salute

The plan had been made for a Saluting Base to be erected in the Pichelsdorfer Strasse, and at 1825 hours Russian time, the leading car of "C" Squadron 11th Hussars rounded the corner and the GOC mounted the Saluting Base. The great moment, for which all had waited so long, had at last arrived. "C" Squadron 11th Hussars, followed by 1st Battalion Grenadier Guards, Canadian Battalion and 131 Infantry Brigade Headquarters roared past the saluting base, while a small number of German civilians stood by with glum looks on their faces.

The big moment was over, but there was still plenty to be done. Accommodation required much hard work being spent on it, both to clean it up and repair it, and in addition there were other ceremonial parades for which preparation had to be made, and many busy days were to be spent in rehearsals, cleaning up equipment, etc.

The flag ceremony. The Union Jack is broken at the foot of Berlin's victory column in the Tiergarten

It was arranged that the first of these parades should be on the 6th of July, when the Union Jack was hoisted on the biggest flagpole which could be found, at the foot of the Franco-Prussian War Memorial in the Grosse Stern. For the parade one company was found from each of 1st Battalion Grenadier Guards, 1/5th Queens, 2nd Devons and the Canadian Composite Battalion. They were formed up facing East on the West side of the Monument, and, after Lieutenant-General Sir Ronald Weekes had inspected the parade, the Union Jack was hoisted, and the first visible sign had been given to the German people that the British Troops were in occupation.

From the 6th of July until the 12th of July, repairs and cleaning up proceeded apace. Accommodation began to improve and it was decided to move forward 5th Royal Horse Artillery in order to take part in the big parade which was being planned in the next few weeks. The Regiment, in fact, moved into Kladow Barracks on the 10th of July. HQ RA was moved forward on the 14th of July and the remainder of Divisional Headquarters on the 18th of July.

Field-Marshal Montgomery decorates Marshal Zhukov

On the 12th Field-Marshal Sir Bernard Montgomery made his first appearance in Berlin since our arrival in the city, when he invested the Russian Commanders, Marshals Zhukov and Rokossovsky, General Sokolovski and Colonel-General Malinin. A small but impressive parade was formed up on the West side of the Brandenburg Gate facing East. A Guard of Honour was provided by the King's Company 1st Battalion Grenadier Guards and a squadron of the 8th Hussars and 11th Hussars lined the route from the Brandenburg Gate to the Saluting Base. The Field-Marshal arrived at 1455 hours with the Divisional Commander and was given a general salute. Punctually at 1500 hours the Russian Commanders arrived at the Brandenburg Gate and were received by the Field-Marshal and another general salute was given. After inspecting the Guard of Honour, during which inspection the Press strove to take photographs from every angle at close quarters, the Field-Marshal invested the Russian Generals and the parade was concluded with a march past the saluting base by the Guard of Honour.

From this day onwards events began to take place in rapid succession. On the 13th of July the first full-scale Divisional Parade, which was in fact a rehearsal for the Victory Parade, took place with magnificent weather and in the perfect setting of the Charlottenburg Chaussee. The parade was a great success, and it was obvious that with a few minor improvements a really impressive Victory Parade could be staged at some future date when required.

The Potsdam Conference. Mr Anthony Eden with Major-General Lyne at Gatow Airfield

On the 15th of July the delegates began to assemble for the Potsdam Conference. The chief British delegates, headed by the Prime Minister, were due to arrive by air at Gatow Airfield, and a composite Guard of Honour formed by the Royal Navy, the Canadian Berlin Battalion and the Royal Air Force Regiment, was provided for the Foreign Secretary, Mr Attlee and the Chiefs of Staff, while for the Prime Minister the same Guard of Honour was augmented by the addition of a Company from the 1st Battalion Grenadier Guards. Throughout the arrivals a Squadron of the 11th Hussars lined the route. At the rehearsal some difficulty was experienced in synchronising the movements of such a varied body of men, and the fact that the Canadian detachment consisted entirely of French Canadians did not facilitate the word of command. However, all difficulties were surmounted and on the day the combined Guard of Honour was a great success.

The hopes that the Victory Parade might take place while the Delegates and Chiefs of Staff were at the Conference were not unfounded and the Prime Minister fixed the date for Saturday, the 21st of July.

The period from the 15th to the 21st of July was one of feverish activity, flag poles and stands being erected, polishing of equipment and last-minute rehearsals. The early hours of the mornings would reveal Commanding Officers holding surreptitious parades to perfect their role, at an hour when no one was about.

The great day arrived and by 0930 hours the stage was set. The troops on parade were found from 131 Infantry Brigade Headquarters, 3rd and 5th Regiments Royal Horse Artillery, 8th Hussars, 11th Hussars, 1st Battalion Grenadier Guards, 1/5th Queens, 2nd Devons, Divisional Engineers, Searchlight Battery and representative elements of the Royal Navy, Royal Air Force and Royal Air Force Regiment. The bands were provided by the Royal Marines, 11th Hussars and 2nd Devons.

The Victory Parade in Berlin

By 0945 hours all the distinguished guests were in their places on the Saluting Base and at 1000 hours the Prime Minister arrived, accompanied by Field-Marshal Sir Bernard Montgomery, the Chiefs of Staff and the Foreign Secretary. As the Prime Minister mounted the Saluting Base, where the Divisional Commander was waiting to receive him, the guns of the 3rd Regiment Royal Horse Artillery roared out a salute from nineteen guns.

As soon as the noise had died away the Prime Minister left the Saluting Base and mounted the leading Half Track which was drawn up in front of the Stand. With him in the same vehicle travelled Field-Marshal Sir Alan Brooke, Field-Marshal Sir Bernard Montgomery and the Divisional Commander, while other distinguished guests were hurried into the seven other Half Tracks which were provided and magnificently turned out by the 1st Battalion Grenadier Guards. At 1005 hours the vehicles moved off down the Charlottenburg Chaussee, which was lined by British Troops. At the Grosse Stern the inspection started. The Parade was formed up with 3rd Royal Horse Artillery round the Monument, then each side of the Chaussee stretching almost to the Brandenburg Gate were 5th Royal Horse Artillery, 8th Hussars, 11th Hussars, Royal Engineers, Searchlight Battery and the massed carriers of the Infantry.

Tanks approaching the saluting base at the Victory Parade

The Prime Minister drove down the Charlottenburg Chaussee towards the Brandenburg Gate, and then back to the Grosse Stern. From there the procession turned North-West where, formed up with their Colours, were the Royal Navy, 1st Battalion Grenadier Guards, 1/5th Queens, 2nd Devons, Canadian Battalion, 131 Infantry Brigade Headquarters and the Royal Air Force and Royal Air Force Regiment.

The whole inspection lasted forty minutes and at 1045 the Prime Minister returned to the Saluting Base, where a five minute interval was necessary before the march past began.

For twenty minutes, guns, tanks and armoured cars roared past the base, led by 3rd Regiment Royal Horse Artillery, 5th Royal Horse Artillery followed by 8th Hussars, 11th Hussars, Royal Engineers, Searchlights with the massed carriers bringing up the rear. Then followed the marching troops headed by the Band of the Royal Marines and the Royal Naval Detachment, 1st Battalion Grenadier Guards, 1/5th Queens, 2nd Devons and the Canadian Battalion. By 1120 the parade was over.

Mr. Churchill opens the Winston Club in Berlin

To some it had seemed too long, to others far too short, but in the hearts of all British men and women present there was a feeling that they had been privileged to witness a spectacle for which they had all longed and one which they would never see again, while for all ranks of the 7th Armoured Division there was a feeling of pride and satisfaction that they had been able to end their long record of achievements by playing their part in the Victory Parade in Berlin.

At 1125 hours the Prime Minister departed with Field-Marshal Sir Bernard Montgomery and the Divisional Commander to open an Other Ranks' Club, which was christened "Winston".

There can be no more fitting way to conclude this Divisional History than to repeat the words spoken by the Prime Minister at this Opening Ceremony:

"Soldiers of the 7th Armoured Division. I am delighted to be able to open this Club and I shall always consider it a great honour that it should have been named after me.

"I have, not for the first time, had the pleasure of seeing your troops march past, and this brings back to my mind a great many moving incidents in these last, long, fierce years.

"Now, here in Berlin, I find you all established in this great centre, from which, as from a volcano, fire and smoke and poison fumes have erupted all over Europe twice in a generation. And in bygone times also German fury has been let loose on her neighbours, and now it is we who have our place in the occupation of this country.

"I feel I can go so far as to ask Field-Marshal Montgomery to signalise this happy event of the great Victory Parade we have had today by giving a whole holiday to all the troops in Berlin, and I hope, Field-Marshal, that you can accommodate this to operational and other necessities.

"Now I have only a word more to say about the Desert Rats. They were the first to begin. The 11th Hussars were in action in the desert in 1940 and ever since you have kept marching steadily forward on the long road to victory. Through so many countries and changing scenes you have fought your way.

"It is not without emotion that I can express to you what I feel about the Desert Rats.

"Dear Desert Rats! May your glory ever shine! May your laurels never fade! May the memory of this glorious pilgrimage of war which you have made from Alamein, via the Baltic to Berlin, never die! It is a march unsurpassed through all the story of war so far as my reading of history leads me to believe. May the fathers long tell the children about this tale. May you all feel that in following your great ancestors you have accomplished something which has done good to the whole world; which has raised the honour of your own country and which every man has a right to be proud of."

The end of the Axis

SHEET 1.

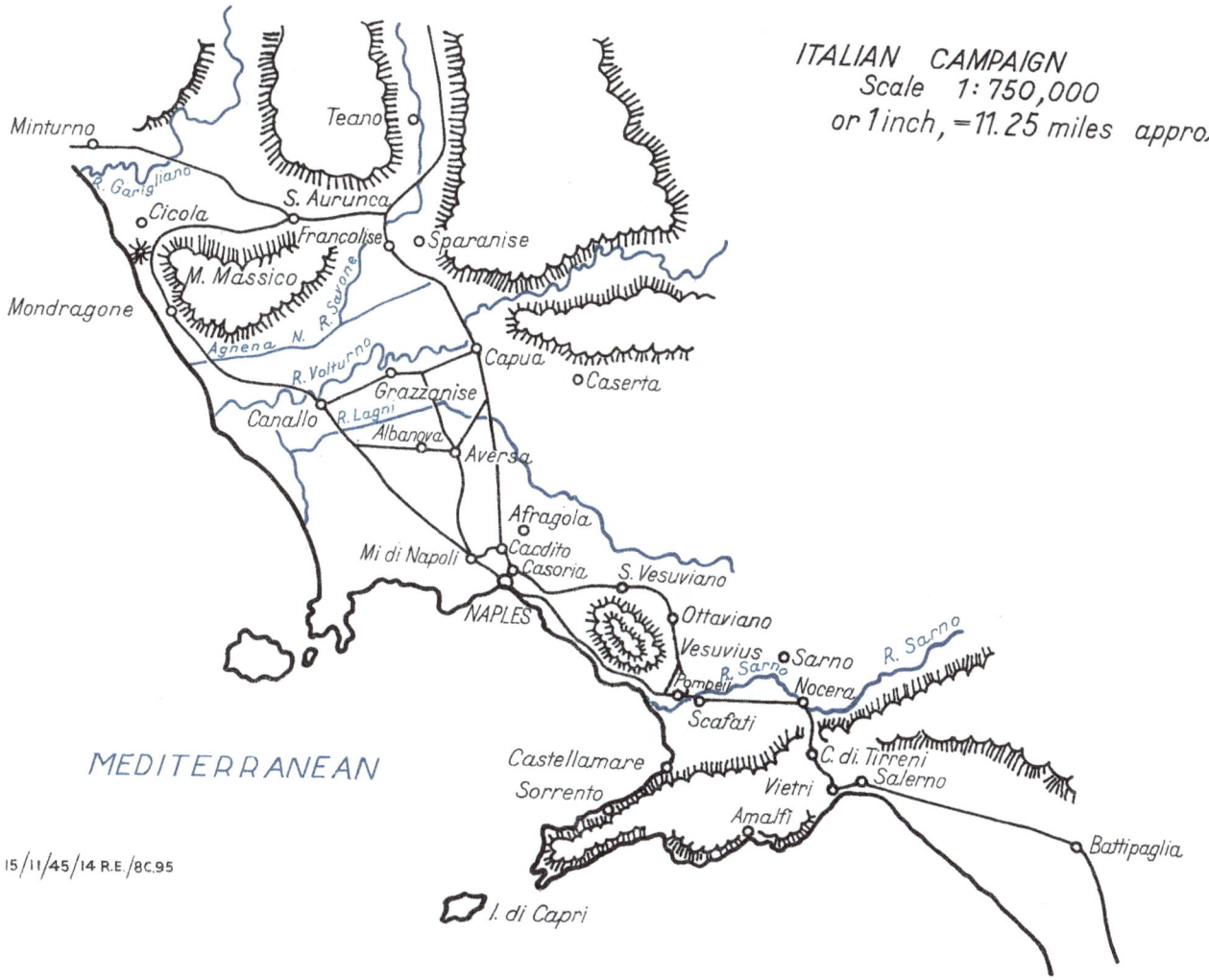

ITALIAN CAMPAIGN
Scale 1:750,000
or 1 inch,=11.25 miles approx

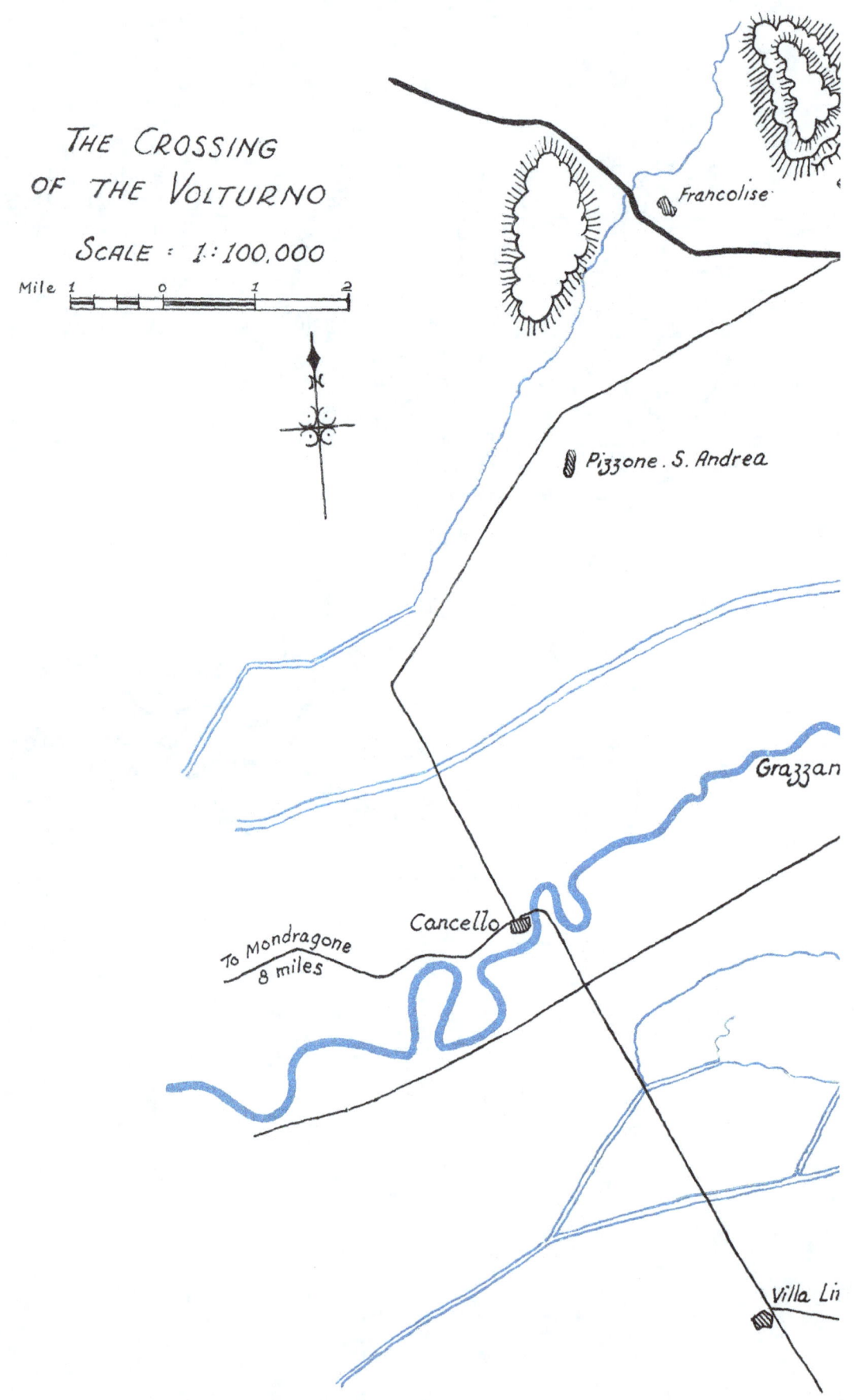

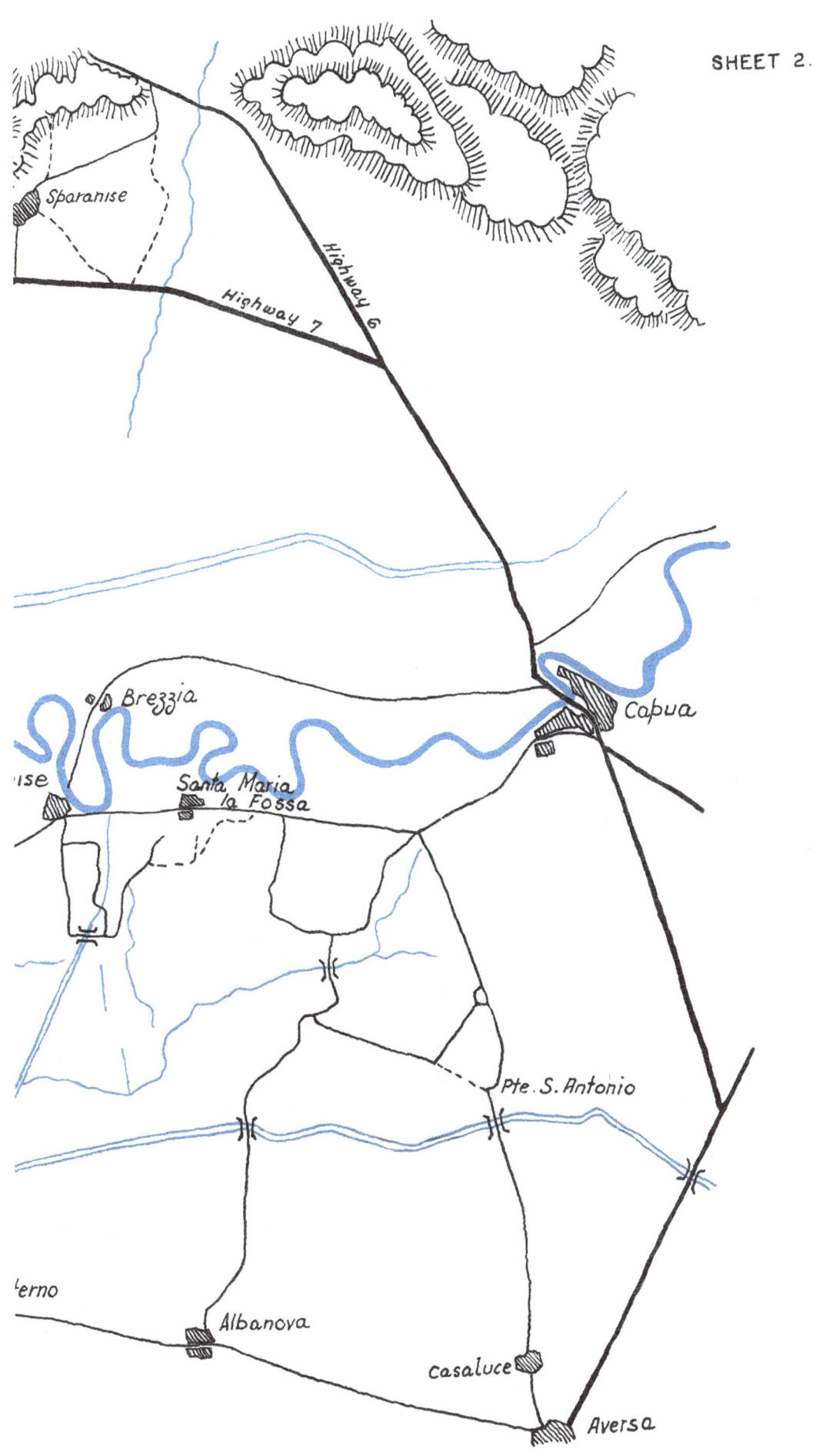

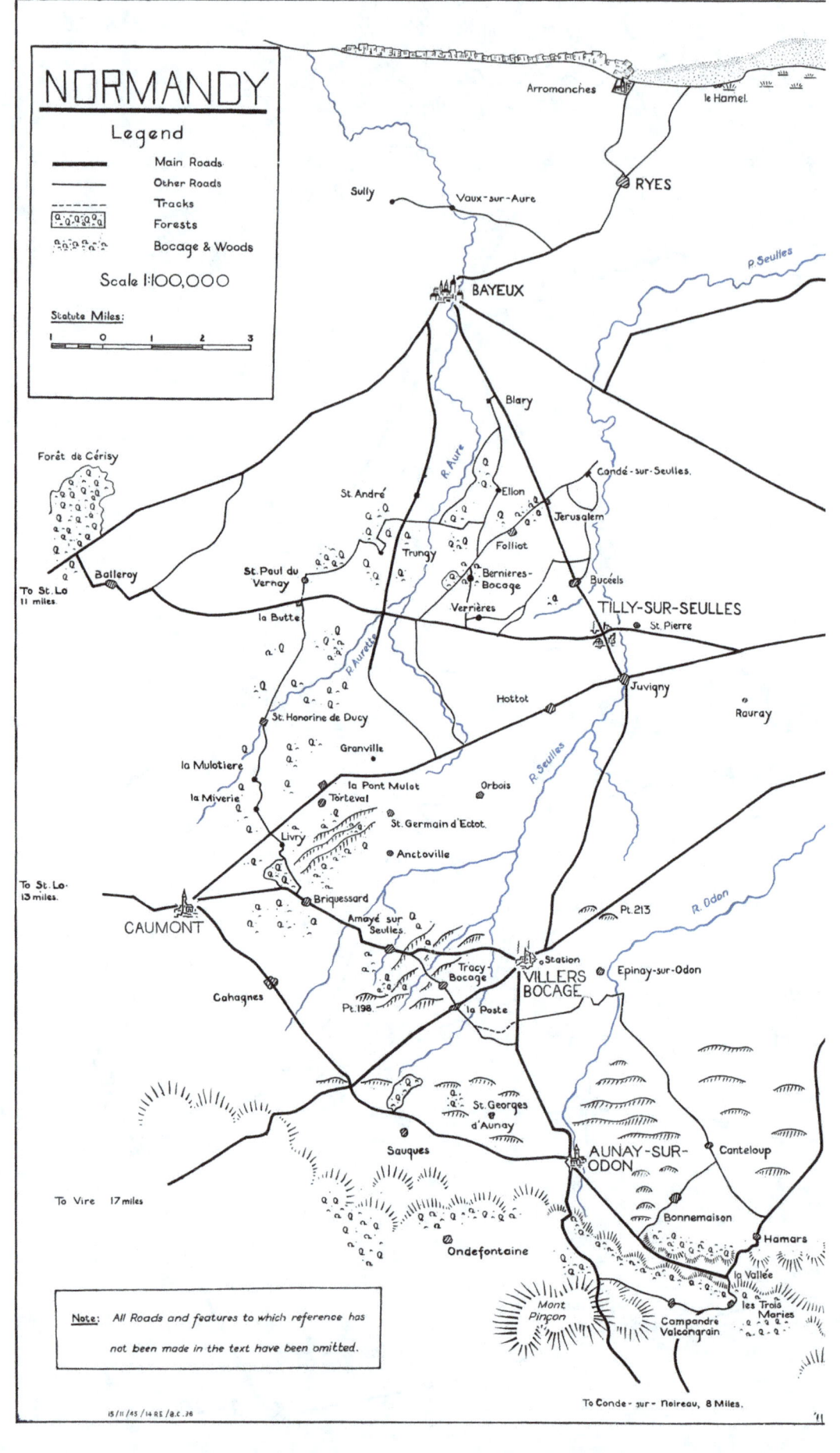

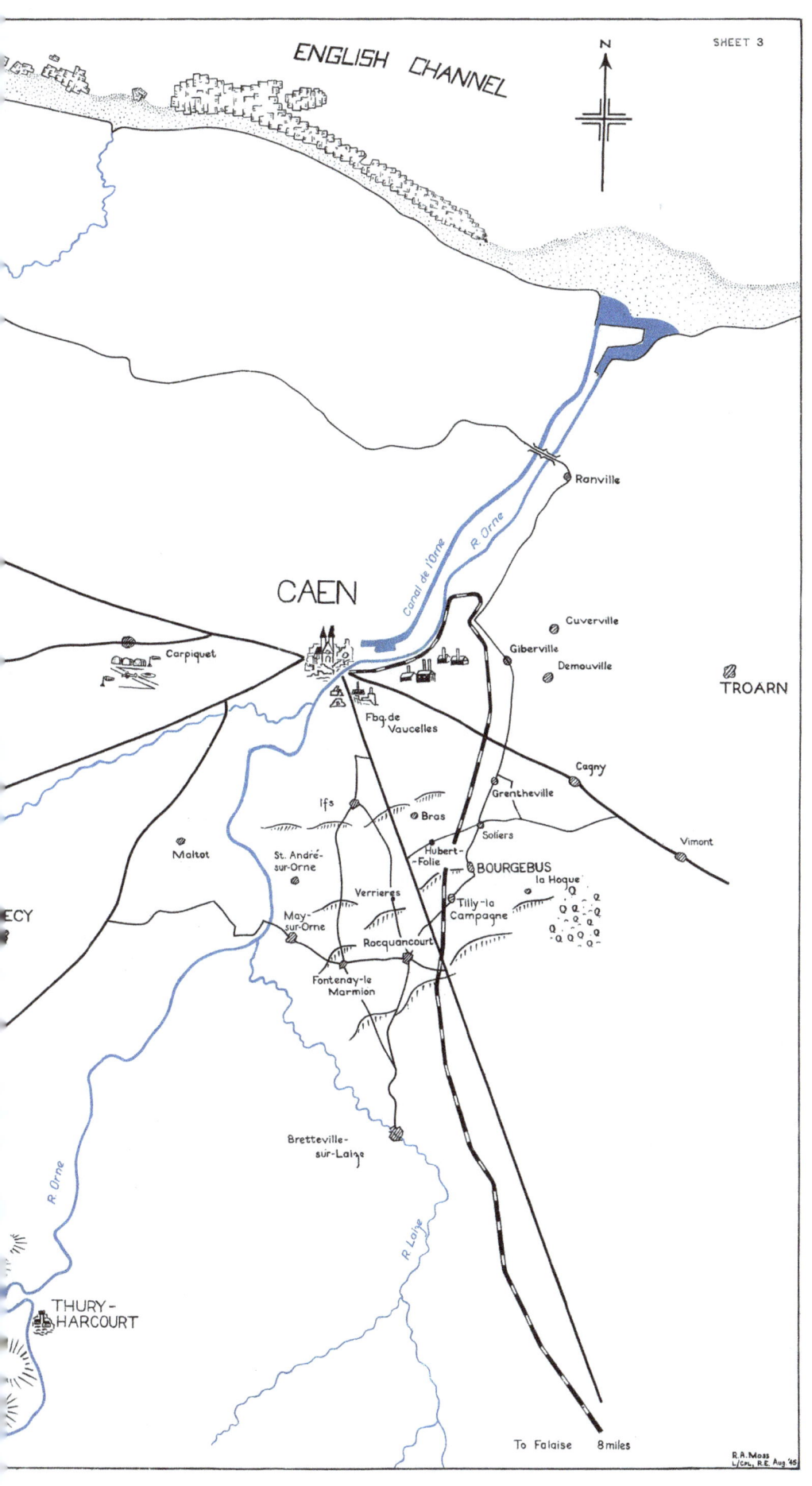

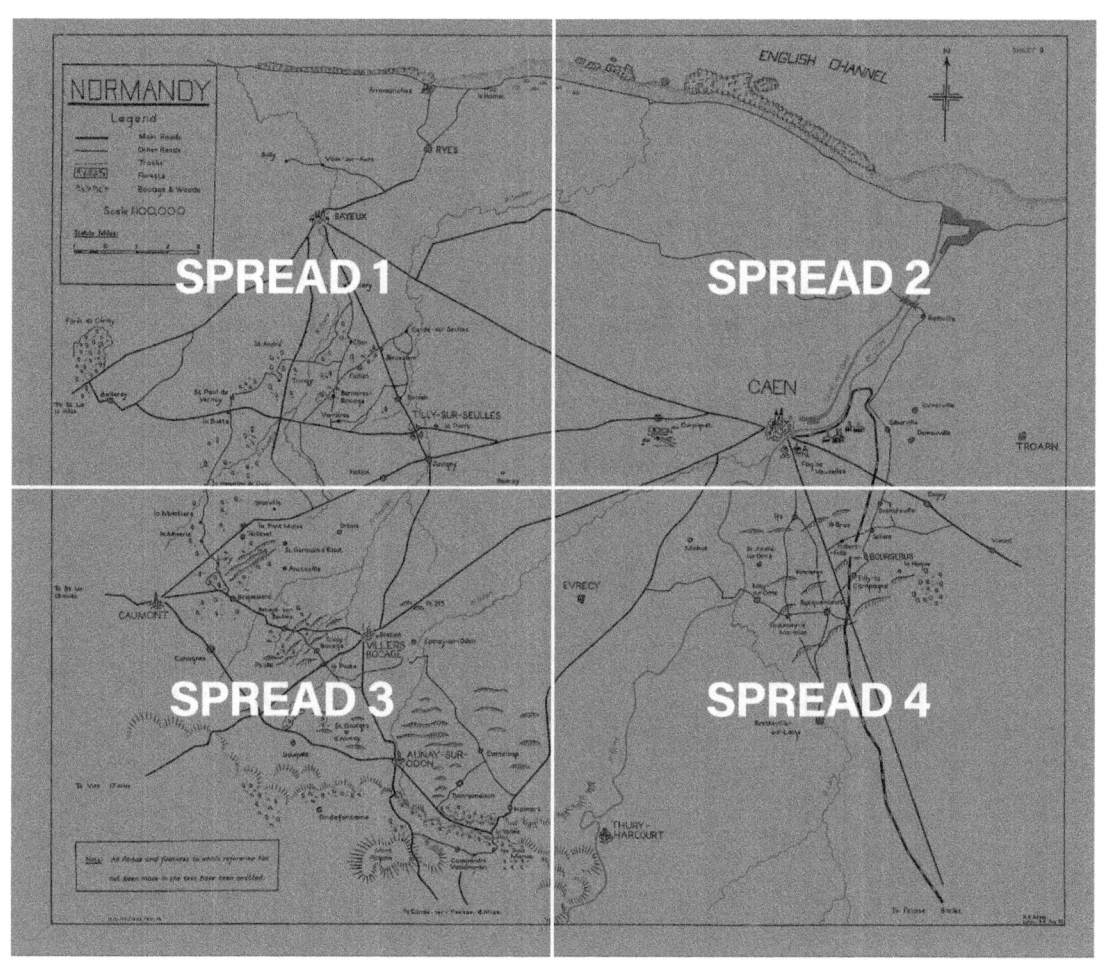

SPREAD 1

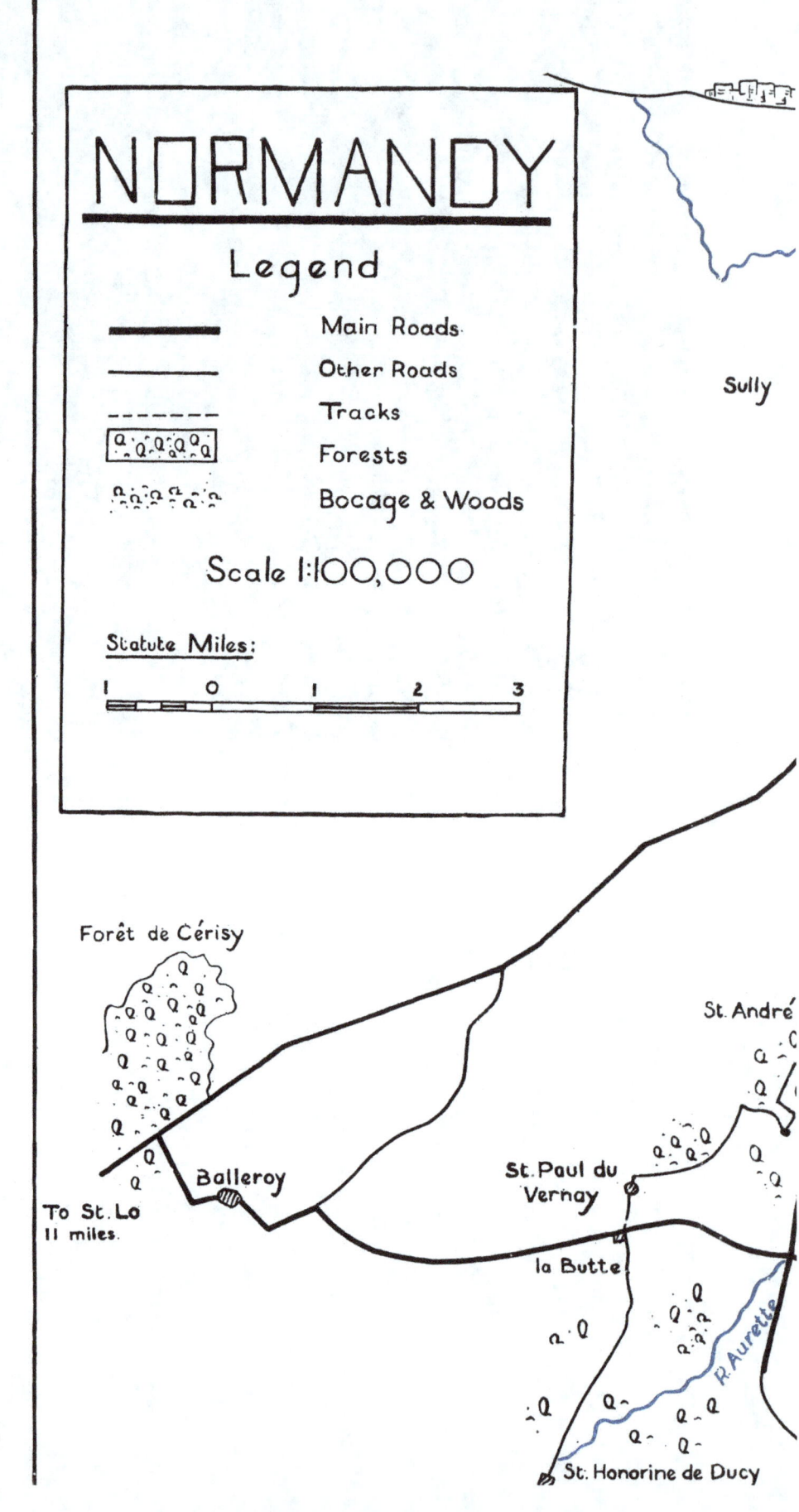

SPREAD 1

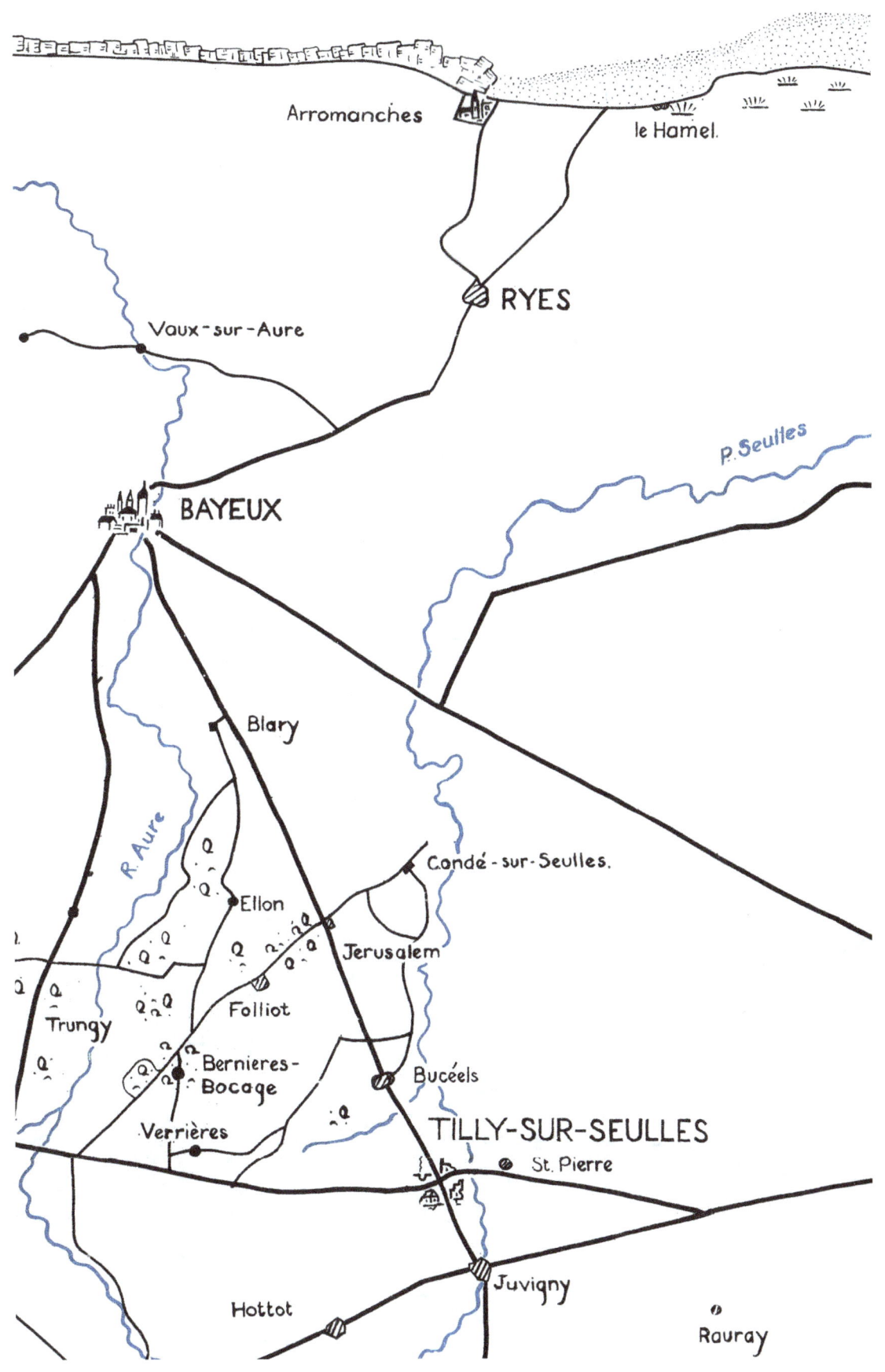

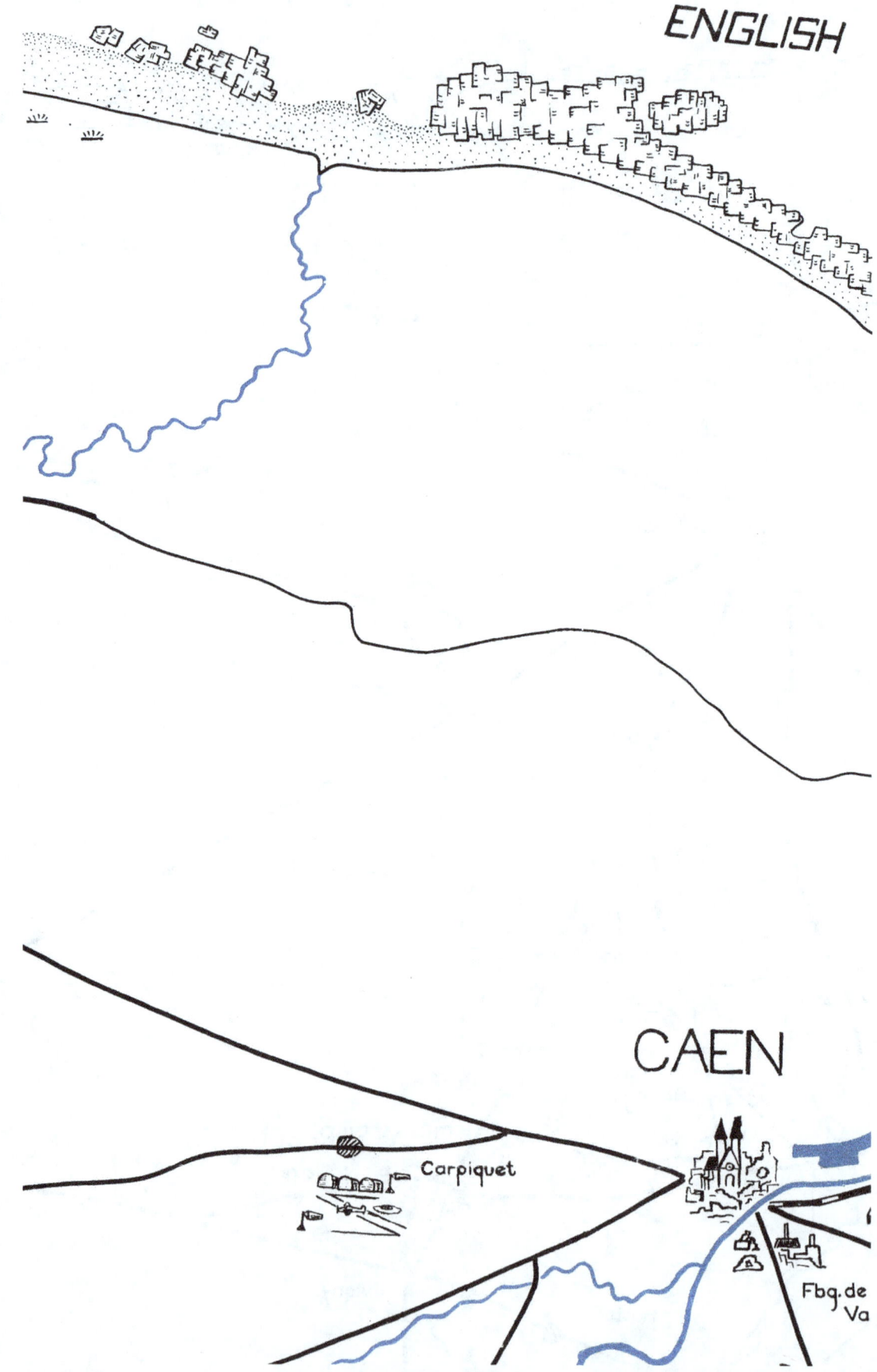

SPREAD 2

SHEET 3

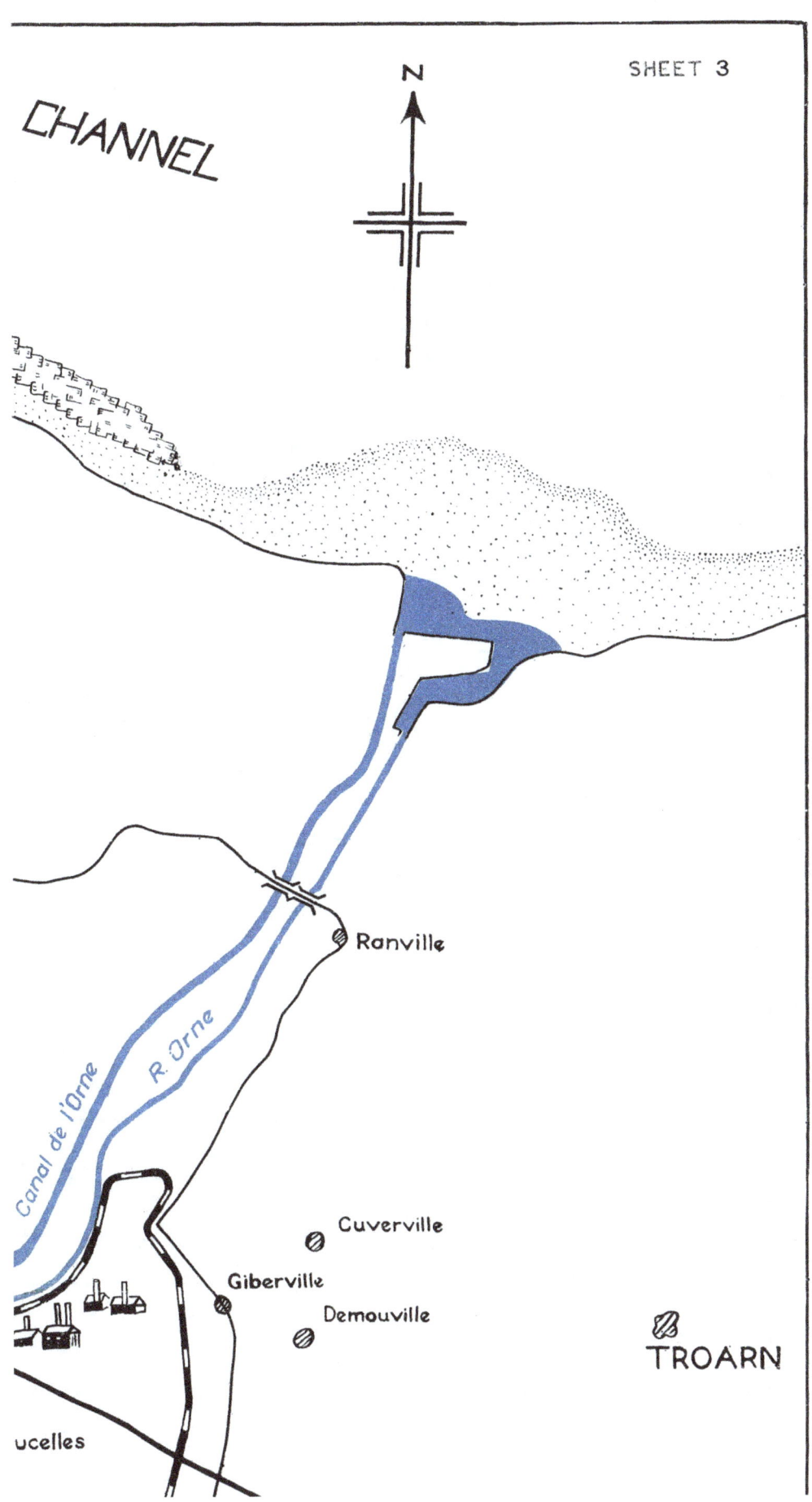

SPREAD 3

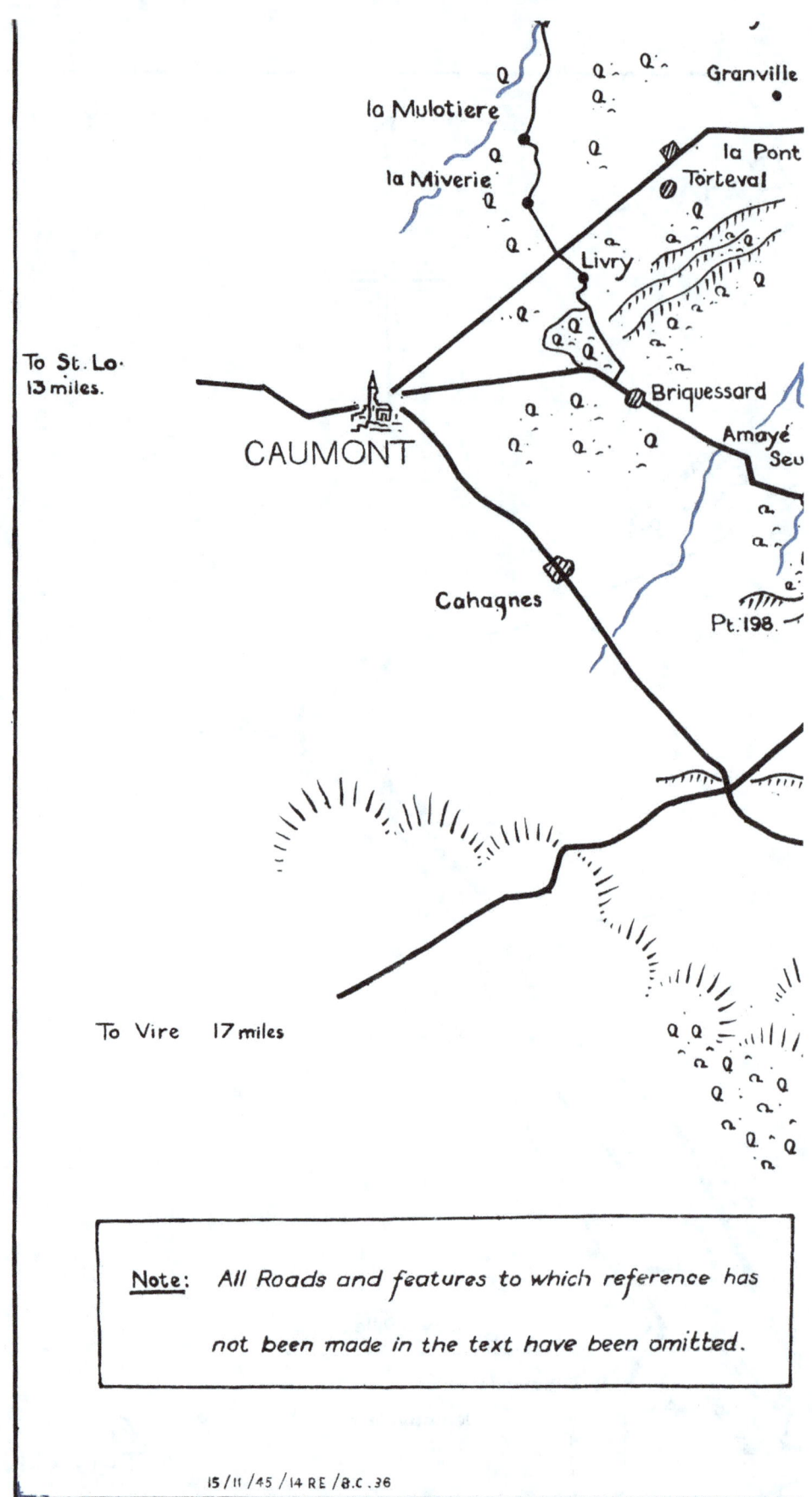

SPREAD 3

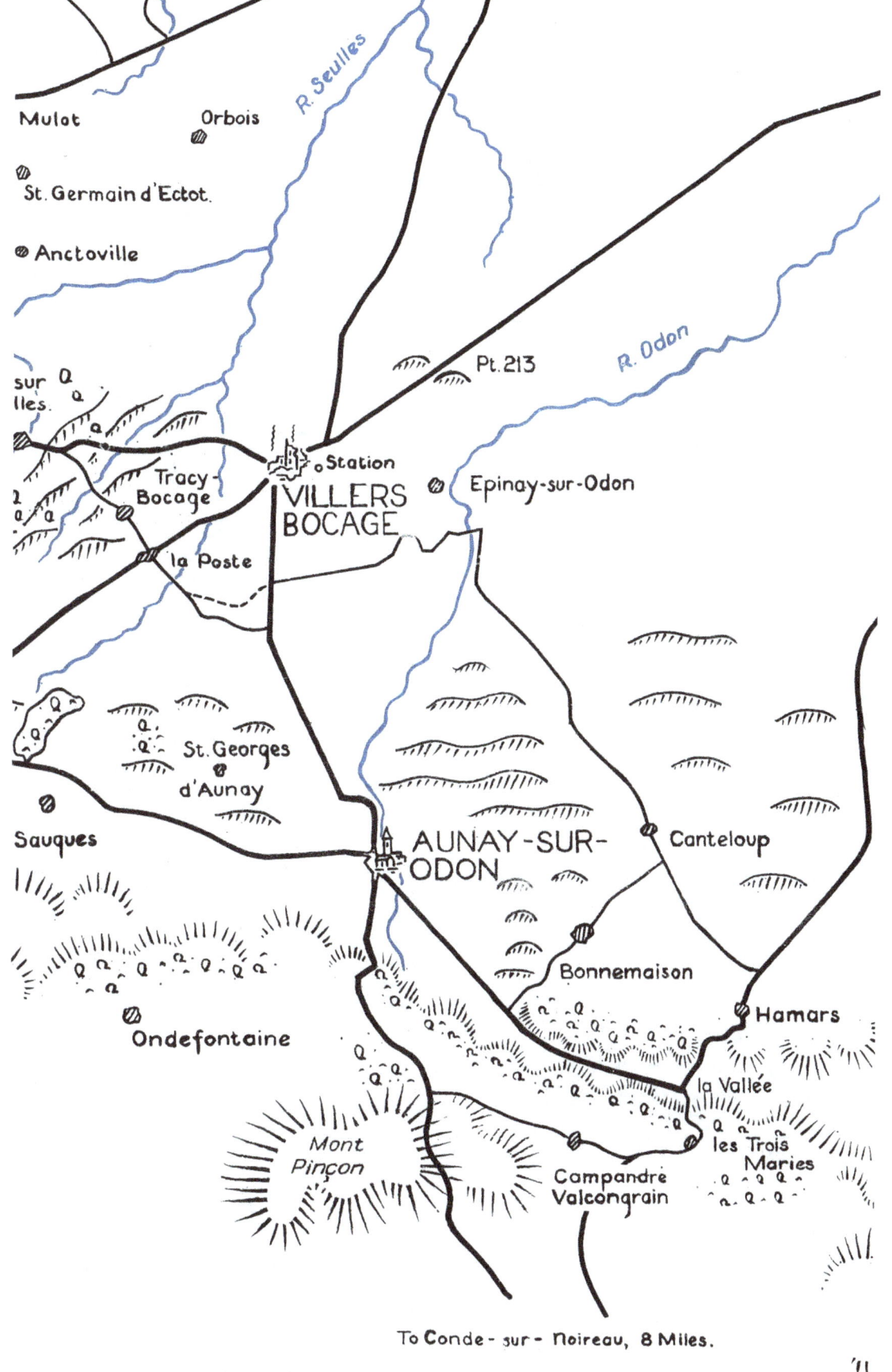

SPREAD 4

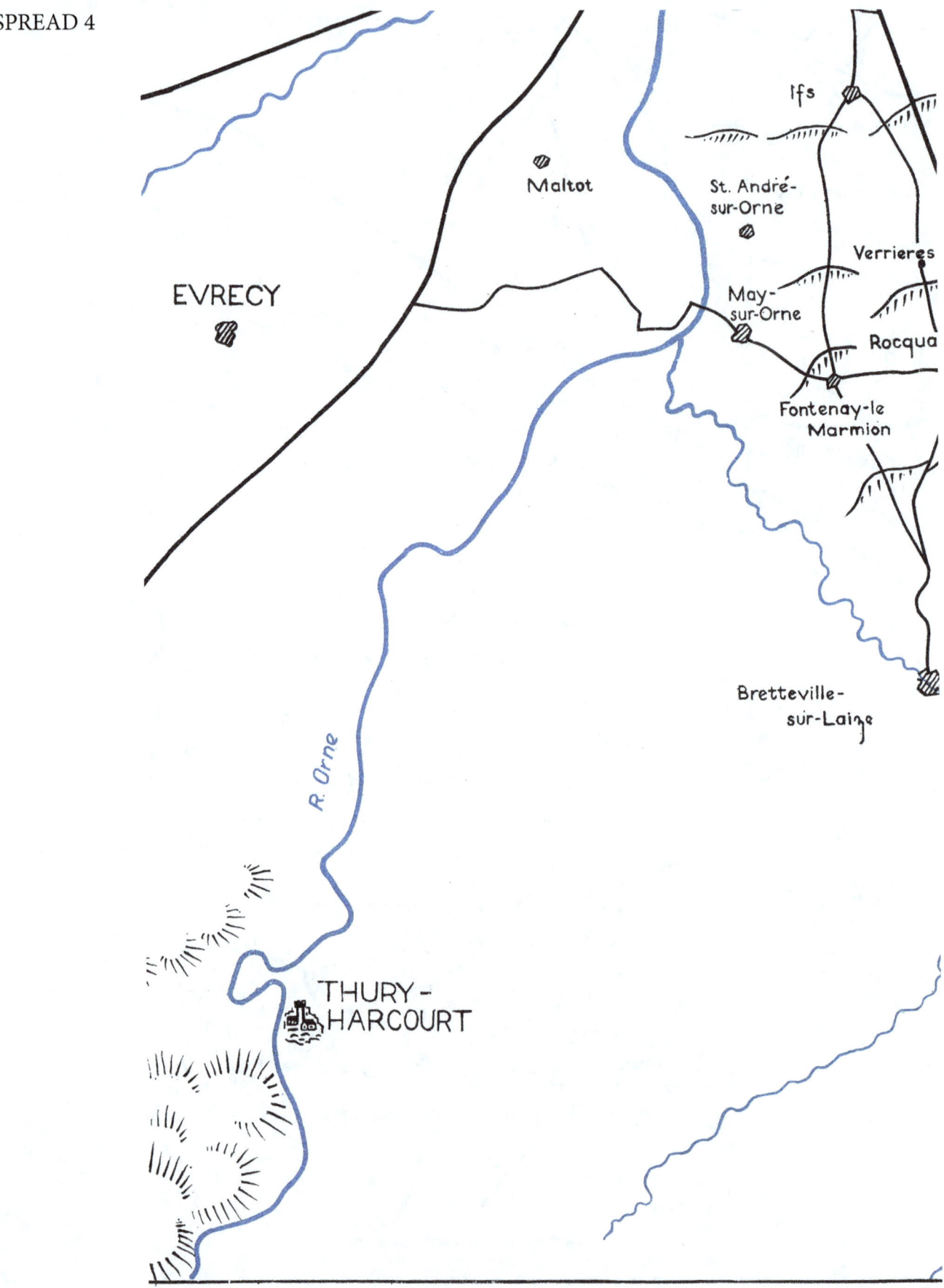

SPREAD 4

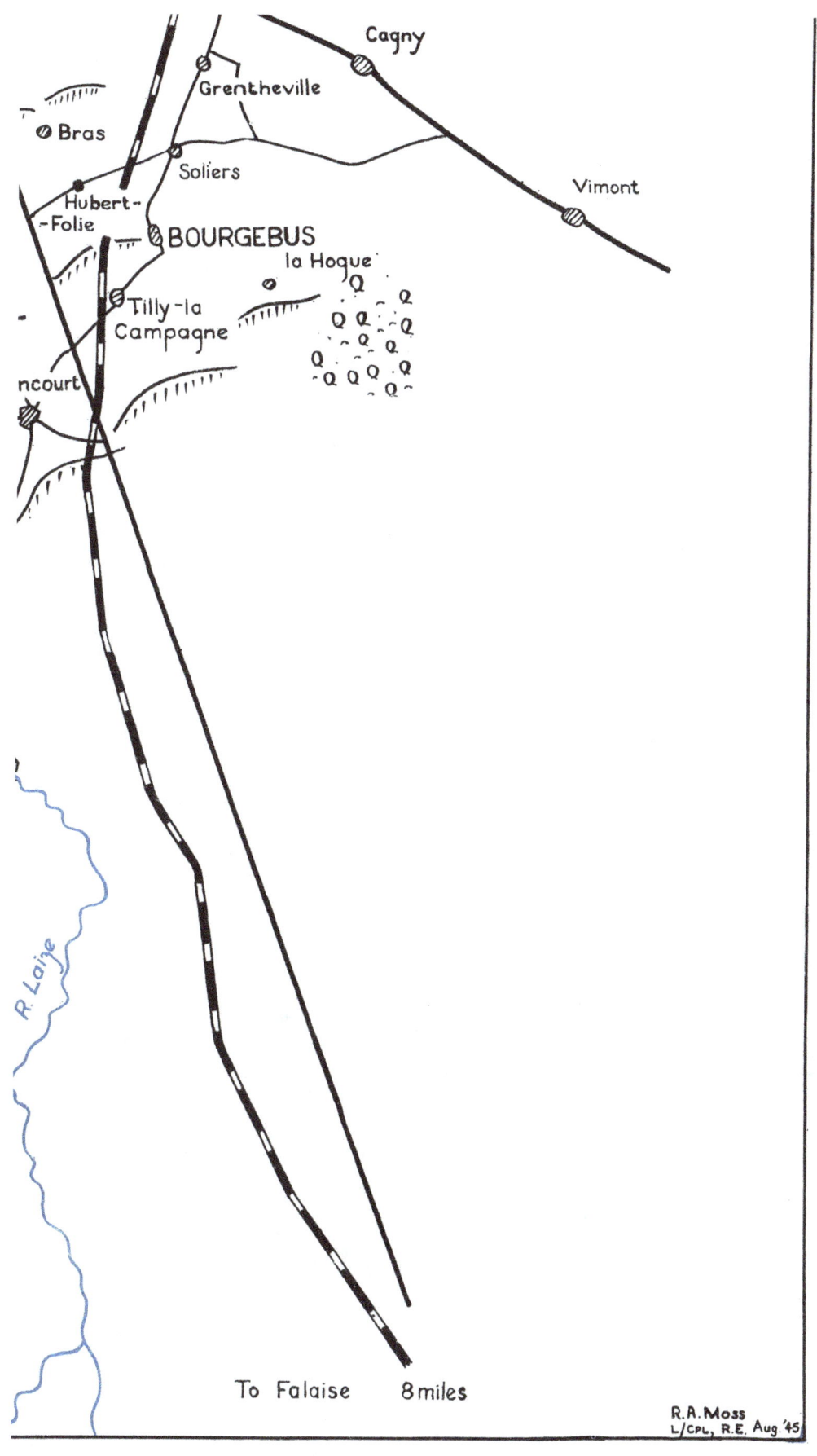

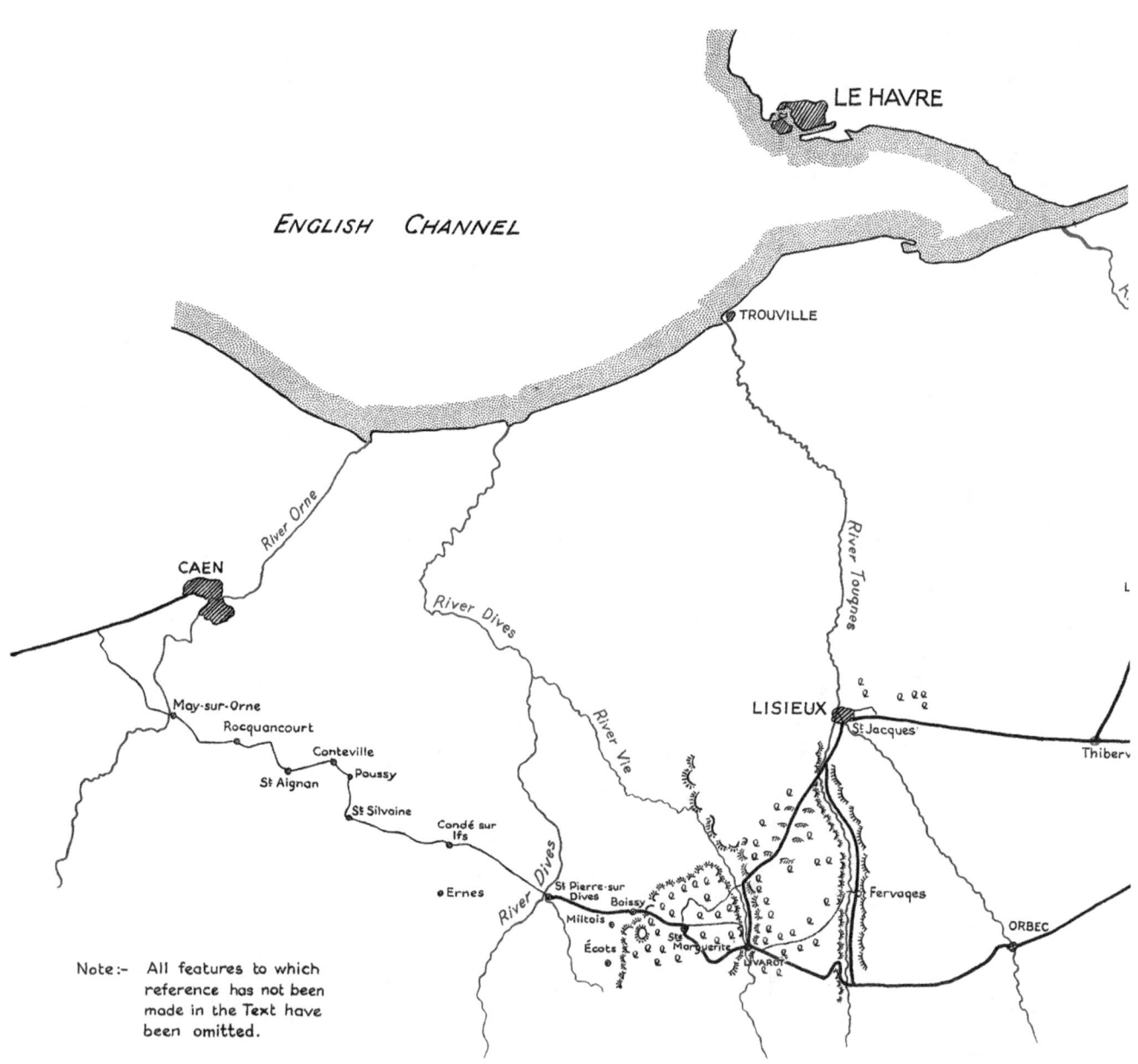

SPREAD 1
SPREAD 2

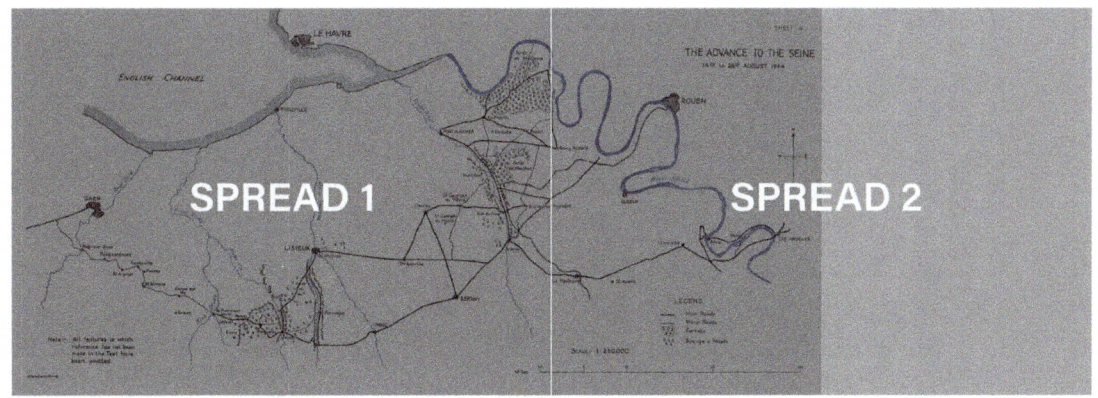

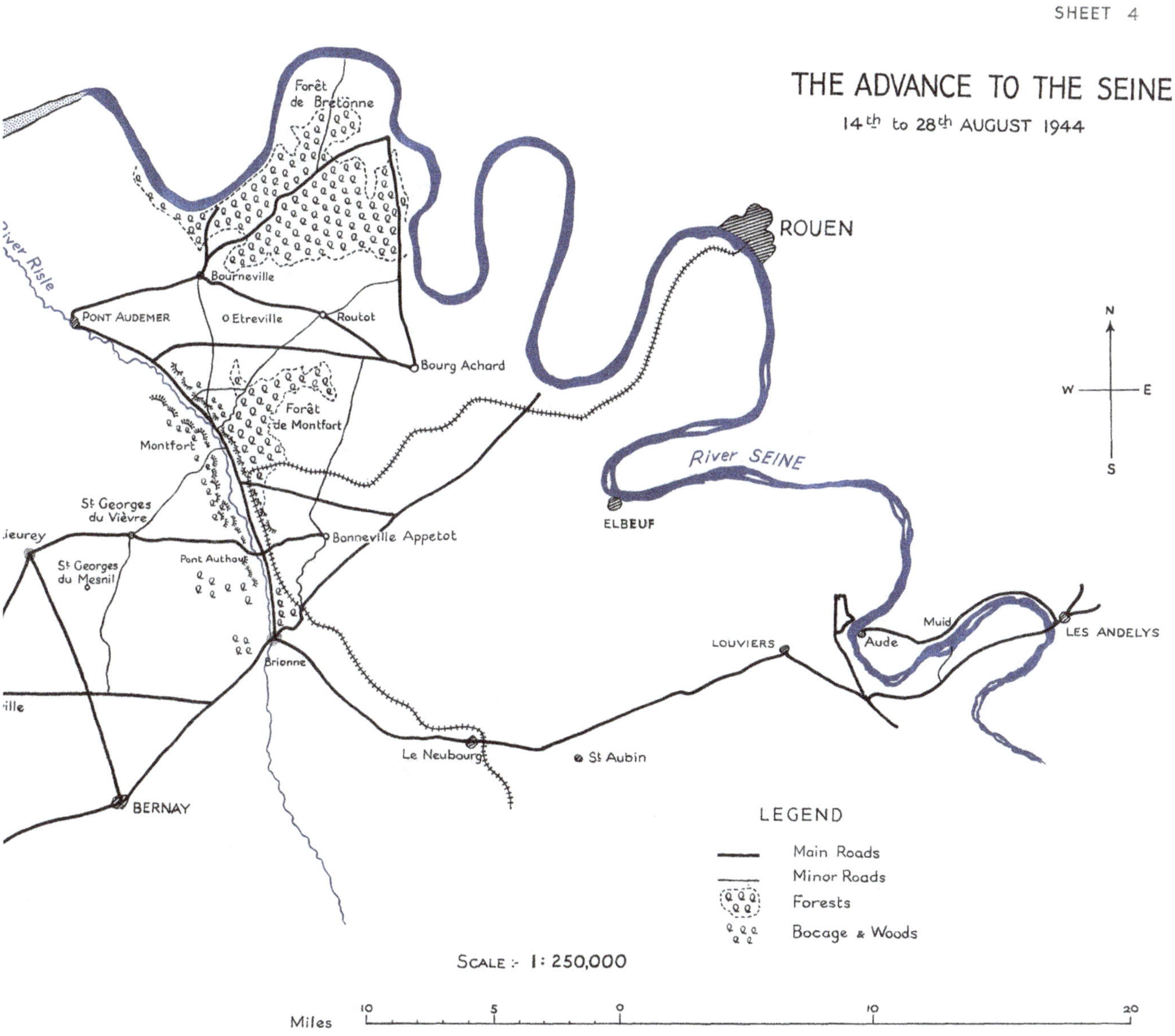
SHEET 4
THE ADVANCE TO THE SEINE
14th to 28th AUGUST 1944
Forêt de Bretonne
ROUEN
River Risle
Bourneville
PONT AUDEMER
Etreville
Routot
Bourg Achard
N
W
E
S
Forêt de Montfort
Montfort
River SEINE
St Georges du Vièvre
ELBEUF
Bonneville Appetot
Lieurey
St Georges du Mesnil
Pont Authou
Muid
LES ANDELYS
LOUVIERS
Aude
Brionne
ville
Le Neubourg
St Aubin
BERNAY
LEGEND
Main Roads
Minor Roads
Forests
Bocage & Woods
SCALE :- 1: 250,000
Miles
10
5
0
10
20

SPREAD 1

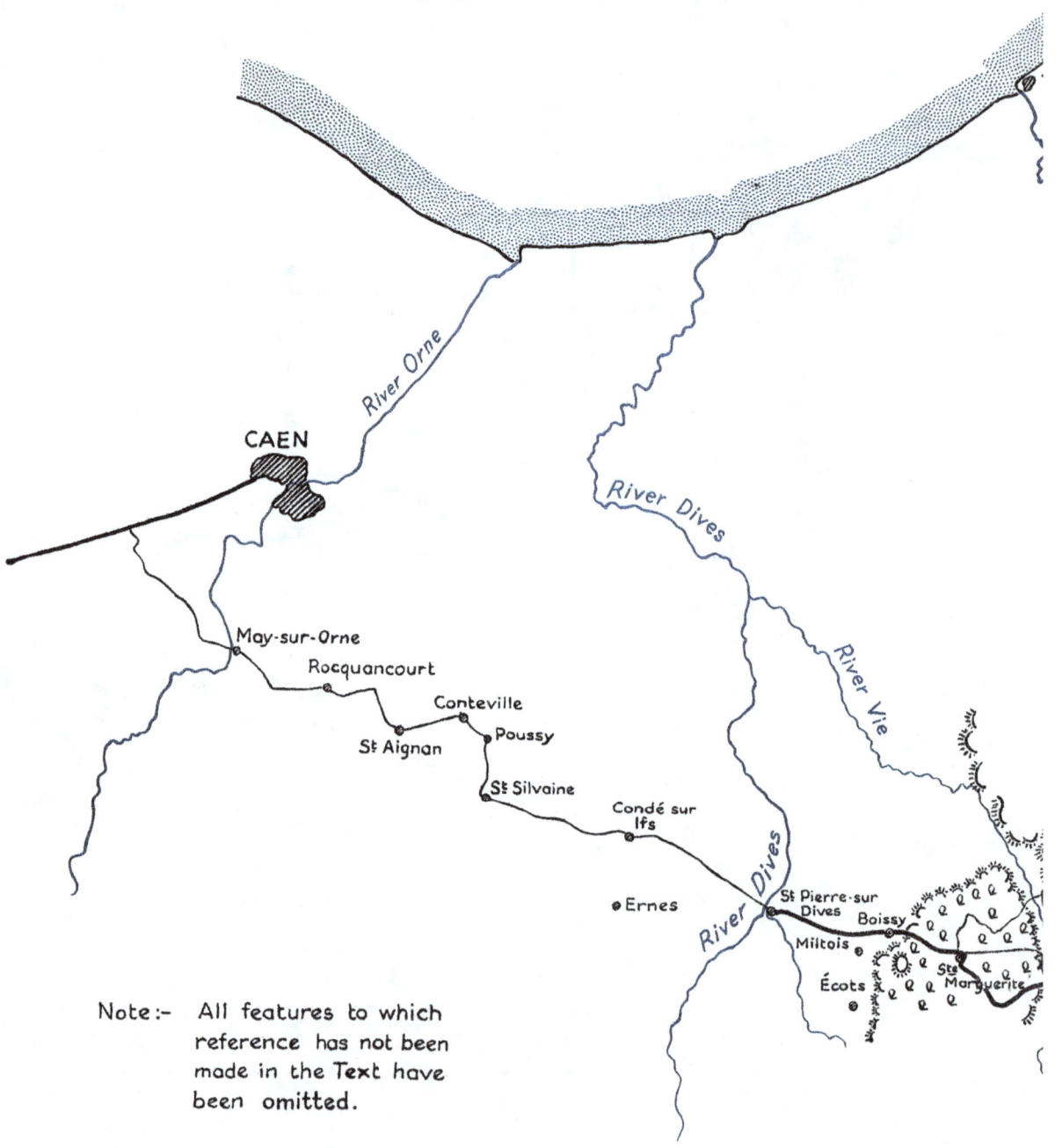

Note:— All features to which reference has not been made in the Text have been omitted.

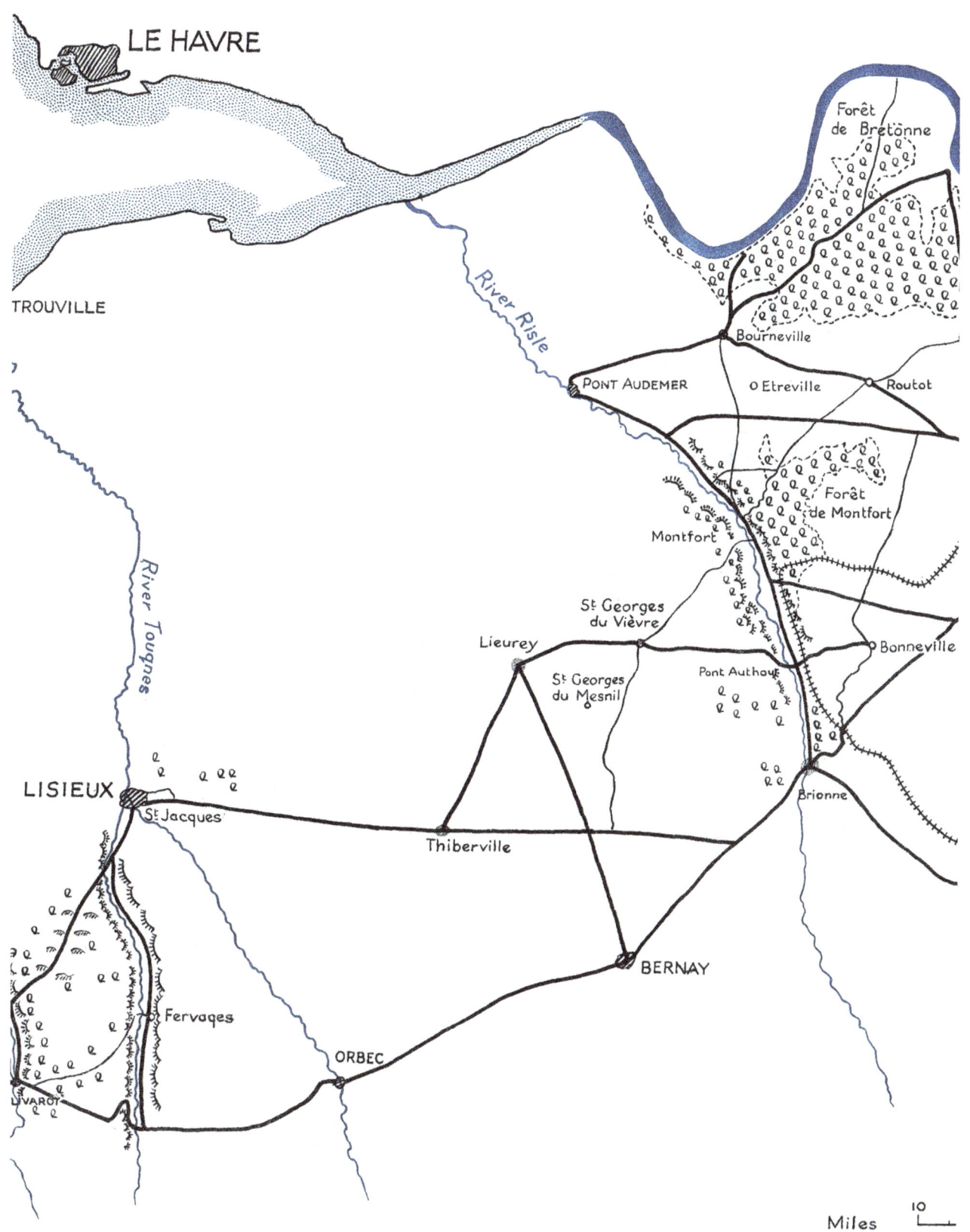

SPREAD 1

SPREAD 2

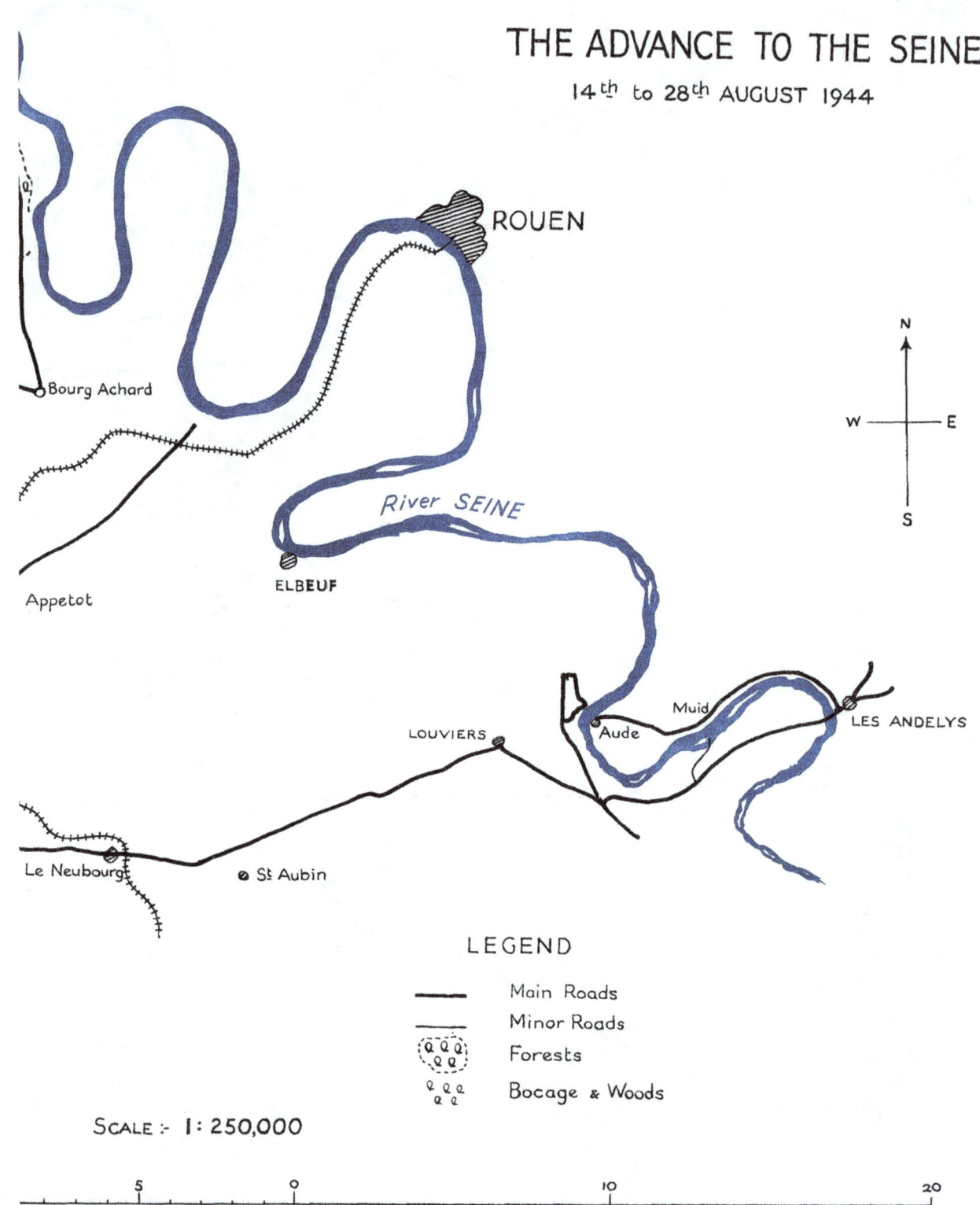

SPREAD 2

THE ADVANCE TO GHENT

29th August - 6th September 1944

SCALE : 1 : 1,000,000   1 inch = 16 miles

LEGEND

——— Main Routes used by the Division

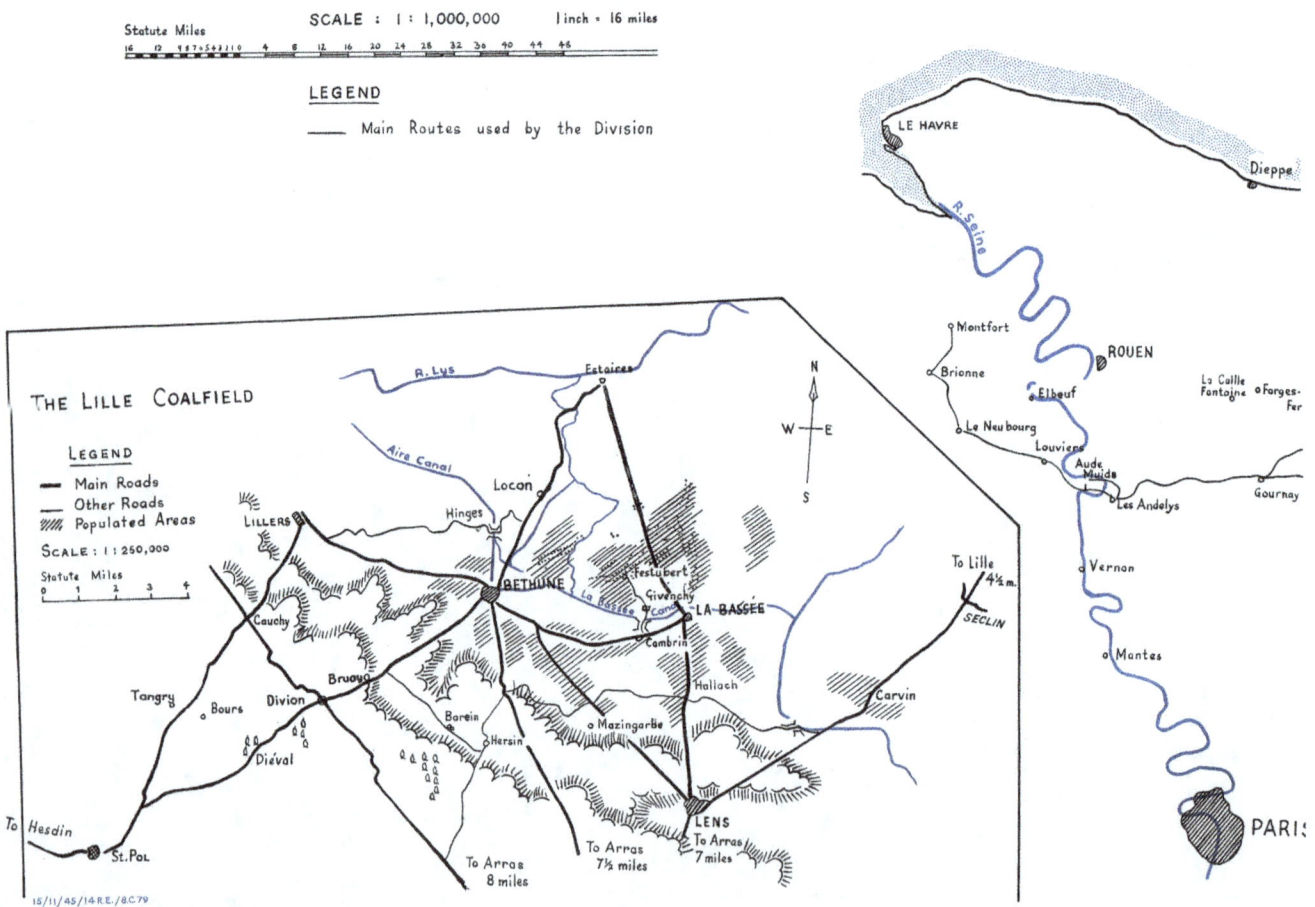

THE ADVANCE TO GHENT
SPREAD 1
SPREAD 2
PARIS

SHEET 5.
N
W
E
S
CALAIS
BOULOGNE
DUNKIRK
OSTEND
WALCH-
EREN
N. BEVELAND
BEVELAND
BRUGES
R. Calanches
R. Authie
Hesdin
Abbéville
Auxi-la Chateau
R. Somme
Cauchy
Lillers
Hinges
Estaires
Bourg
Diéval
St Pol
Locon
Bethune
R. Lys
Frévent
Cambrin
Hersin
la Bassee
Mazingarde
LILLE
LENS
Seclin
Carvin
Domart
Bernoville
Berneuil
Airaines
Conde
Hangest
Doullens
Vignacourt
M-Vidames
Picquigny
Aumâle
Abancourt
Poix
Grandvilliers
AMIENS
ARRAS
Deynze
GHENT
Lokeren
Nazareth
Cruysanthem
Kerkhoven
Picq
Audenarde
Wetteren
St. Nicholas
R. Scheldt
ANTWERP
Lierre
MALINES
BRUSSELS
Beauvais
GHENT
AREA
Scale 1: 250,000
Canal de Stekene
R. Lys
GHENT
L. St Martin
Deynze
of the R. Lys
Lokeren
La Pint
Nazareth
Melle
R. Lys
Wetteren
R. Scheldt
Cruysanthem
To Audenarde
To Audenarde

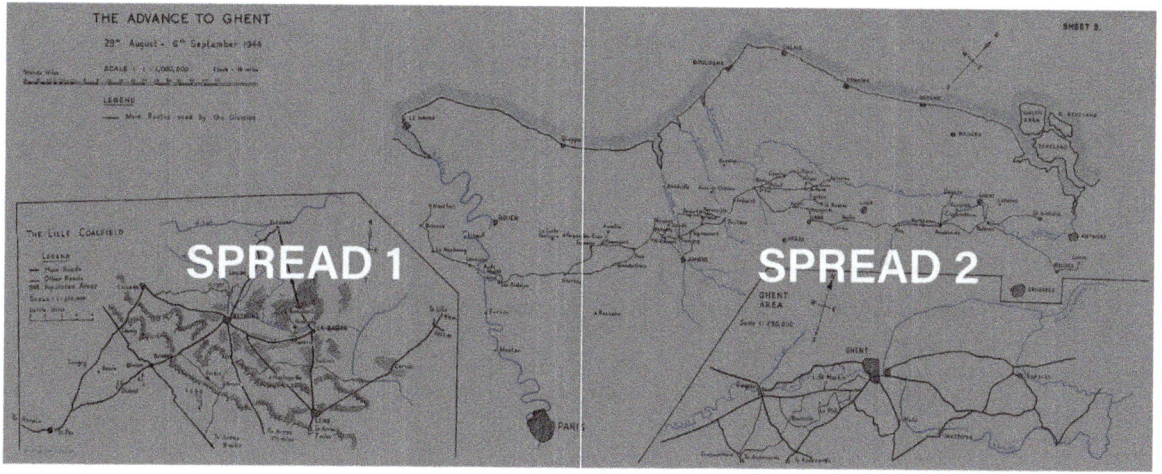

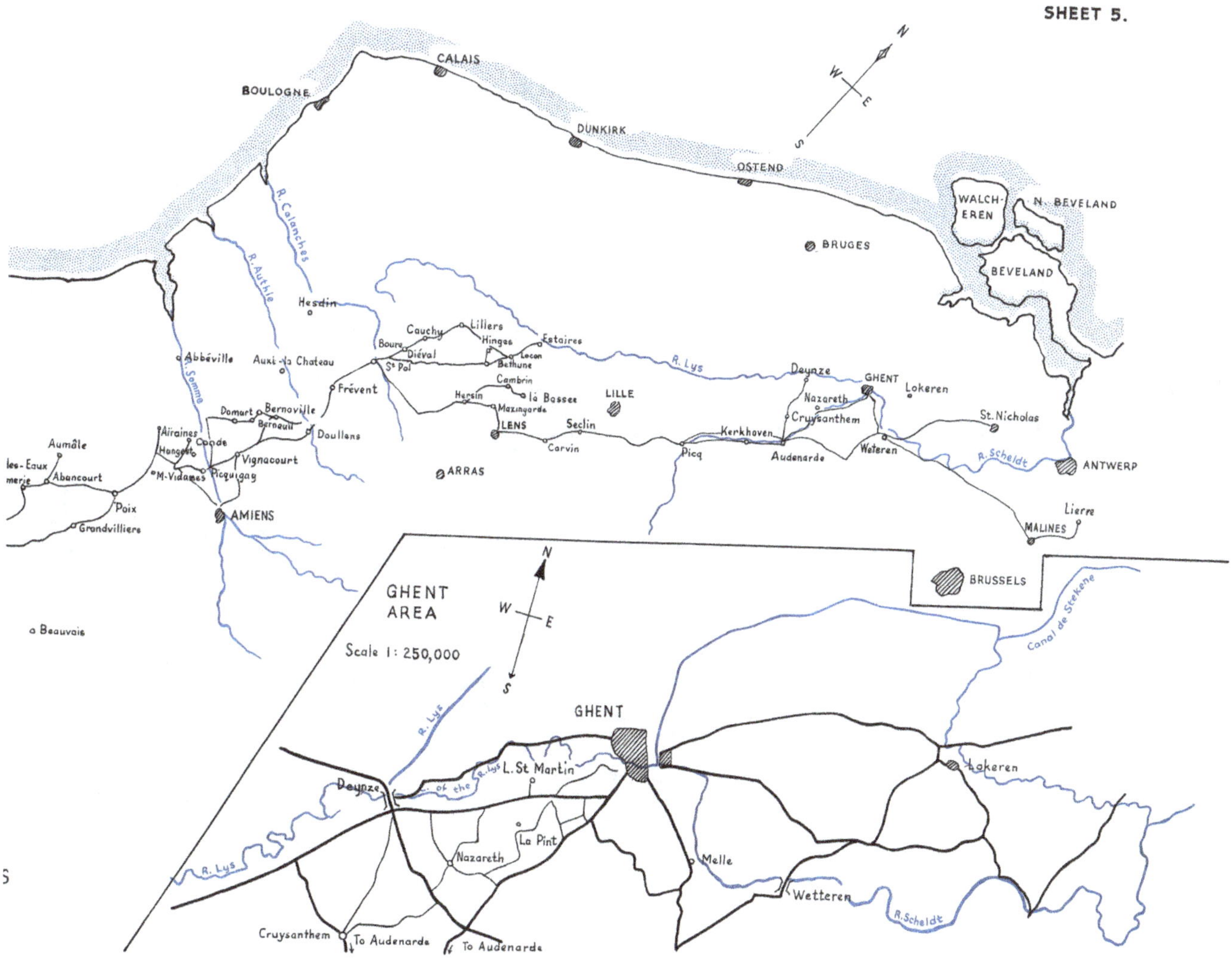

SPREAD 1

THE ADVANCE TO GHENT

29th August - 6th September 1944

SCALE : 1 : 1,000,000 1 inch = 16 miles

Statute Miles

16 12 9 8 7 6 5 4 3 2 1 0 4 8 12 16 20 24 28 32 36 40 44 48

LEGEND

—— Main Routes used by the Division

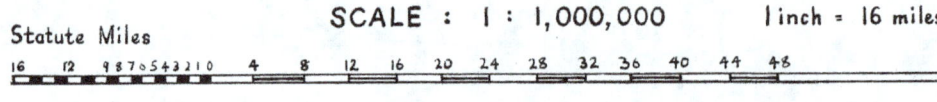

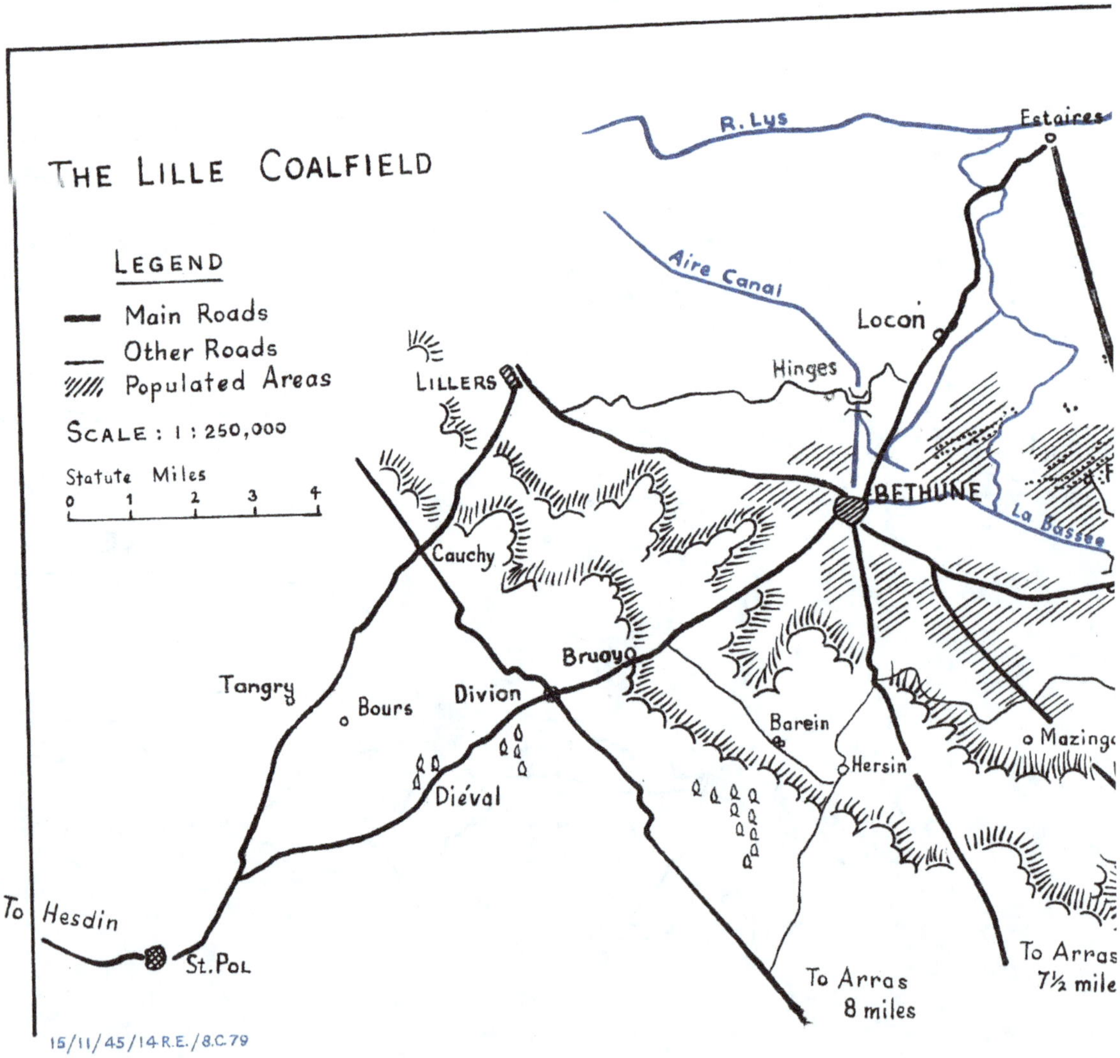

SPREAD 1

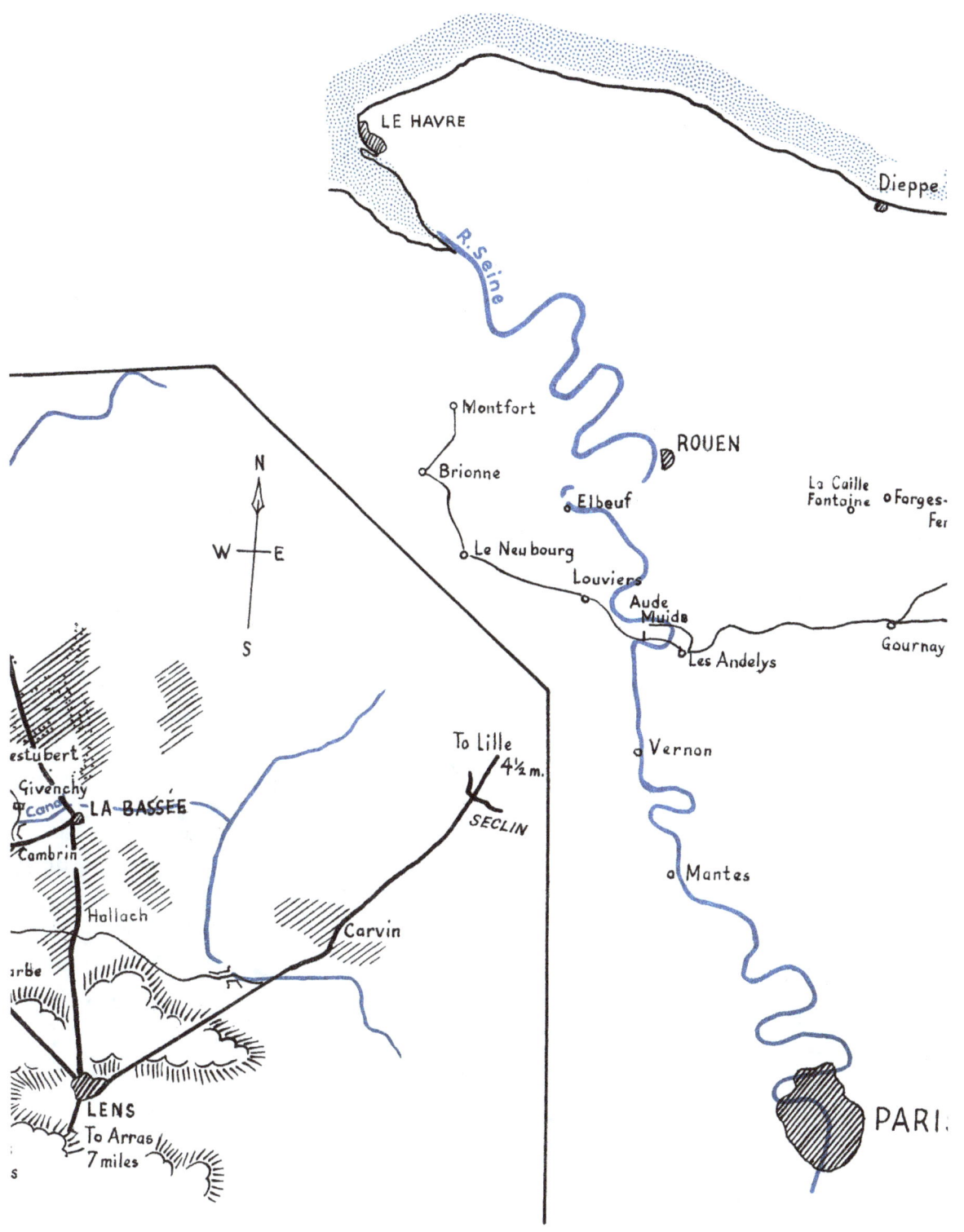

SPREAD 2

SPREAD 2

SHEET 5.

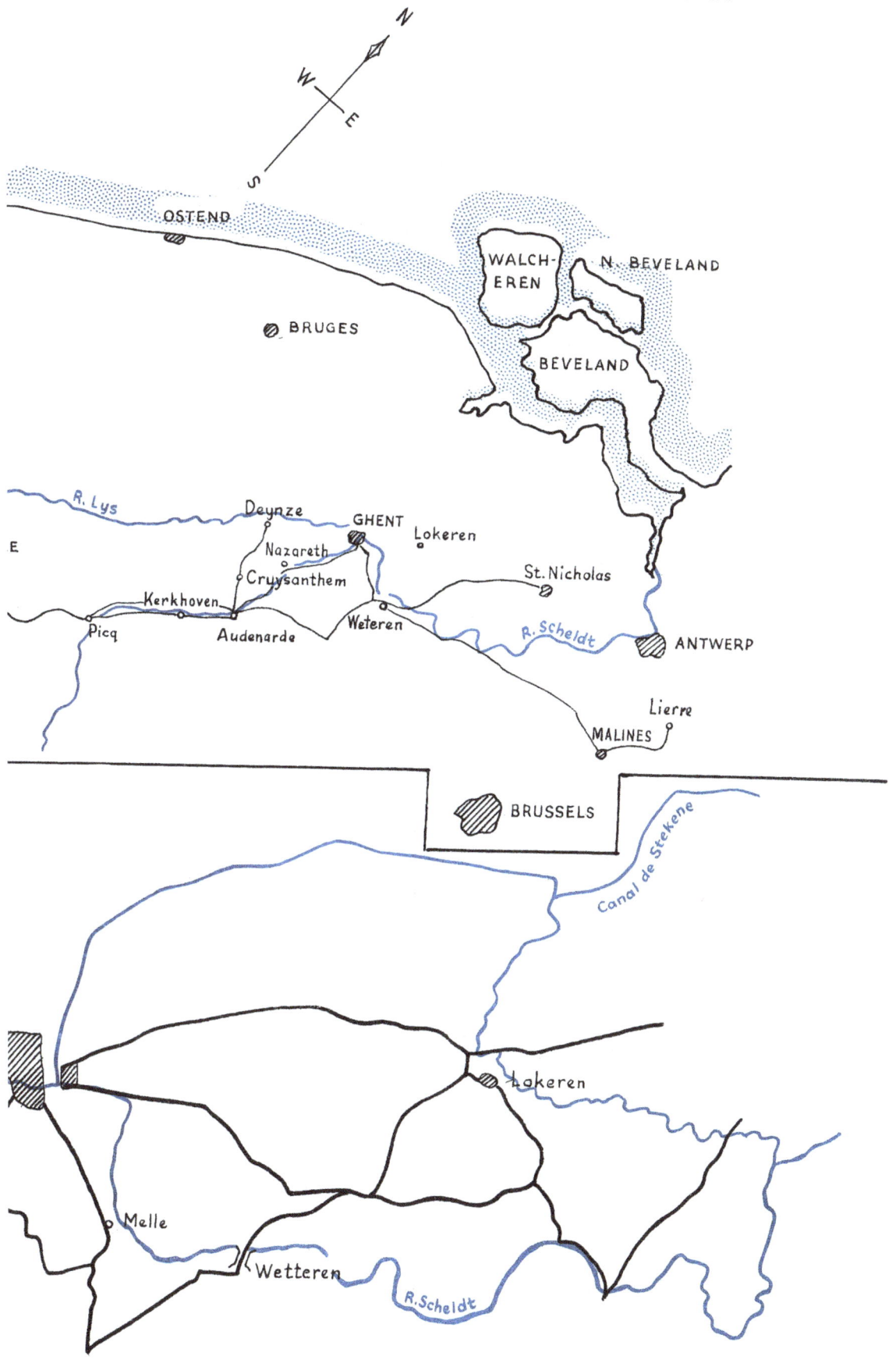

THE LOW COUNTRIES
6th SEP 1944 — 25th MAR 1945

Scale :- 1 : 1,000,000
1 inch = 16 miles

Statute Miles

SHEET 6.

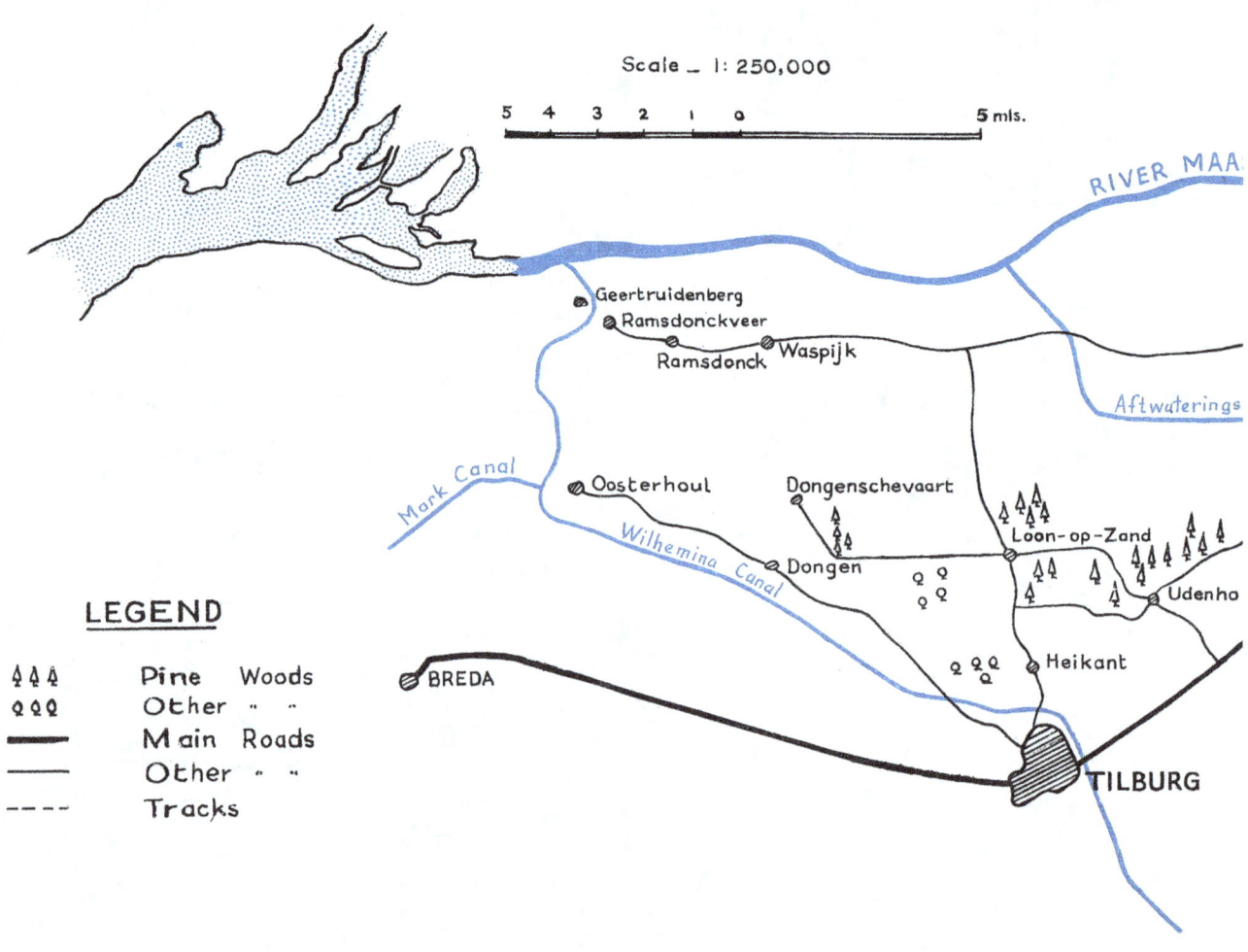

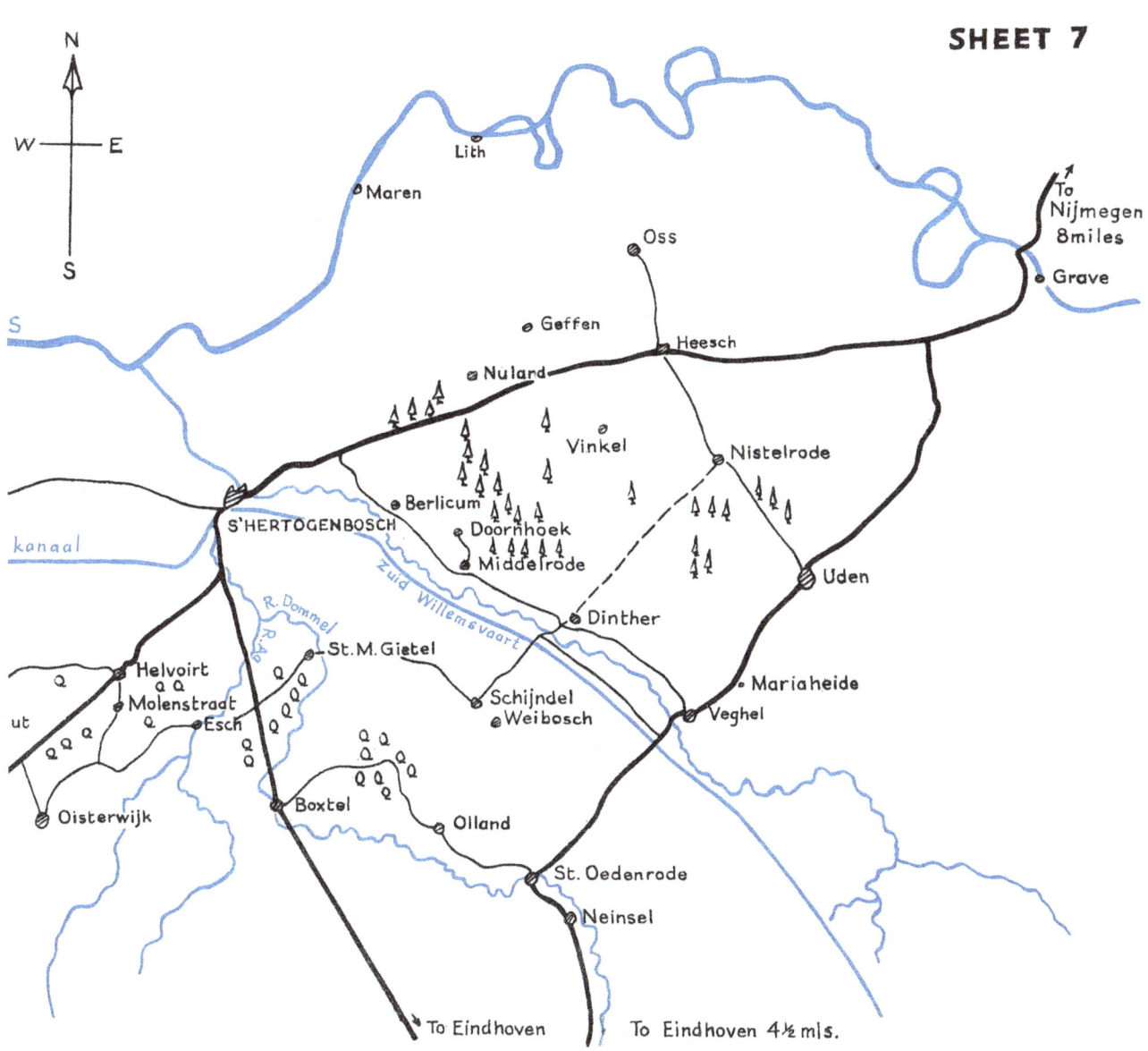

SHEET 7

BELGIUM & HOLLAND 10TH NOVEMBER 1944 — 2nd FEBRUARY 1945

SHEET 8

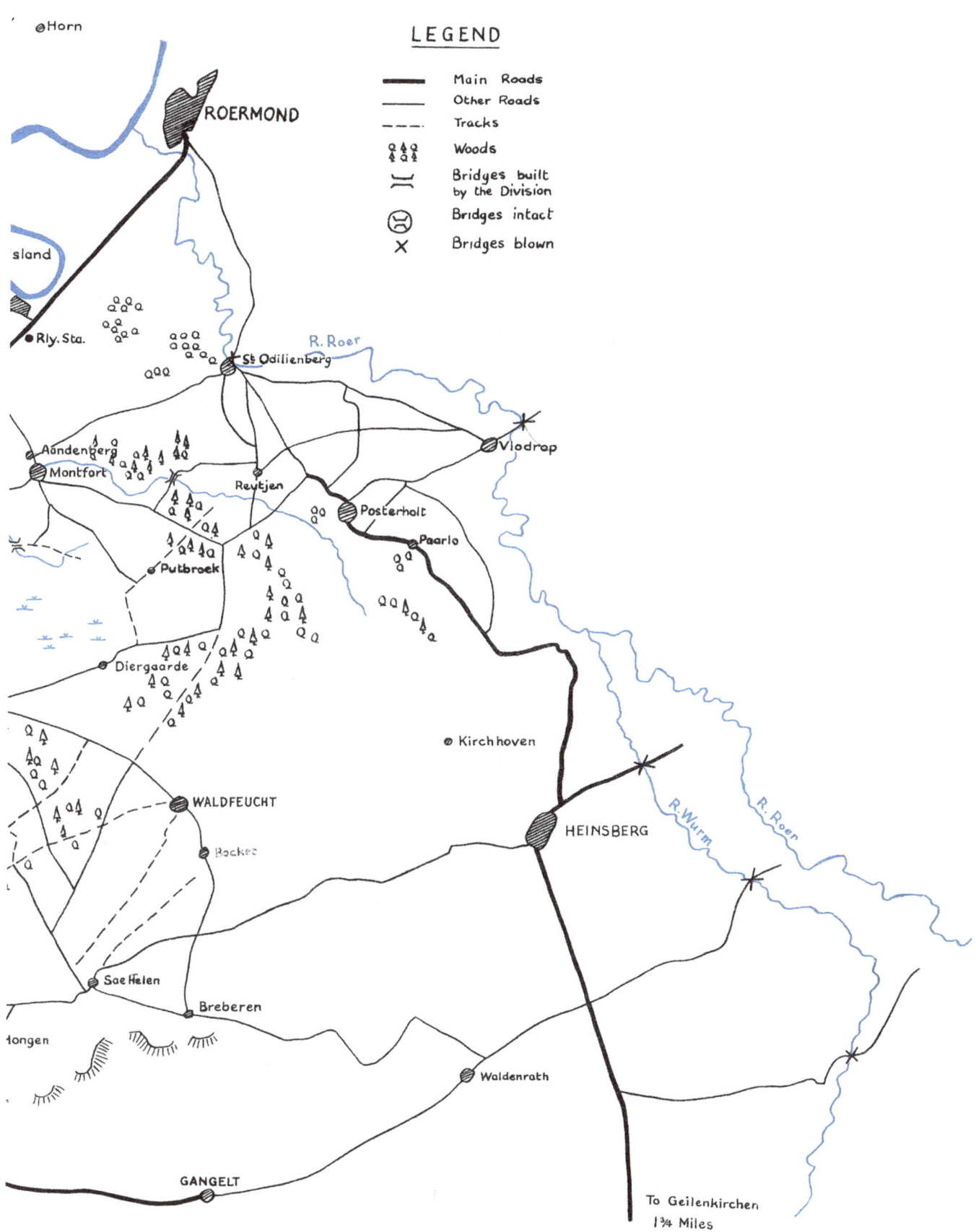

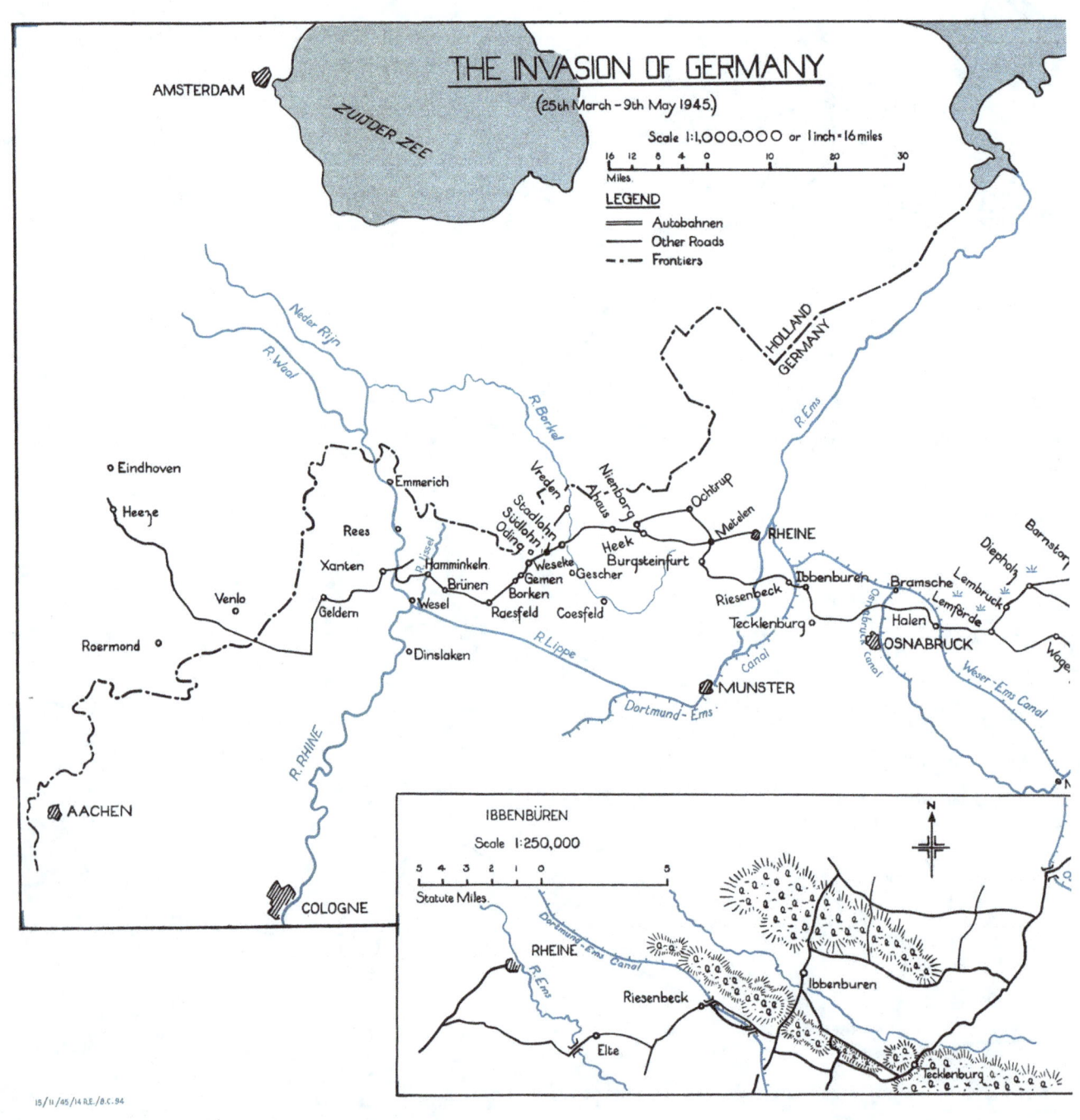

THE INVASION OF GERMANY
SPREAD 1
SPREAD 2

SHEET 9.
NORTH SEA
BALTIC SEA
N
Husum
Freidrichstadt
Heide
Kiel Canal
KIEL
Itzehoe
Pinneberg
R. Elbe
HAMBURG
LUBECK
WISMAR
Bremervörde
R. Weser
BREMEN
Horneburg
Harsefeld
Buxtehude
Moisburg
Hollenstedt
HARBURG
Tostedt
Maschen
Stelle
Winsen
Wildeshausen
Harpstedt
Kirchweyhe
Syke
Twistringen
Bassum
Riede
Schwaförden
Sulingen
Rotenburg
Welle
Bücholz
Jesteburg
Verden
Heber
Schneverdingen
Barenburg
Kirchdorf
Hoya
Rethem
Visselhovede
Ebbingen
Varlingen
Kroge
Lauenburg
Bispingen
LUNEBURG
Nienburg
Walsrode
Fallingbostel
Dorfmark
Soltau
Wietzendorf
R. Weser
Minden
To Lemförde
Uelzen
Celle
HANNOVER
R. Aller
OSNABRUCK
L/Cpl. R.A. Moss, R.E. Oct '45.

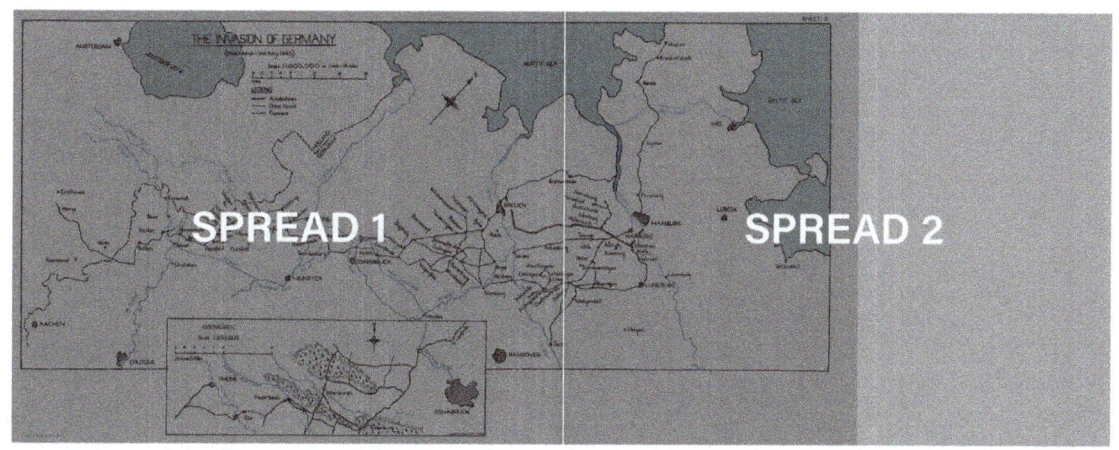

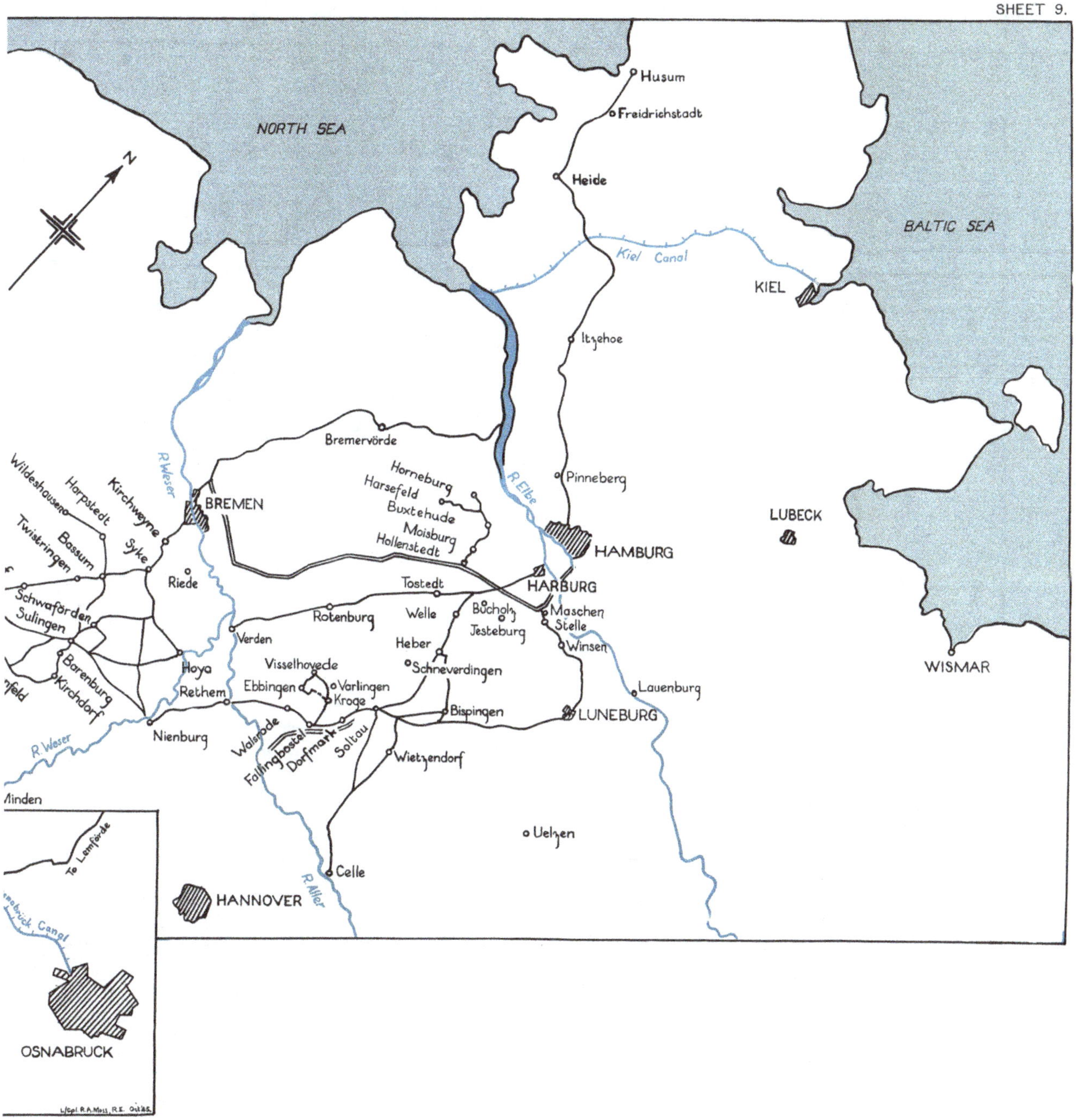

SPREAD 1

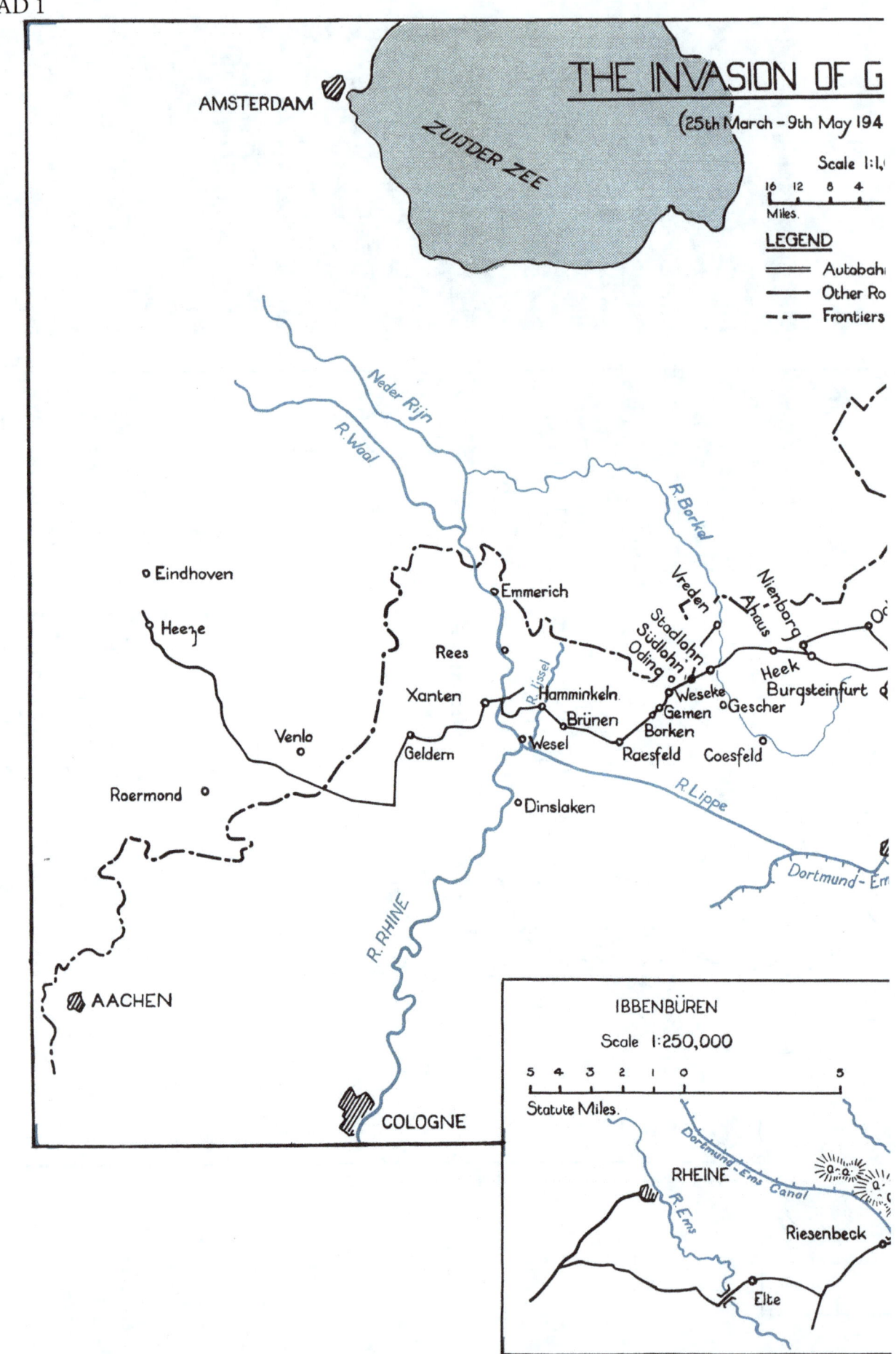

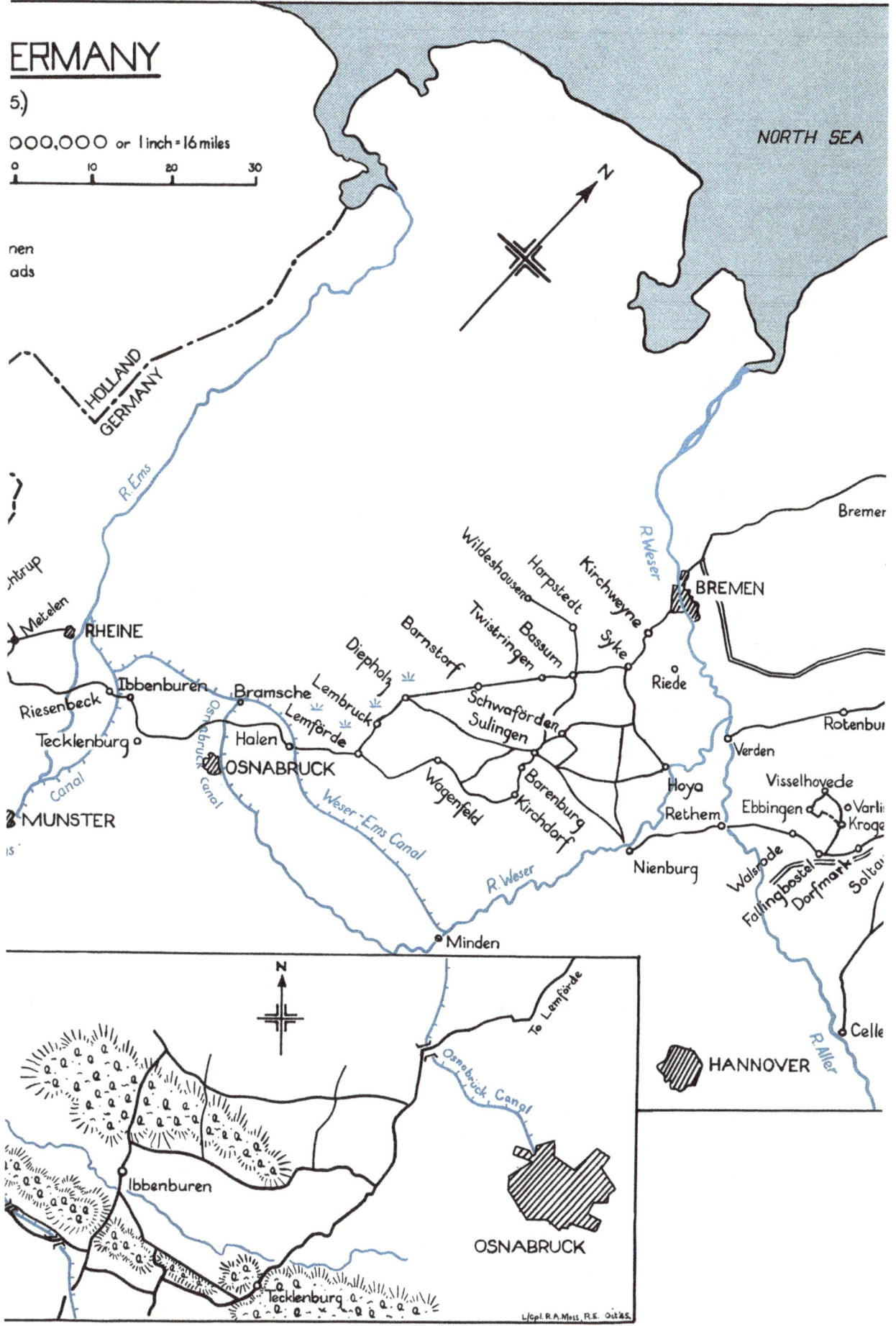

SPREAD 2 SHEET 9.

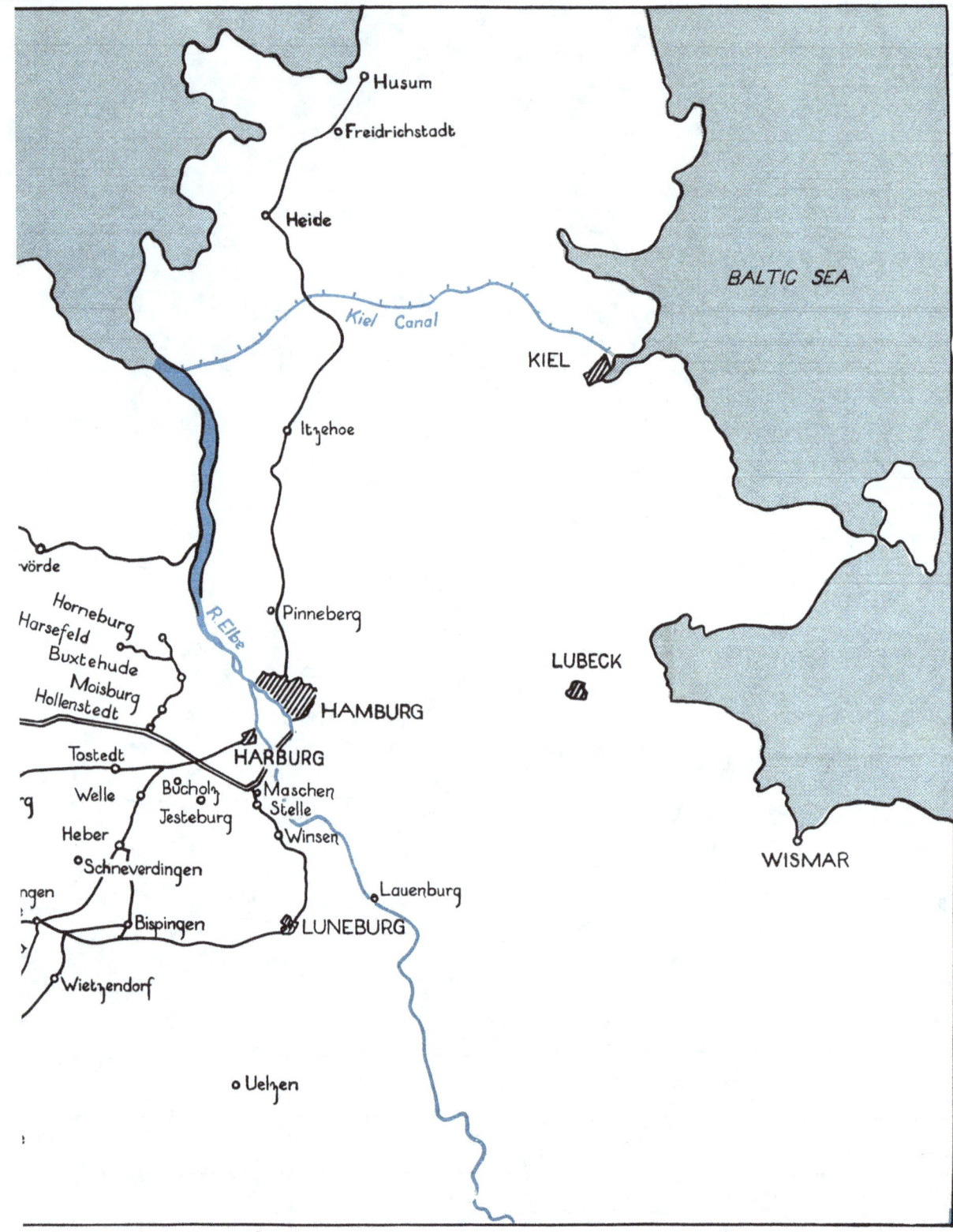

SPREAD 2

THE CROSSING OF THE RHINE
AND AFTER

Scale 1:250,000

Statute Miles:
5 4 3 2 1 0 5

— Main Roads
— Secondary Roads
--- Minor Roads and Tracks
–·– International Boundaries

SHEET 10.

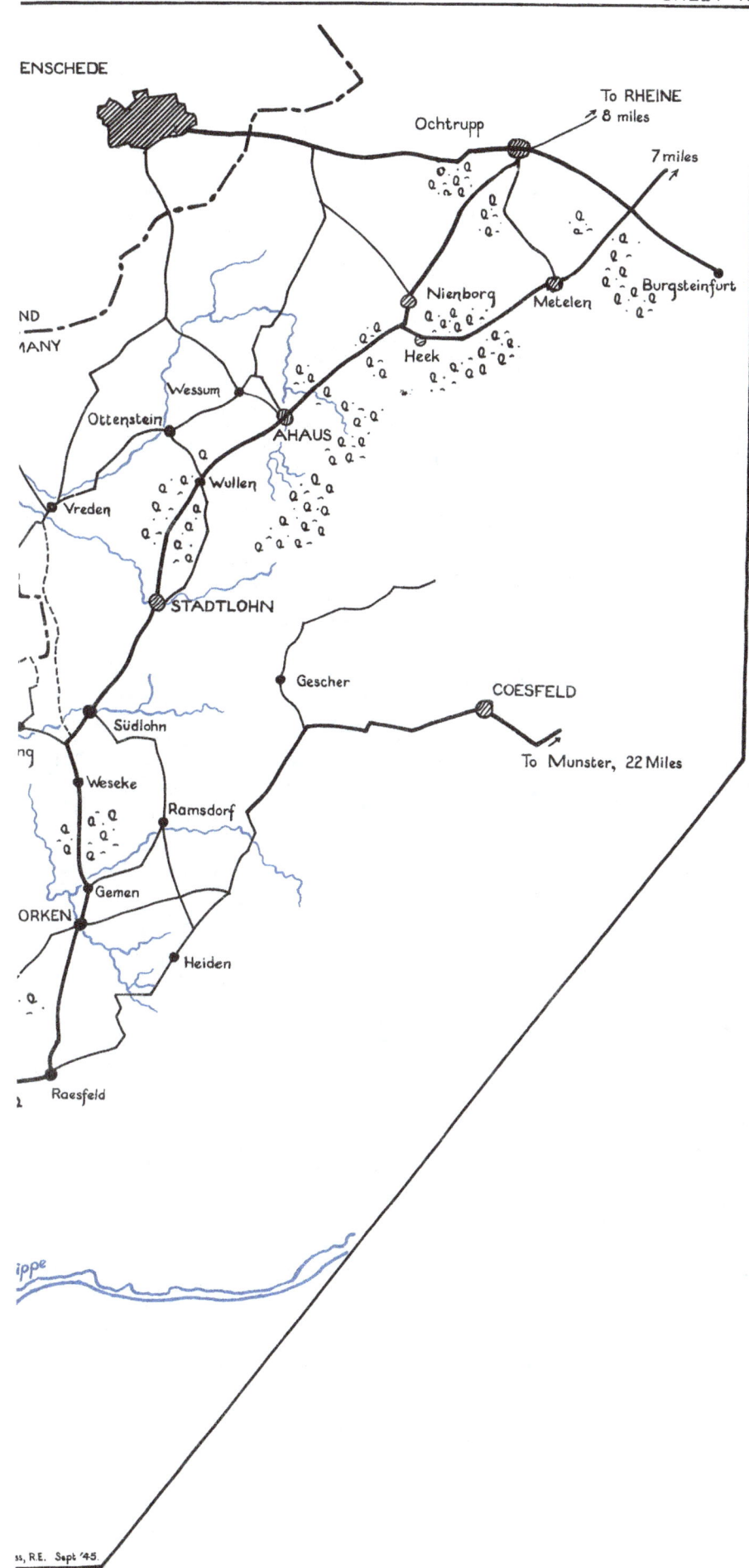

SHEET 11.

THE ADVANCE ON HAMBURG

Scale: 1:250,000

Statute Miles:
10 9 8 7 6 5 4 3 2 1 0 10

LEGEND

- ○= Autobahnen and Junction Points.
- —— Main Roads
- —— Other "
- ---- Tracks
- Forest
- Woods

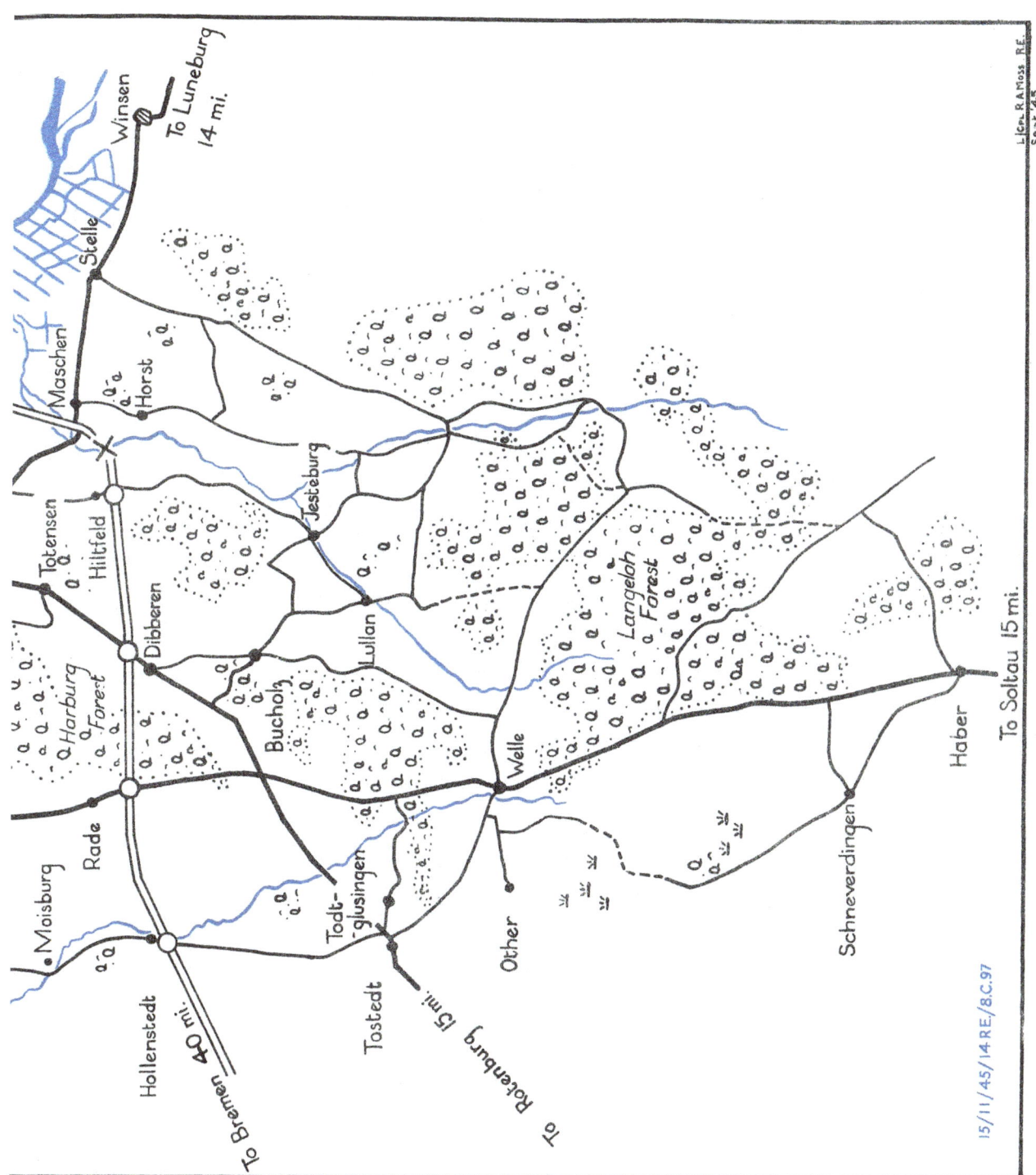

REGIMENTAL HISTORIES OF THE BRITISH ARMY

A selection of N&MP reprinted titles ALWAYS AVAILABLE ALWAYS IN PRINT

Read the real history of The Second World War in the stories of the Regiments, Corps, Divisions, & Battalions that fought it.

NAVAL & MILITARY PRESS
WWW.NAVAL-MILITARY-PRESS.COM

CLUB ROUTE IN EUROPE
The Story of 30 Corps in the European Campaign.
9781783311033

30 Corps was heavily involved in the closing campaigns of the Second World War in Europe, starting when its 50th (Northumbrian) Division landed on Gold Beach on D-day. It helped to clear the Cotentin peninsular in Operation Bluecoat and, after General Brian Horrocks took over command, it took part in Operation Market Garden at Arnhem, and the crossing of the Rhine into the German heartland. A superb unit history of these often difficult and bloody operations.

SEVENTH ARMOURED DIVISION
October 1938 - May 1943
9781474539180

2nd BATTALION SOUTH WALES BORDERS 24th REGIMENT
D-DAY TO VE-DAY
9781474539012

Describing the campaign from D-Day onwards, this excellent contemporary battalion history is divided into two parts. The first contains an outline of the activities of the 2/24th during the campaign in Europe from D-Day to VE-Day, and the second is a detailed narrative of some of the more important actions in which the battalion fought. Complete with a list of awards. Originally printed in Hamburg in 1945.

49 (WEST RIDING) RECONNAISSANCE REGIMENT
Royal Armoured Corps - Summary of Operations June 1944 to May 1945
9781474536677

Rare Reconnaissance unit history that was completed immediately after the war had ended. Following the D-Day invasions, the 49th Reconnaissance Regiment fought as Montgomery's left flank, and played vital roles in the capture of Arnhem, and the liberation of Holland. They are honoured annually in Utrecht to this day. The book is completed with 2 good coloured maps.

THE HISTORY OF THE CORPS OF ROYAL MILITARY POLICE
9781783310951

Excellent history of this corps, almost entirely devoted to WW2 on all fronts, including Middle East, North-West Europe and Burma. Complete with a Roll of Honour.

THE STORY OF THE 79th ARMOURED DIVISION OCTOBER 1942 - JUNE 1945
9781783310395

A magnificent and fully illustrated official history of Britain's 79th Armoured Division - the specialised unit which developed and operated 'Hobart's Funnies', the adapted tanks which carried out a range of tasks on D-day and after ranging from mine clearance to bridge laying. Follows the unit from its formation to victory in Europe.

HISTORY OF THE ARGYLL & SUTHERLAND HIGHLANDERS 7th BATTALION
From El Alamein To Germany
9781781519653

THE ESSEX REGIMENT 1929 - 1950
9781781519813

Comprehensive history of both regular & territorial force battalions, mainly Middle East (inc. Tobruk & Alamein), North-West Europe & 1st Bn. with Chindits in Burma 1944. Rolls of Honour and awards.

HISTORY OF THE IRISH GUARDS IN THE SECOND WORLD WAR
9781474537094

A fine history of a proud regiment; The Irish Guards played their part gallantly during campaigns in Europe, North Africa and Italy during the Second World War, claiming two Victoria Cross recipients during that conflict. The basis of this history was the War Diaries kept by Battalion Intelligence Officers, along with individual records and papers. A Roll of Honour, Honours Awards down to Military Medal, and 22 good maps complete this very good WW2 Regimental.

ALGIERS TO AUSTRIA
The 78th Division in the Second World War
9781783310265

OPERATIONS OF THE EIGHTH CORPS
The River Rhine to the Baltic Sea. A narrative account of the pursuit and final defeat of the German Armed Forces March-May 1945.
9781474538176

THE HISTORY OF THE 51st HIGHLAND DIVISION 1939-1945
9781474536660

The 51st Highland Division fought and lost in France in 1940, was reborn, and fought and won in the North African desert, Sicily and finally in North Western Europe from D-Day to the end of the war. As a division the men earned the respect of friend and foe alike, and this is their story. Amply illustrated with 36 photographs, 18 maps and battle plans (many coloured) that help the reader to follow the course of the conflict. A good index (persons, units and place names) and a statistical battle casualties list complete this good WW2 Divisional History

THE HISTORY OF THE FIFTEENTH SCOTTISH DIVISION 1939-1945
9781783310852

Formed at the outbreak of war in September 1939, the 15th (Scottish) division served in North-western Europe after landing in Normandy soon after D-day on 14 June 1944. It fought on the Odon River, at Caen, Caumont, Mont Pincon, the Nederrijn, the Rhineland, and across the Rhine. On April 10, 1946, the division was disbanded. The total number of casualties it sustained during the 12 months of fighting was 11,772.

THE STORY OF THE ROYAL ARMY SERVICE CORPS, 1939-1945
9781474538251

A complete history of the RASC in all theatres throughout the Second World War. This a model unit history originally published under the direction of the Institution of the Royal Army Service Corps, it is excellently produced, and arranged by theatre of war. The narrative is full with technical information, and the many photographic plates record visually British military vehicles in service situations.

www.ingramcontent.com/pod-product-compliance
Lightning Source LLC
Chambersburg PA
CBHW081841230426
43669CB00018B/2779